THE EVERYDAY LIVES OF CHILDREN WHO HAVE EXPERIENCED DOMESTIC ABUSE
Looking Beyond the Trauma Lens

Brenda Herbert

P

First published in Great Britain in 2026 by

Policy Press, an imprint of
Bristol University Press
University of Bristol
1-9 Old Park Hill
Bristol
BS2 8BB
UK
t: +44 (0)117 374 6645
e: bup-info@bristol.ac.uk

Details of international sales and distribution partners are available at policy.bristoluniversitypress.co.uk

© Bristol University Press 2026

DOI: 10.51952/9781447374701

British Library Cataloguing in Publication Data
A catalogue record for this book is available from the British Library

ISBN 978-1-4473-7467-1 hardcover
ISBN 978-1-4473-7468-8 paperback
ISBN 978-1-4473-7469-5 ePub
ISBN 978-1-4473-7470-1 ePDF

The right of Brenda Herbert to be identified as author of this work has been asserted by her in accordance with the Copyright, Designs and Patents Act 1988.

All rights reserved: no part of this publication may be reproduced, stored in a retrieval system, or transmitted in any form or by any means, electronic, mechanical, photocopying, recording, or otherwise without the prior permission of Bristol University Press.

Every reasonable effort has been made to obtain permission to reproduce copyrighted material. If, however, anyone knows of an oversight, please contact the publisher.

The statements and opinions contained within this publication are solely those of the author and not of the University of Bristol or Bristol University Press. The University of Bristol and Bristol University Press disclaim responsibility for any injury to persons or property resulting from any material published in this publication.

Bristol University Press and Policy Press work to counter discrimination on grounds of gender, race, disability, age and sexuality.

Cover design: Nicky Borowiec
Front cover image: Stocksy/Marusya Wrobel

This book is dedicated to Antony, Madeleine and Ben.
All my love, always xx
And to all the children who lived in Coronation Building,
I hope life was kind.

Contents

List of figures		vi
Acknowledgements		viii
1	Introduction: Now you see me	1
2	Over-researched and under-represented: decolonising the figure of the child	24
3	The everyday life of Mystical	48
4	Taking the fun out of play	69
5	The aesthetics of everyday life	94
6	The art of loving in everyday life	121
7	Conclusion: Floating Matters	152
Appendix		166
References		170
Index		203

List of figures

3.1	Metal cups and bowls	50
3.2	Mystical's artwork	52
3.3	From top left to bottom right: food preparations; Nicole preparing food; dinner table; food with a funny face	55
4.1	A WhatsApp video call	74
4.2	Tic-tac-toe	76
4.3	The playground	79
4.4	The swings	81
4.5	Pool on the balcony	87
5.1	Impromptu activity in the corridor	95
5.2	Knife in the sun	96
5.3	The moth	97
5.4	The lake	100
5.5	Halloween decorations	101
5.6	(Left) Christmas tree; (right) Christmas table decoration	102
5.7	Heart-shaped cakes	103
5.8	Table decorations	104
5.9	Newly decorated room	107
5.10	Jane the doll	108
5.11	Virtual home	110
5.12	Snow!	115
5.13	The magical bench	116
5.14	Everlasting	117
5.15	From top left to bottom right: the trees; the bus; the sky; shopping trolleys	119
6.1	Treasured golf balls	125
6.2	An adventure	126
6.3	Treasure	127
6.4	(Left) The 'golden rool'; (right) the 'golden rule'	130
6.5	(Left) Caring person; (right) caring actions	132
6.6	River of life	139
6.7a	What grown-ups should know	141
6.7b	What I wish grown-ups would ask	141
6.8a	Unlucky rainbow	142
6.8b	Lucky rainbow	142
6.9	Tabitha	145
6.10	Hops	147
7.1a	Floating Matters exhibition	153
7.1b	Floating Matters exhibition close up	153

List of figures

A.1a	Assembling the art pack	167
A.1b	Art pack	167

Acknowledgements

This book would not have happened without my two families. To the children and mothers who participated in the research, thank you for opening your hearts and homes to me. It is such a privilege to share your lives and see you grow. To Antony, Madeleine and Ben – forever my loves – thank you for putting up with my growing piles of books and unread PDFs! I am sorry I still have not tidied up. Thank you for all your hard work, love and support, Antony – I love you very much. Well, Mum, I finally finished my work! Dad, I am sad you didn't get to see the book. Thank you both for all your hard work and love. To Richard, Jonathan and Jennifer – thank you for your love – here's to a future filled with more love, creativity and happiness. Much love to Giancarlo, Emily, Helen, Jo, Alex, Mayuri, Ethan and Aleyna. To Aunty Marie-Claire, Uncle France and Aunty Soon – thank you for everything. Thank you to Linda and Graham for looking after Antony, Ben and Madeleine while I tried to finish this book. Neil, thank you for cheering me on with my research.

To my very wise supervisor, Dr Sevasti-Melissa Nolas, thank you for seeing my potential. I remember nervously asking whether you would supervise me – I am so glad you said 'Yes'. From the beginning, Anita, Chantelle and Charlie, you cheered me on – your friendship and encouragement helped to wipe away many tears. I am here because of your support. Thank you. Zoe and Elina, thank you for reading and believing in my work. Adrien and Vik, thank you for your companionship and holding the writing space, especially during the 'lockdown' period. A special thanks to Dr Lisa Morriss – thank you for holding my worries and heart through some of the trickier moments of the research. Attending your ECR event was one of the best things I participated in during my PhD. To the Friday writing crew, Ariane, Siobhan, Lisa, Kim, Saf and Wahida, thank you for all the encouragement, chat and advice. Those Friday mornings made me laugh and work. Thank you all for showing me that academia can be a caring and kind space. Thank you to the Goldsmiths Sociology PhD group for being so generous. Thank you to Artemis and Luan for your kindness and wisdom. Thank you to Professor Wendy Luttrell, Professor Erica Burman, Dr Fay Dennis, Professor Kiran Grewal and Professor Rebecca Coleman for your wisdom, scholarship and advice, which have nurtured my work.

Mary and Sarah M. – this project would not have come off the ground without you both. You believed in me from the beginning and despite all the ups and downs of work, you kept the faith and advocated for the project. Not enough is said about you both. This book is as much about your work and commitment as it is about mine. Joanna, thank you for being one of my biggest fans. I look forward to working with you more. Toni,

Zoe, Elizabeth and Juliette, thank you for always being ready with a pep talk and wise advice to keep my mind from worrying. To Juliet, Marilyn, Linda, Lidia, Breeda, Sue and Caroline, thank you for cheering me on. Hasret, Linda, Alex, Kelly and Martin, thank you for supporting me from the start and always encouraging me to keep going. Thank you for your radical therapeutic work. Kelly, you are an awesome cheerleader – thank you for all your support.

Thank you to all my friends who kept listening to me talk about my research. Thank you to Katie, Sheridan, Sophie, Eleanor, Ros and Annabel, who kept listening. Thank you to Michelle, Richard J., Maria, Fernando and Donna for supporting me and patiently waiting for the party. Thank you to Tricia and Tine for loving me. An enormous thank you to Tracey, Virginia, Sarah C. and Alisi, who patiently gave me brilliant advice, cheered me on and always listened with an empathetic heart.

A special thanks to the Sociological Review Foundation for awarding me the fellowship to complete this book. A special thanks to Professor Karen O'Reilly for being a brilliant mentor and to Professor Mark Featherstone. Lastly, a big thank you to my editors Isobel Bainton, for your kindness and for seeing the potential in the project from the very beginning, and Rupert Spurrier, for your advice and guidance.

I would like to acknowledge that part of Chapter 2 first appeared in a previous journal: Herbert, B. (2025), 'Beyond the passive and damaged child: using child as method to decolonise the literature on children and domestic abuse', *Annual Review of Critical Psychology* 20. Open Access: https://discourseunit.com/arcp-20-child-as-method-in-movement-work-action-subject-2025/

1

Introduction: Now you see me

'Look, look!' shouts seven-year-old Kyro, as he waves a huge stick that he has found in the playground. The stick is three times as big as Kyro, but he waves it deftly around his head, pretending he is a pirate.

'Brenda! Look!' calls Kyro with excitement.

'Yes, I am, but I just need to show Rosa how to use the camera,' I reply to Kyro, as I look back down to Rosa, his five-year-old sister.

'So how can I see the pictures?' asks Rosa, turning the small digital camera around and pressing different buttons. 'I can't see anything.'

'You have to press this button, and then this one. See?' I explain.

'Yes! Yes! I can see it. Kyro, look, look!' says Rosa as she turns around and runs across the playground clicking the button and taking photographs.

'Brenda, you are not really looking at me!' Kyro calls out in exasperation.

(Field notes, March 2020)

It is the middle of March 2020; it is only a few days before the UK goes into physical restrictions, commonly known as 'lockdown', due to COVID-19 and I am in a playground in London, UK, handing out an art pack to Rosa. The art pack includes paper, stickers, pens, pencils, glue, lolly sticks and a small toy digital camera. I had quickly assembled the art packs as I needed a way to continue my ethnographic study with children who had experienced domestic abuse and social work intervention. I had spent the last week delivering the packs to all the children who had agreed to be part of the project. I was only one month into my ethnographic study when the physical restrictions for COVID-19 were introduced, so I had to adapt my research methods quickly. This book is about the 18 months I spent getting to know ten children through weekly online or in-person visits. The children's ages ranged from five years old to ten years old.

All the children in the study had experienced domestic abuse and social work intervention, but this was not only who they were; this book explores the everyday lives of the children. Existing research on domestic abuse and children highlights the extent and impact of the issue on children's lives and relationships but tends to focus on adversity and damage. It frames these issues from an adult, professional perspective, namely that offered by the disciplines of psychology and social work. There is little research on children's perspective. This has produced a dominant narrative of children as passive and damaged (Callaghan et al, 2017a, 2018). This book challenges this framing to show that children who experience domestic abuse are more than their trauma and abuse. During an 18-month multimodal ethnography in one inner-city London borough, the ten children who participated in this study show their lives in all their fleshy humanness.

Through being attentive to the everyday, we can see how they navigate their lives, how they create fun, beauty and love in the everyday, despite the challenges of having experienced domestic abuse. While this book is based on my PhD multimodal ethnographic research with children in London, the children's lives speak beyond the UK setting and disrupt the Global North/Global South binary which works on the assumption that childhoods in the North are always affluent and childhoods in the South are always impoverished (Twum-Danso Imoh et al, 2019; Twum-Danso Imoh, 2024). The children's lives have commonalities and links with other children globally who have been marginalised through racism and poverty. Their stories show that patriarchal and colonialist social norms are upheld when we see children, who are marginalised, only through the lens of trauma and abuse. In this book I argue that our gaze must shift.

This book is an invitation to imagine an alternative way of working with children by being attentive to their everyday lives. My professional background as a counsellor working with children and young people who have experienced domestic abuse prompted me to undertake this research. Through my everyday work, I noticed that some of the social work practices that were intended to protect children often misjudged their needs, leaving them more marginalised. I often felt that while many social workers entered into the profession to work empathetically with children and families, they were often limited by the system they worked within. Coming from a psychoanalytic perspective, I was initially keen to explore the psychodynamic processes which resulted in these misattuned social work interventions. However, as I researched the social work academic literature, I was shocked to find that there was very limited research conducted with children – they were essentially missing from the production of knowledge about themselves. This led me to question why there was so little research with children and to change my research to focus on children and their lived experience.

Academics and practitioners have long called for more research with children who have experienced domestic abuse to better understand their lived experience and to provide appropriate support (Mullender et al, 2002; Stanley, 2011; Macdonald, 2017; Øverlien and Holt, 2018, 2021). Yet, with a few notable exceptions (McGee, 2000; Mullender et al, 2002; Stanley, 2011; Øverlien, 2014; Katz, 2015; Callaghan et al, 2016a; Øverlien and Holt, 2021), only limited research has been done with children. My analysis of the research literature shows that there has been an epistemic injustice, in that children have not been able to create or contribute to knowledge about themselves, which I discuss in Chapter 2. Using Burman's (2018b) *Child as method* approach, I interrogate the extant literature to draw out the different figures of the child that are present in research, society and practice with children who have been marginalised through social work intervention and domestic abuse. Using these figures of the child, I illustrate how, in ignoring children's knowledge, we uphold a colonialist and patriarchal social order that further marginalises certain children and perpetuates abuse. I argue that this epistemic injustice is not exclusive to children who have experienced domestic abuse in the UK, but there are parallels with children who are marginalised in the Global South. To address this epistemic injustice, I argue that it is important to create knowledge with children about their everyday lives.

Cultural theories of the everyday, which frame my study, offer an opportunity to not only see how the social affects subjectivity but also how children flourish in, adhere to and resist constraints in the mundaneness of the everyday. It is an opportunity to be attentive to how children make meaning of their lives. Childhood scholars (Di Napoli Pastore, 2022; Twum-Danso Imoh et al, 2022) and Black feminists (hooks, 2009, 2016c; Sharpe, 2016, p 4; Williamson, 2017; Emejulu and Sobande, 2019; Quashie, 2021) have argued that it is in being attentive to the everyday that we can go beyond the extreme challenges of the lives of marginalised communities to find how they make their lives liveable. The theoretical framing of the everyday creates a space to see communities beyond the lens of trauma and abuse, to witness them in their fleshy humanness. Indigenous and decolonial scholars Smith (1999), Mohanty (2003) and Tuck (2009) have long argued against 'the damage narrative' that has dominated research in Indigenous and marginalised communities, which in turn further oppresses and 'others' them.

In order to address this epistemic injustice and research beyond the narrow lens of trauma and abuse, an 18-month multimodal ethnography with ten children in one London borough was carried out. The multimodal ethnography enabled children to choose which mediums and modes they wanted to communicate through – it provided different ways of seeing, listening, playing, feeling and thinking. It did not confine children to one mode of communication, and indeed we played with methods. The longitudinal aspect of ethnography meant that children were able to create knowledge over a period rather than being given only a singular opportunity. I returned to the children to clarify and explore their ideas and stories. Given the time and word constraints of the book, I chose to focus on the children; therefore, there is only very limited information about mothers and professionals.

In this chapter I give a brief overview of the research, practice and policy landscape of domestic abuse and children. I argue for the need to go beyond the lens of trauma and abuse to address the epistemic injustice in order to support the needs of children. I demonstrate how studying the cultural theories of the everyday allowed me to create knowledge with children, so that children could be seen in their fleshy humanity rather than as passive and damaged victims of domestic abuse alone. I summarise the methodological approach that I chose for the research and give a summary of the knowledge created with the children, and I make a case for shifting the gaze. The chapter concludes with an overview of the whole book and a reflection on what undergirded my approach to the research.

But first, before I delve into outlining my theoretical and methodological framework, I will introduce the children and their mothers. In line with the ethos of centring the children in this book and reorientating our gaze away from the colonial and patriarchal framing of children and childhoods, the children present themselves and their mothers in their own words.

Children and mothers in their own words

Ten children in total chose to be part of the research project. All were living with their mothers and siblings only. They had experienced domestic abuse from their fathers and were all living apart from them.

All the children in the study had at least one parent whose heritage was from another country, one that had been colonised by Britain or another European country. The families came from Ireland, Mauritius, Algeria, Afghanistan, the Philippines, Jamaica, the Democratic Republic of Congo and Chile. I have not placed the countries with the children so as to protect their identity.

In line with my agreement with the mothers and children, their real names are not used. While there are ethical reasons why real names should be used in research (Lomax, 2015; Kara, 2018, p 99; Gordon, 2019), the mothers and some children were keen to remain anonymous due to ongoing interactions with social services and reasons of safety. As part of the ethos of creating with children, I asked each of the children what name they would give themselves and how they would describe themselves. In the following paragraphs are their descriptions – the length varies according to how much the children wanted to let you (the reader) know about themselves.

The children

Mystical is a seven-year-old boy. He says he is short with long and curly hair. He is interested to know how birds fly with feathers (he already knows how they glide), how giraffes got to have such long necks and how cheetahs can run so fast. Mystical doesn't like lava and fire because they can burn you. He doesn't like school dinners and only eats their fish and chips. He doesn't like the rice especially because it is cold. This happens because the school keeps their back door open so that children can go out to play after they finish their meal, but this means that the dinner gets cold quickly. Mystical really hates cold rice. Mystical's favourite colours are blue, yellow, white and black. His favourite game is Pixel Gun 3D (it's a bit like Minecraft). Mystical lives with his mother, Nicole, and his brothers in a flat.

JoJo Siwa (named after the greatest singer in the world!) is nearly seven. She has her hair in two buns. Her favourite food is mashed potatoes and her favourite colour is pink. JoJo Siwa loves to play with her dolls, toy kitchen and to play games, especially a game called 'President'. Her favourite toys are her unicorns, toy cars, Barbie dolls and toy kitchen. She likes to eat sweets the most and dislikes burger sauce but likes ketchup. JoJo Siwa has three older sisters. She lives with her sister Esmeralda, another older sister and her mother, Stardust, in a flat. Her eldest sister is away studying.

Esmeralda is eight years old and has long hair. She loves to eat noodles and her favourite colour is blue. She likes chocolate but does not like sweets and juice. Esmeralda would like to be a dentist when she grows up (that is partly why she doesn't like sweets and juice, as they are not good for your teeth). Her favourite toys are her unicorns. Esmeralda lives with her younger sister JoJo Siwa, her mother, Stardust, and one older sister. Her eldest sister is away studying.

Elsa is five years old. Her favourite colour is blue, and her favourite toy is her Shopkins (tiny miniature figures). She loves to eat cookies and loves to draw. Elsa does not like to eat apples. Elsa lives with her brother Pogi and her mother, Ann, in a flat.

Pogi is ten years old and describes himself as Asian. His favourite colour is purple. He loves to eat pizza but does not like school dinners. His favourite toy is his Xbox and he likes to play games on it. He doesn't like school, and he is interested in money. Pogi lives with his sister Elsa and his mother, Ann, in a flat.

Tdrommie is eight years old. He likes the colour blue and his favourite food is cheeseburgers. He doesn't like potatoes, custard, mushrooms and mustard. He doesn't have a favourite toy but loves to play Minecraft. Tdrommie's favourite place to be is his home. He lives with his mother, Stacey, two older brothers, one older sister and one younger sister in a flat.

Sagittarius is a ten-year-old girl. Her favourite colour is purple. Her favourite foods are noodles, fried chicken and pasta. She does not like anything about mushrooms – the texture, the taste, everything about mushrooms is horrible. Sagittarius's favourite toy is a white fluffy dancing llama called Boppy. She likes to play games, Roblox with her friends and board games with her mother and sister – these include Cluedo, Guess Who and Connect 4. Sagittarius is interested in unicorns, very interested in different types of animals (all of them actually) but especially hamsters, dogs and cats. Sagittarius says, 'when I am with my best friend, we tell each other jokes and act silly; when I am with my sister and mother, I do silly dances and joke with them'. Sagittarius lives with her mother, Marta, and her sister in a flat.

Katie is a ten-year-old girl. Her favourite colours are blue, pink and purple – she is less keen on green. She is interested in ballet and art. Her favourite foods are her mother's rice and lamb dinners. She does not like watermelon or pizza. Katie likes books by David Walliams and likes to watch films, and sometimes likes to watch princess films too. She lives with her mother, Bella, her maternal grandfather and three siblings.

Rosie is a five-year-old girl. Her favourite colours are pink and blue. Her favourite food is chips; she does not like to eat tomatoes. Rosie likes to do cartwheels and loves gymnastics. She lives with her mother, Summer, and her brother Kyro.

Kyro is a seven-year-old boy. He likes the colour purple and likes roller-skating. His favourite food is spaghetti and he doesn't like to eat cauliflower and sweetcorn. Kyro lives with his mother, Summer, and his sister Rosie in a flat.

The mothers

A key element in making this project work was the cooperation of mothers, whose permission I needed before I approached the children. Mothers were key in supporting me to keep in contact with children over the period of physical restrictions for COVID-19 and were enthusiastic about their children participating in the project. Seven mothers took part in the project.

Marta loves plants and animals. She loves cooking, good food and books, although she tends to fall asleep now while reading. She likes music from the 80s and 90s as well as classical music. Marta doesn't like spicy food but loves sweets and desserts (any!), as well as vegetables and salad. She doesn't eat lamb or rabbit. Her favourite colours are purple, lilac and navy blue.

Stardust is interested in different cuisines and loves to cook. She doesn't eat meat, Brussels sprouts or asparagus. Her favourite colours are black and red – her least favourite is green. Stardust loves to watch horror films and to read books by Stephen King; she really likes the book *One Rainy Night* by Richard Laymon.

Summer's favourite colour is purple, and she is interested in ice skating. She likes to eat spaghetti bolognese and does not like to eat avocados. She likes to watch *EastEnders*, horror films and old-school musicals. Summer likes to listen to R 'n' B and reggae music.

Bella's favourite colours are pink and red, but she is not too keen on dark colours. She is interested in cooking, baking and, according to her children, she 'makes the best birthday cake'. Bella likes to eat vegetables, healthy food and homemade bread. She doesn't like pizza. She loves *The Lion King* both as a film and a play. At the moment she is reading the theory test book for her driving test.

Stacey likes the colour pink. Her favourite food is pizza and her favourite day is Saturday. She likes to watch *EastEnders*, and her children make her happy.

Nicole likes to sing, dance, cook and clean. She also likes to watch horror films as well as Bollywood films. Her favourite horror film is *Annabel*. She eats anything and likes fried rice. Her favourite colour is blue.

Ann likes cooking and eats a variety of foods – her favourite is sushi. Her favourite colour is pink, and she is not too keen on dark brown as a colour. Her favourite TV programme is a Korean Netflix series. She used to read lots of books, but since having children she doesn't read as much. Ann likes stories that are true to life. Her faith is very important to her and she likes Christian music and books that give hope and courage.

The children also gave their pets pseudonyms. All other persons referred to in this book have also been given a pseudonym.

Domestic abuse and children

All the children in this book had experienced domestic abuse and social work interventions in the UK. In this section, I will set out the landscape with regards to domestic abuse, how it relates to children and its consequences. Firstly, I will define what I mean by the terms 'child' and 'domestic abuse'. While I acknowledge and explore in the book (see Chapter 2) how the meaning and category of a 'child' is heavily contested as to what it means and who can inhabit this position, for this book I use the UK government's definition of a child in England:

> As anyone who has not yet reached their 18th birthday. Child protection guidance points out that even if a child has reached 16 years of age and is:
>
> - living independently
> - in further education
> - a member of the armed forces
> - in hospital; or
> - in custody in the secure estate

they are still legally children and should be given the same protection and entitlements as any other child.

(Department for Education, 2018)

For this book, the use of the term 'domestic abuse' rather than 'intimate partner violence' or 'woman abuse' is used to emphasise that the abuse happens in the home, a domestic space. Home is the place where a child resides and is socialised (Conkbayir, 2014). The word 'abuse' rather than 'violence' is used to include the non-physical aspects of abuse. The term 'domestic abuse' is commonly used by professionals and families, and for a level of ease in communication, it is the term I will use throughout. (For a detailed debate about the use of the different terms, please see Holden, 2003; Sloan-Lynch, 2012; Walby et al, 2016; Walby and Towers, 2018; Myhill and Kelly, 2019.) While I acknowledge that domestic abuse can be experienced and perpetuated by any person regardless of their gender or identity, in this research the survivors of domestic abuse were all women and children, and the perpetrators of the abuse were all men. This is a reflection on the concept of domestic abuse being seen primarily as predominantly (but not always) perpetrated by men towards women (Hester, 2013).

It is worth noting that official definitions of 'domestic abuse' in the UK made no reference to children as victims until the Domestic Abuse Act 2021. Up until then, the presumption in law was that domestic abuse happens in an intimate dyad between two adults, usually a male perpetrator and a female victim. For example, the Children Act 2004 says that children's needs must be taken into consideration as they are 'witnesses' to domestic abuse and affected by it, and not because they are direct victims. It was not until activists, practitioners and academics campaigned for children to be recognised as being survivors/victims of domestic abuse in their own right that this was reflected in the Domestic Abuse Act 2021.

The disregard, in law, for children as direct victims prior to the Domestic Abuse Act 2021 resulted in policies and services that predominantly focused on adults, with more focus on women than men (Callaghan et al, 2015; Fellin et al, 2018). It rendered the experience of children as secondary to that of their parents, and consequently the resources to support them became secondary to adult services. As Callaghan (2017a, p 222) writes, children's care is a 'bolt on to specialist domestic violence services'. Support for children can often stop once mothers have ended their engagement with services, regardless of whether children still need the provision (Callaghan et al, 2017a). Children's needs are either folded into those of their mothers or seen as completely separate; either way, the complexity of children's everyday lives and relationships are not acknowledged (Cairns and Callander, 2022). Recognising what children actually experience in domestic abuse is an important step in understanding them and providing an appropriate service (Mullender et al, 2002; Øverlien, 2011; Stanley, 2011; Holt, 2015, 2017; Stanley and Humphreys, 2017).

The story of harm

The lack of inclusion of children as victims/survivors of domestic abuse is surprising considering that the research literature nonetheless portrays children as 'damaged' and 'passive' recipients of abuse (Callaghan et al, 2015, 2017a, 2018; Katz, 2015). The evidence of the negative impact of domestic abuse on children has been led by quantitative research in psychology and medicine (Øverlien, 2010, p 81; Callaghan, 2015). The research has generally used a biomedical model, where the focus has been on the physical and biological impact of domestic abuse on children. Numerous studies have demonstrated the negative effects of domestic abuse on children (Edleson, 1999; Mullender et al, 2002; Levendosky et al, 2003; Eriksson et al, 2005; Evans et al, 2008; Holt et al, 2008; Stanley, 2011; Holt, 2015; Guedes et al, 2016; Kimball, 2016; McGavock and Spratt, 2016; Icheku and Graham, 2017; Fernández-González et al, 2018; Stanley et al, 2018). Negative effects include challenges to children's mental health over their lifetime (Mezey et al, 2005; Bogat et al, 2006; Peltonen et al, 2010; Taillieu et al, 2016; Mersky et al, 2017), difficulties in their intimate and peer relationships (Ehrensaft, 2008; Black et al, 2010; Siegel, 2013), increased risk of physical ill health (Bair-Merritt et al, 2006), educational challenges (Koenen et al, 2003; Byrne and Taylor, 2007; Willis et al, 2010), increased risk of criminal behaviour (Gilbert et al, 2012), and vulnerability to enter future abusive relationships or for themselves to be abusive in their intimate relationships (Stanley and Humphreys, 2015; Latzman et al, 2017; Kimber et al, 2018). While the studies recognise and chart the extent of the harm of domestic abuse, what is missing from the majority of the literature are the views of children themselves. The studies cited have generally had limited, if any, focus on the interplay between domestic abuse, social factors, individual subjectivity and intersubjectivity.

Domestic abuse, safeguarding and social work intervention

The narrative of harm and damage has led to domestic abuse being framed, in the UK, as a safeguarding issue for children which can warrant social work intervention (Holt, 2017; Stanley and Humphreys, 2017; Ferguson et al, 2020). All the children who participated in my research had experienced social work interventions. For this book social work intervention is defined as the direct work done by social workers to protect children – what Ferguson (2011, p 2) calls the 'action, movements, talk that needs to go on to ensure that, as far as possible, children are safe'. Children who have experienced domestic abuse and social work interventions tend to be assessed as being in significant need which requires support from a social worker. This can mean that they are deemed either (i) child in need (CIN), meaning the family are voluntarily working with social services to support them, or (ii) child protection (CP), where there is such significant concern about the child/ren's wellbeing and safety that the local authority has a statutory obligation to monitor and support the family to improve the situation (Ferguson, 2011, p 35). Typically, once a child is on the CP register, the aim is for the social worker to work with the family to improve their wellbeing and safety so that they can move down to being classified as a CIN. If there are significant concerns, there may be a plan to remove the child/ren from residing with the parent and place the child/ren under the care of the local authority. This could mean being placed in foster care, and if the risks continue to be considered high by the local authority and court, being placed for adoption, long-term fostering or residential care.

Domestic abuse continues to be the most common reason cited for why a child is deemed to be a 'CIN' in social work assessments (Department of Education, 2021). In the year ending 31 October 2021, domestic abuse, which includes harm to either a child or a person in the home, was the reason given for why 43.5 per cent of children were found to be in need at the end of their assessment (Department of Education, 2021). In 2020–21, according to government statistics, there were approximately 168,960 episodes where domestic violence was cited as a factor for referral to social work. These figures clearly show that domestic abuse is a major factor in the lives of children who come to the attention of social workers. Ofsted (2017) says 'it is the most common factor in situations where children are at risk of most harm'. In addition, serious case reviews identify domestic abuse as a chief characteristic in families where children die or are subject to serious assault (Brandon, 2008; Stanley et al, 2018). Responding effectively to domestic abuse is clearly a priority to keep children safe, but historically children's knowledge about domestic abuse has largely been ignored in both practice and research and children have been portrayed as primarily passive and damaged.

Another observation about the literature on domestic abuse is that it fails to take account of children's social, economic and political environment (Etherington and Baker, 2018). There is a gap in both quantitative and qualitative research about how social injustices can affect children's experience of domestic abuse (Featherstone et al, 2018; Ferguson et al, 2020). While feminists have continuously linked domestic abuse to wider social determinants, this has not been the case for children (Featherstone et al, 2018, p 127). There is little exploration of how ethnicity, race, poverty, gender, and physical and/or mental disability can intersect and affect children's vulnerability to, and experience of, domestic abuse, even though children in this group are disproportionately represented in the social care system and in serious case reviews (Featherstone, 2016; Firmin et al, 2016; Harris, 2016; Bywaters et al, 2017b; Featherstone et al, 2017; Bernard and Harris, 2018; Firmin, 2018). Furthermore, the economic policies of austerity from 2010 to 2019 have decimated support systems and services for domestic abuse survivors, placing families under more stress and harm (Walby, 2015; Sanders-McDonagh et al, 2016; Bywaters et al, 2017a; Ferguson et al, 2020). Not only were families affected financially (Featherstone, 2016; Bassel and Emejulu, 2017; Hall, 2017, 2019), but the services they relied on were diminished (Sanders-McDonagh et al, 2016; Hall, 2019; Jupp et al, 2019), which placed them under further social work surveillance and risk (Bywaters et al, 2017a, 2017b; Featherstone et al, 2017; Gupta, 2017; Fahmy and Williamson, 2018; Grant et al, 2018; Ferguson et al, 2020).

Not only were services reduced during this period, but social work service review (Munro, 2011) and research (Munro, 2004; Parton, 2011; Peckover, 2014; Peckover and Golding, 2017; Featherstone et al, 2018) increasingly criticised social work practice for turning into a tick box exercise, with safeguarding decisions being made due to risk aversion rather than the needs of the family. The management style in social work has been heavily criticised for pushing a certain neoliberal ideology that individualises and psychologises safeguarding issues, without considering the socio-political context that influences the wellbeing and safety of children (Bunting et al, 2018), thus contributing to the ongoing harm of children (Featherstone, 2016; Bywaters et al, 2017a; Ferguson et al, 2020).

The combination of domestic abuse being recognised as a safeguarding issue, the reduction in funding and the management style in social work have had negative effects on families (Featherstone et al, 2018; Ferguson et al, 2019). The increase in awareness and responsibility for social workers to tackle domestic abuse was not matched by an increase in adequate resources for families. This has led to what feminist academics have argued – families being stigmatised and pathologised within the system, with mothers being penalised for not keeping their children safe despite their lack of resources and control over the perpetrator (Radford and Hester, 2006; Hughes et al, 2011; Callaghan, 2015; Stanley and Humphreys, 2017; Stanley et al, 2017). Mothers and children who were already racially marginalised in society were further financially marginalised, and despite limited resources were held more responsible for 'failing to protect' their children (Emejulu and Bassel, 2018, p 113). For example, mothers were criticised for not being able to parent their children safely because they did not speak English, but all English as a second language (ESOL) classes had been cut from the local services in the local area, so there were no places for them to learn English (Emejulu and Bassel, 2018, p 113). It is important to note that poverty is both gendered and racialised, with the majority of families below the poverty line being lone-parent, Black and minoritised families (Featherstone et al, 2018, p 13) and often placed under more surveillance for the risk they may face rather than getting the support for the injustices which put them at risk (Featherstone et al, 2018, p 14).

The figure of the child and epistemic justice

In this book, I illustrate how epistemic injustice and the mobilisation of different figures of the child, especially the passive/innocent child, are intrinsically linked to uphold patriarchal and colonial social norms. I demonstrate how the policing of children's contribution to knowledge creation is crucial to upholding inequality and does not keep the embodied child safe.

In terms of domestic abuse, the views of children are often missing from reviews or research (Mullender et al, 2002; Stanley, 2011; Callaghan et al, 2018; Øverlien and Holt, 2018, 2021; Stanley et al, 2018). Serious case reviews (investigations into the reasons why a child has died or been seriously abused or neglected) and research show that the voice of the child/young person is often misunderstood or ignored (Brandon, 2008; Sidebotham et al, 2016; Macdonald, 2017; Stanley et al, 2018; Morrison et al, 2020). However, there is growing awareness that children are capable of providing credible data from a young age (James and Prout, 2015; Holloway et al, 2018). At the same time, international conventions such as the United Nations Convention of the Rights of the Child 1989, particularly Article 12, and its enshrinement in the UK Children Act 1989 and 2004, now make it a legal requirement to involve children in issues that affect them. In the field of domestic abuse, there has been a growing understanding that children can provide valuable insight and knowledge about living with domestic abuse.

Although limited, the qualitative research conducted with children has moved the discussion to recognise that children are not passive witnesses to abuse but are knowing subjects and actively targeted by the perpetrator (Callaghan et al, 2015; Katz, 2015). In-depth qualitative interviews with children have highlighted the adverse impact on children but also how they are active agents in surviving their experience of domestic abuse (Mullender et al, 2002; Radford and Hester, 2006; Øverlien, 2011, 2013, 2017; Katz, 2014, 2015; Callaghan et al, 2015, 2016a; Fernández-González et al, 2018). These studies not only report the behaviour of children but also tell of the children's experience of domestic abuse and focus on their feelings about what happened in the home. These studies have highlighted how children actively resist domestic abuse and make use of their space and relationships to protect themselves from its adverse effects.

While there is a growing knowledge about children's experiences of domestic abuse, there is little knowledge about their childhoods and everyday lives.

Children in these circumstances are often seen through the narrow lens of having experienced abuse, with little attention paid to their dreams, desires and gaze upon the world. In other words, much of the research on children replicates ideas already prevalent within social work. Where children have been included in research, the primary focus has been on either their experience of domestic abuse or the evaluation of services. While these things are important, the children continue to be viewed through the narrow lens of abuse and trauma. There is little attention paid to other aspects of their personhood.

Observing this shortcoming of the research literature, I felt disorientated and began to search for answers as to why children were being excluded from research. In doing so, I had to look further afield than the social work literature on domestic abuse. I turned to the work of Erica Burman's (2018b) *Fanon, Education, Action: Child as Method*, as well as the work of Black, Indigenous and decolonial feminists bell hooks (1987, 1990, 2004, 2016a), Beth Richie (1996, 2012), Eve Tuck (2009, 2010, 2013), Linda Tuhiwai Smith (1999), Sylvia Wynter (2003) and Chandra Mohanty (1984, 2003), who inspired me to imagine a different research than the one I had initially planned. Burman's (2018b) *Fanon, Education, Action: Child as Method* (henceforth *Child as method*) provided me with the framework and courage to adopt a different approach, to imagine otherwise. In the next chapter, I use this framework to review the literature on the figure of the child and its impact on children who have been marginalised globally.

This book takes up the call to problematise the 'Global North' and 'Global South' binary often presented in childhood studies (Twum-Danso Imoh et al, 2019) – with the Global North being post-industrialised countries in Western Europe, North America and Australia, and the Global South being the other countries generally located in the southern hemisphere (Twum-Danso Imoh et al, 2019, p 2). By being attentive to the everyday lives of children who are marginalised in the UK, I draw links with children who are marginalised in the Global South, showing that childhoods in the Global North are not just ones of affluence but that children who are marginalised in the Global North and South share a commonality of being pathologised and viewed as 'lacking'. Twum-Danso Imoh et al (2019) criticise the current practice of researching affluent childhoods of the Global North to contribute to the theorisation of race, gender and class, while the research in the Global South focuses on marginalised children and 'saving' them. They argue that this means that some children are excluded from creating knowledge and there is no recognition of the different childhoods in both world areas. I argue that despite numerous calls by scholars for more research to be done with children who have experienced domestic abuse, there continues to be limited research with children beyond the lens of abuse and trauma. This follows the pattern of research with children in the Global South, where the focus can be on research *about* rather than *with* (Twum-Danso Imoh et al, 2019).

I explore how ignoring children in the creation of knowledge is a political act that upholds a patriarchal and colonial social order. I will argue that 'the child' is used as a political trope and that in order to move forward in the area of protecting children, we need to decolonise our thinking about the child and their participation in society. Drawing on Burman's (2018b) *Child as method* approach, I critique the different figures of the child that circulate in the discourse on protecting children and set out why it is important to not only listen to children's voices but to situate their embodied experience in their political, socio-economic environment. Chapter 2 argues that there is limited knowledge created with children about their views and their lived experience beyond abuse and trauma, an epistemic injustice that this research seeks to address through researching the everyday lives of children who have experienced domestic abuse and social work intervention.

Cultural theories of the everyday

The cultural theories of everyday life (henceforth, 'the everyday') offer a theoretical approach to explore the lives of children who have experienced domestic abuse and social work interventions. Such theories take us beyond the narrow lens of trauma and abuse, by allowing for a more nuanced look at how the wider society, the family and the child are intertwined, and allows the child's relational agency and materiality back into the analytical frame.

The study of the everyday is not new. Social theorist Henri Lefebrve (1974), who focused on workplaces, argued that the everyday is made up of repetitions, routine and regularity. Cultural theorist Michel de Certeau (1984, 1996) offered a different perspective, writing that although people had routines and rules, structures and tradition, by being attentive to the everyday you could see how individuals rebel and resist the overriding structures.

Meanwhile, feminist sociologists (Oakley, 1990, 2019; Federici, 2012) have called to be attentive to the everyday for it can highlight the unpaid and unappreciated work of women, highlighting how housework can be oppressive and gendered – linking the political and the personal. Black feminists (hooks, 1990, 2016a; Sharpe, 2016; Bassel and Emejulu, 2017; Williamson, 2017; Quashie, 2021) argued that in being attentive to the everyday, you can observe how Black and marginalised communities build community and support. hooks (1990, 2016c) argued that homemaking can be a form of resistance and love. Childhood scholars (Di Napoli Pastore, 2022; Twum-Danso Imoh et al, 2022) and researchers with marginalised communities (Al-Mohammad and Peluso, 2012; Zeitlyn, 2012) have also argued that it is in paying close attention to the everyday lives of communities that we can see how children and families are more than the challenges that they face. Twum-Danso Imoh et al (2022) argue that it is a way of seeing beyond the extreme of children's lives. While the everyday routines, rituals and homelives of children are scrutinised by social workers, there is limited research with children about their everyday lives.

Viewed from the perspective of theories of everyday life, the home takes on a meaningful guise beyond its materiality. The physical home is what social workers scrutinise in order to assess whether a child is safe (Ferguson, 2011, p 53), where abuse can happen, but the home is also where everyday routines, rituals and traditions take place. The threshold of the home can act as a barrier to the outside world. Social workers have to negotiate crossing this threshold to assess family life. As a researcher conducting my study during COVID-19 restrictions, I used the doorstops/thresholds to drop off art packs and communicate with children safely. The doorway can be a physical barrier that keeps family members within or outside the home, and social and economic policy and impact can influence what goes on behind closed doors. The under-occupancy penalty, more commonly known as the 'bedroom tax', for example, or housing policies more generally, can have an effect on how many rooms families are able to afford and what housing is deemed appropriate (Greenstein et al, 2016).

From this perspective, home is not only a physical space but also a relational one – it is where family life is practised (hooks, 1990, 2009; Massey, 2004a, 2005; Hall, 2019). Alexander et al (2015) write how relationships in the home can make it feel risky or safe. For example, in the case of domestic abuse, children can feel like they are walking on eggshells when the perpetrator is in the home, or feel safe when they have their friends round. Who is in the home can change the dynamic and space. Routines and practices can create safety and comfort. The everyday ritual of food preparation, play and celebrations can foster a sense of belonging and meaning (Highmore, 2010). Routines can also mark the ebb and flow of the day, like eating breakfast, washing, eating and sleeping, giving an insight to the temporal flow of everyday life (Highmore, 2004, p 304).

Home can be a sensory place that entails the physical, relational and embodied aspect of home (Pink, 2004, 2015). Objects can hold memories of different times, people and places (Miller, 2008). A soft toy can comfort a child, as it reminds them of the grandmother who gave it to them (Callaghan et al, 2016a, p 16) or a flag that symbolises belonging (Luttrell, 2020, p 63).

Key to the everyday life of children is play. Play allows children to express themselves, build relationships, and create knowledge and meaning in the everyday (Di Napoli Pastore, 2022). Play is not only entangled with relationships but with material, sensorial, social and political contexts. Being attentive to play is a way of centring children's knowledge and the meaning making of children which disrupts the tropes of the passive and damaged child present in the literature on domestic abuse.

Important to this book is hooks's (1990, p 42) argument that the everyday of homemaking is a place where Black and marginalised children can return home to feel nurtured, loved and humanised. Black feminists have long argued that the home is the everyday place where Black and marginalised groups resist and rebel against the dominant patriarchal, racist and imperialist social order (hooks, 1990, 2016c; Emejulu and Bassel, 2018) and is a place where love and care can flourish (hooks, 1990, 2009, 2016c). In the childhood studies literature, it is also often demonstrated that children are very much aware of the care that their mothers show and can themselves too be homemakers (Cheney, 2017; Vizard et al, 2019; Luttrell, 2020).

While the home has been presented as a place of risk and fear in the literature on domestic abuse, there is limited research as to how children build a home away from the perpetrator. How and what do they do to create a home? In being attentive to the everyday lives of children, we can highlight both children's agency and the constrictions under which they live. We can see beyond the extremes of challenges that they face and go beyond the tropes of childhood and see them in their humanness.

The reluctant ethnographer

The study of the everyday calls for a methodology that is attentive to the small and large moments of life, the rhythms, flows and structure to create knowledge of how children make meaning of their lives. Scholars have argued that it is in paying close attention to the everyday that we can go beyond the narrow lens of oppression and trauma and see how marginalised communities resist and make life liveable (hooks, 1990; Al-Mohammad and Peluso, 2012; hooks, 2016c; Di Napoli Pastore, 2022; Twum-Danso Imoh et al, 2022). For my project, not only was it important that the methodology was able to be attentive to everyday life, but it also had to be able to be 'attentive' to the way children communicate and express themselves to create knowledge about their everyday lives (Clark, 2011; Twum-Danso Imoh and Okyere, 2020; Nolas and Varvantakis, 2021). A major unexpected factor was that the methodology and methods had to navigate the physical restrictions of COVID-19. In the following paragraphs I outline how I was drawn to multimodal ethnography and how I conducted research during COVID-19 restrictions. I give a brief overview of my methods and reflect on navigating my positionality, ethics and challenges.

I was a reluctant ethnographer, but after analysing and reflecting on the research literature, I knew that an ethnographic study would enable me to be attentive to the minutiae of the everyday lives of children. I realised that ethnography would be the most suitable methodology to answer my questions of how children make meaning of their everyday lives and would allow the research to go beyond the narrow confines of the domestic abuse and trauma lens. Studying the cultural theories of the everyday through ethnography can allow for social structures and systems that affect subjectivity to be seen (Scott, 2009; Highmore, 2010; Back, 2015; Hall, 2019) as well as to understand how people resist and are creative within their social and economic constraints (Emejulu and Bassel, 2018; Di Napoli Pastore, 2022; Twum-Danso Imoh et al, 2022). I wanted to pay attention to the complex stories of the children's lives, and how they are interconnected with the material, social, structural and human and non-human aspects of life, and the longitudinal aspect of ethnography would help facilitate that.

However, ethnography alone does not make the research project 'accessible' to children. To do so, I took inspiration from the Connector's Study (Nolas et al, 2017, 2018; Varvantakis and Nolas, 2019; Varvantakis et al, 2019), a three-year multimodal ethnography that looked at the relations between childhood and public life in three cities (Athens, Hyderabad and London), and developed my methodology to create an ethnographic approach for working with the children.

The attraction of multimodal ethnography is that it works across different mediums and modes – visual, sensorial, text, sonic, digital, in-person – and allows children the flexibility to choose the medium and mode in which they prefer to express themselves (Clark, 2011; Dicks, 2014; Nolas et al, 2018; Varvantakis and Nolas, 2019). Multimodality lends itself to working with children, especially young children, as it is not dependent solely on verbal expression but is attentive to the signs that are made though different modes like movement, gestures, dance, songs, jokes, objects, gaze, facial expression and speech (Nolas et al, 2018; Varvantakis and Nolas, 2019). In my study, play and photography were the main modalities in which children documented and communicated about their everyday lives. They were invited to use any (or none) of the contents in the art pack to illustrate what was important to them. With consent from the children and their mothers, we decided to meet via a WhatsApp video call once a week to keep in contact. During these video calls, children would chat, play, sing, joke, watch television – documenting to me their everyday lives, rhythms and routines. As COVID-19 physical restrictions eased, I would spend time outdoors in playgrounds, parks and at children's homes to find out more about their everyday lives. This would involve walking, playing, joking, talking, dancing, drawing, art and craft and photography (see the Appendix). I visited each child once a week, either in person or online, for 18 months. Together, the children and I created knowledge about the cultural theories of their everyday lives.

Recruitment for the project was done through a local London borough in which I had previously worked. Social workers, teachers and other professionals were able to refer families who had experienced domestic abuse to the project. Consent was first sought from the parent and then the child. There were ten children and seven mothers who participated in the project.

All ten children lived only with their siblings and their mothers. All lived in social housing and were from a lower socio-economic background. All the children had either one or both parents who were born in a country that was colonised by Britain or another European country.

Multimodal ethnography in itself does not address epistemic injustice; also required are reflexivity and an ethics of care (Lomax, 2012, 2015). My many social roles, as a mother, as a therapist, as a researcher, as someone who grew up in social housing and as a former social care staff member, all came into play during the research project. At times it felt that the different roles clashed, and I was also deeply aware of the power imbalance that the roles gave me in relation to the children and their families. The families were already experiencing social work interventions – did they think participating in the research affected this positively or negatively? Did they feel they had to participate in the project? During the research, it was the relationships that I built up with the children and their families which helped to navigate and steer the project. With opportunities also came vulnerabilities: at times I struggled to navigate safeguarding issues, particularly where I felt that the families were not receiving the service that they were entitled to – this is written about in Chapter 3. In these situations I tried to practise a feminist ethics of care, going beyond what is merely safe to what will make the family flourish (Tronto, 1993; Lomax, 2015; Puig de la Bellacasa, 2017). At times I also had to challenge my own thinking; a key example was my attitude towards play. Initially, I had tried to use the methods that I thought children would find interesting, but as the research project progressed, I acknowledged that play was important for its own sake for the enjoyment the children experienced, and that it did not need to be made to be 'productive' – it was important in and of itself.

I hope I have not flattened the children in this book. Motivated by the lack of research with children beyond their experience of abuse, I did not want to replicate ideas already prevalent within social work. I found solace and encouragement in Thomas Stodulka's (2017) ethnography *Coming of Age on the Streets of Java*. Stodulka wrestles with trying to carry out research with children that goes beyond the oversimplification of the label 'street children' used by the mass media and the project-orientated agendas of non-governmental organisations (NGOs). What he finds early on is that this same oversimplification affects and is replicated in social and cultural science research (Stodulka, 2017, p 19). Stodulka (2017, p 19) notes that: 'The pressure to publish with all speed and the difficulties to conduct research with street related persons and communities beyond the brokerage and the open houses of NGOs can result in methodological rapid assessments that create analyses that are strikingly similar to media and NGO-discourses.' I too wanted to go past the rapid assessment of children in social work and therapy. I wanted to research their everyday lives to explore who they were, what their everyday lives were like beyond the frame afforded by the gaze of the social worker and what their dreams, worries, frustrations and joys were. In order to do that, I needed to spend time with the children and their families and hence my turn to multimodal ethnography. While there have been numerous ethnographic studies with social work professionals (Ferguson, 2016b; Ferguson et al, 2020; Jeyasingham, 2020; Leigh et al, 2020), to my knowledge there have been no ethnographic studies with children who have experienced domestic abuse and social work intervention in the UK. I wanted to present a 'rolling film' of their lives rather than a limited 'snapshot' (Ferguson et al, 2020), and it was 'hanging out' with children over time that, I reasoned, would allow me to get a more dynamic sense of their lives, loves, hopes and dreams. Ultimately, I wanted to shift the gaze on to the children.

Shifting the gaze

'Brenda! Look!' was a phrase that I often heard throughout the 18-month ethnography, whether it was my online meeting with the children or a face-to-face visit. The children wanted to show me things and to be seen. For children who have been marginalised or have experienced abuse, it is the professional's gaze, the social worker's gaze, the psychologist's gaze, that is given attention, and little attention is paid to their gaze beyond what abuse and violence they have seen, and even then their knowledge has not always been valued (see Chapter 2). In this section I explain the methodological need to shift the gaze to focus on the child's gaze.

The gaze that has been dominant is the adult's gaze that looks upon children through a deficit model lens (see Chapter 2). In many respects it has been a colonial gaze that has been cast on the children – the eye of one who wants to control, not always one of love and curiosity, and not a gaze that champions epistemic justice, which I explore further in Chapter 2. There is much connection between how colonisers frame and framed Indigenous communities and the way in which children who are marginalised have been framed (Cannella, 2004; Liebel, 2020).

Black feminists and decolonial and Indigenous scholars (Tuck, 2009; Campt, 2012, 2017; Smith, 2012; hooks, 2015; Hartman, 2021) have long argued how the gaze, or the look, can be imbued with power. Who gets to look, and whose gaze counts? In *Wayward Lives, Beautiful Experiments* (2021) Saidiyah Hartman writes of the gaze of authorities that tries to punish and police the lives of Black and poor communities. She explains that the photographs taken by the welfare services coerced the Black poor families into the line of visibility and thus surveillance by the authorities, reminiscent of the days of slavery and the plantations, that to be made 'visible was to be targeted for uplift or punishment, confinement or violence' (Hartman, 2021, p 21).

Hartman (2021, p 19) writes that she is tired of looking at the 'white sheets draped on the clothes line' that are present in the photographs in the welfare reports. Instead Hartman (2021, p 19) searches for the stories of 'the riotous Black girls, and troublesome women and queer radicals' that have escaped the social work gaze in the archives. In this book, I am very much interested in the children who *are* caught in the social work gaze. I am interested in what they put on their washing lines, what they say when they talk back to the social work gaze – to the official statutory documentation of their lives, the archiving of their lives. In her book *In the Wake*, Christina Sharpe (2016, p 119) powerfully reorientates our gaze by redacting the photographs of two Black girls, Delia and Drana, so that we only see their eyes. Sharpe is not interested in the photographer's gaze but wants to follow the girls' gazes. What are Delia and Drana looking at? What interests them? Likewise, I want to know what interests the children in my research. I want to follow their gaze.

To decolonise the gaze does not only mean giving a camera to a child, although that is important, but also includes engaging with the child and challenging our preconceived thoughts. It is not about mastery but of '*looking with, through, and alongside another*' (Campt, 2023, p 8, emphasis in the original). Campt (2023, p 172) writes how she does not see the Black gaze as describing the viewpoint of Black people/artists, but it is a 'viewing practice' of reckoning with the precarity of Black life, and a gaze that transforms precarity into 'creative forms of affirmation'. Likewise, I ask you, the reader, to engage with the lives of the children and see how they create a liveable life despite the hardship and injustices they experience. This engagement calls for the use of all our senses, not only our sight. In line with Campt (2017, 2023), I call for readers to not only look at the pictures but to listen, to imagine, to feel – to involve body, spirit and mind.

Building on Campt's work, I go beyond photographs, videos and installations, to walk, play, talk, sing and dance with the children, and together the children and I create knowledge about their everyday lives. I practise what Wendy Luttrell (2020, p 225) calls 'collaborative seeing'. This is where attention is paid to what participants have to say about their pictures or their art. Luttrell highlights the importance of this when she tells the story of Terrance, who had a photo of him in a shop buying sweets. When Luttrell (2020, p 225) showed his photographs to teachers as part of their training, they interpreted the photo from the position of 'a kid in a candy store' to something more foreboding like stealing in a shop. For Terrance, the picture represented his caring duties of helping his younger cousins with their homework, as sometimes he would stop at the shop on his way home to buy his cousins some sweets to encourage them to finish their homework (Luttrell, 2020, p 226). If Luttrell had not paid attention to Terrance's story of the picture, she would not have been able to explore his caregiving with him.

Introduction

This highlights the importance of co-reading as a form of epistemic justice (Fricker, 2009; Smith, 2012), because if we were to only hear from the teachers in Luttrell's group, we would have had a different interpretation of the photo and no real understanding of the story of Terrance.

Thus, I have tried not to flatten out the children through my writing but have tried to allow them to dance, play and jump off the page (McCarthy, 2021a, p 1). I have worried that in trying to be reflexive in my writing, I would appear to be constantly jumping in front of the children (Bell, 2014, p 148) – I hope that this is not the case. Ethnographic writing has long been criticised for presenting the coloniser's view as the *truth* (Pandian, 2019, p 22), but I hope that is also not the case in this project. I have tried to practise epistemic humility (Parviainen et al, 2021), and where possible tried to go back to the children and double-check my interpretations and understanding.

It is in the writing that I have started to make sense of the data I created with the children (Page, 2017; Jusionyte, 2020). Following in the practice of Geertz (1972), I have used thick description to help analyse the data. Thick description involves writing detailed descriptions or vignettes of situations and encounters that not only describe but also interpret the meaning of these encounters (Jusionyte, 2020). For this research project, I started with an interaction that I had with a participant and wrote about it. This then prompted me to reflect back on the occasion and continue to write to draw out the meaning of these encounters. Discussion of my work in supervision meetings and in reading groups with peers expanded and challenged my original analysis too. Strathern (1999, p 6) calls these 'ethnographic moments' an example of the 'relation which joins the understood' (that which has been understood in the field) to the 'need to understand (that which is observed at the moment of analysis)'. The two locations interacted throughout the research project.

It is through trying to capture what is seen, heard, smelt and felt through different modes such as text and visual and audio recordings that I have tried to realise the multidimensional side of the children's lives (Pink, 2011, 2013, 2015; Pink et al, 2016). For it is the conversation between these different media – body, text, material, sense, culture – that underpins multimodal ethnography. It is the connection made that allows for a more contextual sensing of participants' lives (Miller, 2005), which involves a playful and embodied approach to methods. I have often tried to use my body as a way of knowing, as Holmes (2022, pp 117–18) writes that the body is 'not just a site where consumption is displayed and identities represented, but also a material means through which everyday personal life is produced, experienced and negotiated'. Being aware of bodies was important in the research, as often there were limitations on how close our bodies could be due to COVID-19 restrictions – in this sense it was both symbolic as well as material.

So when Kyro calls out 'Benda, you are not really looking', he is right. I am not really looking. I am distracted; I may glance up and see him, but

I am not really looking. I am not engaging with what he is doing and trying to do. Throughout this book there are other examples of where the adults fail to 'really look' and see the children. Where the adults have not been able to shift their own gaze from trauma and abuse and 'really look' at the embodied child before them. But the children 'return the gaze', as Himani Bannerji (1993) writes, for they offer analysis of the injustice that they experience and explore how they make sense of their world. In many ways, the children are returning the gaze of the professionals, and talking back to the violence of their social work reports and what is being archived about them in their social work reports.

I appreciate that this book may be a difficult read for practitioners, especially in the area of social work and psychology, who come to their work wanting the best for children. But I ask, as a practitioner myself, that we need to reflect on and interrogate the colonial and patriarchal roots of the figure of the child that dominate much of our practice and disciplines in order to imagine a more holistic way of working with children.

Summary of the book

The summary of the book is as follows: Chapter 2 explores how the figure of the child is used to uphold a patriarchal, imperialist and colonialist social order using Erica Burman's *Child as method* as an analytical tool. The chapter concludes that the epistemic injustice of not creating knowledge with children should be addressed through being attentive to the everyday lives of children. Chapter 3 is an ethnographic account of my relationship with one of the children in the study, a seven-year-old boy, Mystical, and his mother, Nicole, and their experiences of social work interventions in their lives. It is emblematic of some of the families' everyday lives within the CP system. Chapter 4 is attentive to the importance of joy and fun in the everyday lives of children, and how children searched for fun. I reflect on how the children and their mothers prioritised play and the importance of pleasure in making meaning and creating knowledge in everyday. Chapter 5 focuses on beauty and aesthetics in the everyday lives of children. I am attentive to how children found beauty in the everyday and how the aesthetics in the home fostered a space for celebration and care. The children's focus on aesthetics through their photography opened up a space for a creation of knowledge that was not limited to abuse and enabled them to be seen in their humanness, beyond the frame of the damaged child. Chapter 6 discusses how love is important in the everyday. It explores how children and their families created a sense of belonging, nurture and care in their everyday, and how love was an important aspect of their sense of wellbeing. The children did not only see themselves as recipients of care and love but as givers of love and care too, disrupting the narrative of passivity. I draw heavily on the work of bell hooks (2016a, 2016b, 2016c) to analyse relations, practices of homemaking and care. Chapter 7 is the concluding chapter of the book where I reflect on what knowledge was created and the research process, and consider what this could contribute to future research and practice.

One last note before I begin

The approach I ultimately adopted in this book was sparked by an unexpected personal encounter with my own childhood, and being confronted with an outsider's (mis)interpretation of the home I grew up in. I have written about this before (Herbert, 2025), but I think it is important to do so again. It was before the start of the school term in 2015 and I had taken my two children to the Science Museum. As we were leaving, we came across an art exhibition by Shelter (a charity working to combat homelessness in the UK). Always enthusiastic about photography, we entered the exhibition. There was no one there. I remember clearly my children running ahead, as I slowly started to view the photographs. As I approached the second photograph, my heart started to beat very fast, sour bile rose up through my throat, I felt dizzy and I started to sweat. I blinked and looked again. Yes, there it was before me, a picture of my childhood home with the slogan 'Slums of Britain' above it. I called my children and we left immediately. I was shocked; I felt violently robbed of my story and could not view the exhibition any further. Yes, we lived with poverty and racism, but there was more to our lives than that. There was nothing to indicate the care we showed each other, the food, the street parties, the neighbour who let us use their landline, the man who would chase away children who were harassing me on my way home from school, our excitement at watching trains go by from the rooftops of the buildings. We experienced an array of feelings – love, joy, boredom, sadness, excitement, anxiety, hope and fear, among many others things – not only despair. In trying to raise awareness about homelessness, Shelter and Nick Hedge had painted my childhood home as derelict and hopeless, and my family and neighbours as passive subjects. Too often we can render people passive in their own lives in the name of addressing injustice. It was this misrepresentation of my childhood home that guided my research approach to create knowledge with children, so that, I hope, they will not feel robbed of their story and find themselves unrecognisable as passive victims in the research about their lives.

2

Over-researched and under-represented: decolonising the figure of the child

There are lots of people in the room. Many trying to juggle holding a small plate of food and a glass. I am at an after-talk reception. There are lots of students and researchers milling around. I don't know anyone but have managed, despite my shyness, to talk to a couple of people. The chair of the talk is very good at including everyone and works her way around the room and seems to be able to have a little conversation with everyone. After a little while, she joins my tiny group of two and after polite introductions and reflections on the talk, she gently asks me, 'so what is your research about?'

'It is with children who have experienced domestic abuse,' I reply. In some ways, I know what to expect next, because it has happened many time before. The host tilts her head sideways and in a soft voice says, 'Oh gosh, that must be very depressing!'

I want to say, 'No, the children make me laugh and think, but you are right, it is the way society and the system treats them that is enraging and sad.' But I hold that thought, as the host quickly turns away and asks my companion what he is working on.

(Field notes, November 2022)

I write this vignette because it symbolises much of how children who have experienced domestic abuse are portrayed and what emotions it evokes in people. When facilitating training with professionals, I used what I call 'the gingerbread person' exercise to enable participants to reflect on their perception of children who have experienced domestic abuse. I draw two large gingerbread figures on flipchart paper. On the first paper, I ask them to write down all the words they associate with children who have experienced domestic abuse. I then ask them to do the same on the other gingerbread figure but this time for words they associate with children in general. Often these two lists of words are very different, with words like 'sad', 'depressed', 'angry', 'lost childhood' for the gingerbread figure that represents the child who has experienced domestic abuse. On the other gingerbread figure, the participants would often write 'funny', 'joyful', 'playful', 'carefree', 'laughter'. The exercise is crudely binary, but it enables the participants to reflect on how easily they stereotype children who have experienced domestic abuse, as well as identify their idealised image of childhood – a place where there is little of life's challenges or distress. On deeper reflection, the participants often start to wonder why the child who has experienced abuse would often only be seen through the lens of trauma, and yet the children they worked with were always more than that. The purpose of the exercise was to reorientate the professional's gaze away from only seeing children who have experienced domestic abuse through the lens of trauma and abuse, and to see the other aspects of their personhood.

When I started my literature review for my PhD thesis, I became lost, for I could not find or see the children in the research studies. Much of the research had been done from a psycho-medical model stating how children were affected by domestic abuse, or through the lens of adults – professionals or parents/carers. Any research done with children was predominantly interviews about their experience of domestic abuse or evaluation of services. There was little about their personhood beyond abuse. In essence, the children themselves were missing from their own research about their lives. While much has been written about children and the harm of domestic abuse (Devaney, 2008; Stanley, 2011; Stanley et al, 2017; Fernández-González et al, 2018), little is known about the personhood of the children themselves. Qualitative research has illustrated how children are not passive recipients of harm but at times resist and are knowledgeable of the patterns and severity of abuse (Alexander et al, 2015; Katz, 2015, 2016; Callaghan et al, 2017a). Yet, despite Mcgee (2000) and Stanley (2011) calling for more research with children, there is still limited research done with children who have experienced domestic abuse. While it is important to research the negative effects of domestic abuse and how best to support children, to only focus on the abuse dehumanises and pathologises children because nothing is known about their personhood beyond the remit of domestic abuse and trauma. The image of the passive and/or damaged child is not isolated to children who have experienced domestic abuse, but it is one that is applied to other children who are marginalised in society globally, as I argue later.

In this chapter I draw on Burman's (2018b) *Child as method* approach to analyse the social work literature on domestic abuse and children. Using this, I identify three tropes of childhood – the passive child, the early years child and the fugitive child – and discuss how they are mobilised to uphold patriarchal and colonialist social orders. I argue that 'the child' is used as a political trope and that, in order to move forward in the area of domestic abuse, we need to decolonise our thinking about the child and their participation in society. In addition, I use *Child as method* to interrogate the tropes of the child soldier and the traumatised child to illustrate the commonality in how marginalised children in the Global South are dehumanised and pathologised, and how support programmes for them often depoliticise the issues affecting children's lives. I argue that the binary of the Global North/Global South childhoods must be dismantled to take into account the complexities and pluralities of children's lives. I explore how children's views are not only ignored but that the idea of protecting children is not apolitical. I draw parallels between how research in both world areas can pathologise and dehumanise children who are marginalised in society, and show how researching with children can create knowledge about the wider impact of inequalities on their lives. I draw on Black feminist and decolonial scholars' work to argue for researching with children and being attentive to the everyday. The chapter will argue how being attentive to the mundanity of the everyday lives of children can enable them to create knowledge about their lives that is beyond the narrow remit of the patriarchal and colonial portrayal of the child and childhood.

Child as method

The question of why and how narratives of damage and passivity dominate the literature, when there is little known about the children themselves, preoccupied my thoughts. While there has been much critique of social work practice in cases of domestic abuse (Featherstone et al, 2018; Ferguson et al, 2020), I was left confused because the literature seemed to be repeating the pattern of social workers' responses to domestic abuse – being event-focused and ignoring children's knowledge and lived experiences (Stanley et al, 2011). Since I was left disorientated by the social work literature on domestic abuse and children, I had to turn to literature outside of the field of social work to make sense of it.

A pivotal moment in my research was reading Burman's (2018b) *Fanon, Education, Action: Child as Method*. Burman's analytical approach has its roots in the text from poststructuralist and postcolonialist studies *Asia as Method* (Chen, 2010) and *Border as Method* (Mezzadra and Neilson, 2013). *Child as method* is not a research method per se but an analytical approach that draws on the ideas of revolutionary psychiatrist and decolonial theorist Frantz Fanon and brings together diverse disciplinary and research approaches to understand how child/childhood/children are understood. Here, 'child' is figured as a trope (Castañeda, 2002; Burman, 2018b, p 22), 'childhood' as a social condition or category, and 'children' as the living embodied entities occupying these positions and practices (Burman, 2018b, p 23). Burman's approach offers a framework to reorientate the focus away from the traditional sources of power and knowledge (in this case, adults) to attend to the local (in this research, the child). Using *Child as method*, I interrogate the social work literature around children and domestic abuse to show how the child/childhood/children are utilised to uphold certain ideologies and power relations.

Frantz Fanon, who Burman (2018b) draws on, was born in Martinique on 20 July 1925 and studied medicine in France. He travelled and worked in hospitals in Algeria and Tunisia, where he wrote and reflected on his life as a Black man and the impact of colonisation. He wrote the classics *Black Skin, White Mask* (2017 [1952]), *A Dying Colonialism* (2007 [1959]), *The Wretched of the Earth* (2001 [1961]) and *Toward the African Revolution* (1988 [1964]). Burman (2018b) draws four tropes of childhood from Fanon's writing – the idiotic child, the traumatogenic child, the therapeutic child and the extemic child – and explores how these are used to uphold and reinforce colonial and imperialist social order. Burman has also used a *Child as method* approach to analyse the discourse on Brexit (Burman, 2018a) and post-socialist childhood memories (Burman and Millei, 2022). A *Child as method* approach has also been used to analyse an educational setting (Pierlejewski, 2020, 2021), a legal gender setting (Cassel, 2024) and a migration setting (Christinaki, 2025). In the next section, I use Burman's (2018b) *Child as method* analytical framework on the literature on domestic abuse and children, arguing that there are three dominant images of children that are mobilised: the passive/innocent child, the early years child and the fugitive child. Using this approach, I interrogate the prevalence of the three childhood tropes that are often used to symbolise children who have experienced domestic abuse. I explore the political beliefs and assumptions that they are based on and how they are mobilised to uphold certain ideologies and power relations.

The passive child

One prominent position that children hold in the literature on domestic abuse is that of the passive child. It underpins several social work practices, as well as socio-legal, cultural and media systems, having huge impacts on how children are perceived and meaning that their participation in society is unwelcomed (Burman, 2018b, p 39). It operates on the colonial and paternal idea that children are empty vessels, and knowledge flows from the 'knowing' adult to the child, something Freire (2000 [1968]) describes as a 'banking model of education'. This paternalistic attitude allows adults to keep a privileged position, as I will discuss later in this section. In the literature on domestic abuse, it is the passive child that is most present. The child is seen as a passive witness to domestic abuse and is damaged by it and yet, as noted in the previous chapter, has only recently been acknowledged as a victim of domestic abuse in the law. Their abuse is not documented; for example, there is limited data on the frequency and severity of domestic abuse towards children, of their relation to the perpetrator and of the monitoring of coercive abuse towards children (Howarth et al, 2015; Katz,

2016; Latzman et al, 2017). There is still a level of unknowing about what they actually experience, as most research is undertaken by speaking to adults (usually mothers and professionals) (Cater and Øverlien, 2014; Callaghan et al, 2017a). While research and analysis of domestic abuse of women have become more sophisticated (see the work of Walby et al, 2016; Walby and Towers, 2017; Myhill and Kelly, 2019), there is less documentation and analysis about children's experience of domestic abuse (Cater and Øverlien, 2014; Haselschwerdt, 2014; Callaghan et al, 2015; Haselschwerdt et al, 2016; Katz, 2016). This lack of analysis is a symptom of the fact that children's lived experiences of domestic abuse are not generally explored.

Yet children do experience domestic abuse and are not passive witnesses (Cater and Øverlien, 2014; Alexander et al, 2015; Callaghan et al, 2015; Katz, 2015; Callaghan et al, 2016a; Øverlien, 2017; Øverlien and Holt, 2021). Holden's (2003, p 152) taxonomy of exposure to domestic abuse lists some things that children experience. They include: children intervening verbally or physically to stop their mothers getting assaulted; children themselves being threatened or physically assaulted; children being forced to join in an assault on their mothers; children hearing and/or seeing a physical assault on their mothers; children seeing the initial effects of an assault, for example, bruises; children experiencing the aftermath of any assault, such as the depression of their mothers; and children hearing the retelling of an assault either from their mothers or through overhearing adult conversations. Children experience coercive control by perpetrators, even after they no longer live with them (Callaghan et al, 2015; Katz, 2015, 2016). When children have been asked about their experiences, they are able to be articulate about the severity, type and frequency of the abuse (Mullender et al, 2002; Øverlien, 2010, 2017; Stanley, 2011; Callaghan et al, 2015; Katz, 2015; Callaghan et al, 2016a). At times, this has been more accurate at predicting risks of an escalation of violence than their mothers' accounts (Haselschwerdt, 2014). In this sense, children are not passive witnesses of domestic abuse but knowing subjects.

Quantitative studies of domestic abuse and children have been criticised because the data generated focuses on the challenging behaviour and impact of domestic abuse and not on the children's lived experience of domestic abuse. This means that issues such as how children negotiate their space and shape their subjectivity and identity are not explored. The studies have become increasingly criticised over the last ten years for portraying children as passive recipients of the ill-effects of witnessing domestic abuse (Øverlien, 2011; Katz, 2014, 2015; Alexander et al, 2015; Callaghan et al, 2015). A major criticism has been that children do not merely 'witness' domestic abuse but are actively defending, negotiating and creating their space within their experience of it (Callaghan et al, 2015; Fernández-González et al, 2018). This growing discourse criticised the previous quantitative research for not acknowledging children's agency and for pathologising children who had experienced domestic abuse. The proponents of this view argue that while the quantitative studies give some knowledge of the impact of domestic abuse, they do not give the context in which the children experience it, and give little or no further advancement in understanding the protective factors, resilience and relationships that the children adopt (Katz, 2014, 2015; Callaghan et al, 2015, 2016a; Fernández-González et al, 2018). The data generated also focused more on what the adults thought about the impact on children rather than what the children themselves thought of the experience (Øverlien, 2011, 2013; Alexander et al, 2015; Callaghan et al, 2015).

In contrast, in-depth qualitative interviews with children have highlighted the adverse impact of domestic abuse on children but have also revealed that children are active agents in surviving their experience of it (Mullender et al, 2002; Radford and Hester, 2006; Øverlien, 2011, 2013; Katz, 2014, 2015; Callaghan et al, 2015, 2016a; Øverlien, 2017; Fernández-González et al, 2018). They not only report the children's experience of domestic abuse and their behaviour but also focus on their feelings about what happened in the home. These studies have highlighted how children actively resist domestic abuse and make use of their space and relationship to protect themselves from its adverse effects.

Despite the persistent call from researchers (Mullender et al, 2002; Stanley, 2011) and children (Crowley, 2015; Houghton, 2015; Holt, 2017; Macdonald, 2017) for professionals to listen to children, there are still gaps in research and practice. As highlighted earlier, children's voices are still missing in domestic homicide reviews, despite the fact that they had lived with the abuse and may have been present at the murder (Stanley et al, 2018). Another example is that in court cases regarding contact post-separation, if children say they do not want to see their fathers, the focus will be on changing their minds rather than changing the fathers' behaviour (Macdonald, 2017). The reasons why children are continually ignored will be further explored later in this chapter.

Decisions are taken and research is done mostly without the children, as children are seen as having no agency or subjectivity of their own, and not being capable of contributing to knowledge about themselves. Here, again, we can see how children are seen as fragile and passive. Social work practice has long been criticised for not hearing the voice of the child: Mullender (2002) noted that children's voices were not being heard, and several years later Stanley (2011) reported the same. More recently, Lefevre et al (2017) have shown the importance of building trust with young people to support communication, and researched the best practice for listening to children (Lefevre et al, 2008; Lefevre, 2018). Today, the issues still remain, as children's voices are not being heard in serious case reviews (SCRs) regarding a parent's domestic homicide (Stanley et al, 2018). Yet, children have consistently said that they want to have their say about their care and the care of their families (Holt, 2017; Lamb et al, 2018).

It is a paradox that children who have experienced abuse are deemed too fragile to talk about it for fear of being traumatised (Stanley et al, 2018). In some cases, the children have already experienced one of the worst aspects of domestic abuse, that of parental homicide, and often want their thoughts to be taken seriously (Stanley et al, 2018). Parents too can act as very cautious gatekeepers to children, not wanting them to participate in research or being reluctant to ask them about their experience of domestic abuse (Cater and Øverlien, 2014). Here, it can be argued that in not listening and/or working with children, researchers are mired in ethical hypochondria and timidity (Back, 2012, p 27), instead of being critically attentive to how we, as researchers, can be complicit with power and reproducing the social order.

The passive child is also seen as innocent. The image of the innocent child, or what Anne Higonnet (1998, p 23) calls the romantic child, is prevalent in the Global North. However, children have not always been seen as innocent. Historians suggest that up until the 17th century, children were considered to be mini-adults who needed correction and discipline, especially those born into the Christian faith where they were seen as being born into/with sin (Higonnet, 1998, p 8). With the Enlightenment, pictures of children came to symbolise and consolidate the new cultural ideal of child and childhood – that of innocence. The child was deemed to be innocent of adult wants and desires, and their minds were supposed to be blank (Higonnet, 1998, p 8). There was a 'Romantic insistence on innocence, a need to define children in terms of what adults were not: not sexual, not vicious, not ugly, not conscious, not damaged' (Higonnet, 1998, p 224). Children were to be depicted as 'naturally' innocent.

Childhood study theorists and feminist scholars have long warned that this innocent image or positioning of children is a double-edged sword, as often protection of children is reliant on them being seen as innocent and any form of knowledge or sign of agency is seen as deviant and leaves them open to blame for the abuse inflicted upon them (Bernstein, 2011; James, 2014; O'Dell et al, 2017; Garlen, 2019). This can be seen, in particular, in cases of sexual exploitation and abuse, where girls' agency was taken for consent (Woodiwiss, 2014, 2018). Woodiwiss (2014) argues that social workers and professionals need to divorce agency from blame – just because someone has agency and may make decisions that put them at risk of abuse does not make them responsible for the abuse. Separating blame and agency has proven difficult for social workers, especially in the case of sexual exploitation (Woodiwiss, 2014, 2018).

The inability to separate blame and agency can also mean that work with children can become authoritarian in its inadvertent desire to return them to a place of 'innocence'. In her study of the 'rehabilitation' of children who have offended, Ellis (2018) shows that the professionals had trouble recognising and valuing the girls' agency and aimed to return the girls to a place of childhood 'innocence'. But this idea of 'innocence' was neither one that the girls had experienced nor wanted. Ellis (2018) found that professionals did not understand the fact that the girls' vulnerability was not because of their agency but was a result of the social and economic inequality that placed them at risk of further exploitation. The girls' strategies to survive were interpreted as 'putting themselves at risk' by the professionals (Ellis, 2018, p 162). Instead, Ellis (2018) argues that what the girls needed was not to be returned to a place of 'innocence' to keep them safe but to gain an awareness of how their socio-economic inequality brought with it risk of further exploitation. The girls were adopting tactics to survive in a hostile and exploitative environment.

Callaghan et al (2017a) also note how professionals reacted angrily towards the suggestion that children who had experienced domestic abuse had agency, for they associated blame with agency too. Here we can see how caring professionals have invested in the political trope of the innocent child, how it governs their practice and how difficult they find it to balance agency and vulnerability. The child must remain passive and unknowing in order to be protected.

The early years child

The early years child is mobilised politically and is a powerful symbol in the world of social work and domestic abuse. It is one which people across the political spectrum cling to, from social workers working with domestic abuse to government officials. It is the symbol of the damaged child that needs to be fixed – a cornerstone of early years policies and therapeutic care (Featherstone et al, 2014; Meiners, 2016; Burman, 2018b). This infant determinism is strongly represented in the new enthusiasm for adverse childhood experiences (ACEs), which include domestic abuse (Gillies et al, 2017; Featherstone et al, 2018). This is the belief that given the right start in life, all children can thrive and grow up to contribute to society.

However, the emphasis on the early years ignores the adversity that can affect people at any stage of their lives. It also assumes that damage is inevitable. More telling is that the focus on early years and ACEs ignores and underestimates the effects of socio-economic and political injustices and abuse which can affect wellbeing throughout life. Racism, economic disadvantage and other discriminations are not registered as adversities on the ACE list (Featherstone et al, 2014, 2018). The discourse acts as a mandate for governments and the state to intervene in the lives of families, particularly marginalised communities, in order to improve the lives of children (Gillies et al, 2017). Instead of tackling the injustices that families face, parents are sent on parenting classes and families are placed under surveillance (Crossley, 2018). In lieu of providing more resources to support families, policy makers and funders have embraced neurobiology with its focus on the development of children's brains; such a focus has allowed attention to be deflected from social and economic injustices which contribute to the prevalence of abuse (Featherstone et al, 2014; Featherstone, 2016; Gillies et al, 2017). Attachment and neurobiology theories are mobilised to promote intervention in the early years of life (Featherstone et al, 2014). While it is important that abuse is stopped as early as possible, the narrative that neurobiology and attachment theories propagate in the public sphere is that damage done in the early years is the most profound and damaging for life (Enlow et al, 2012; Callaghan et al, 2017a, 2017b). Hence, this emphasis individualises and psychologises abuse and recovery. The reality is that we can be affected by abuse and trauma at any stage of our lives, and we can also recover from trauma (Wastell and White, 2017).

Theories of attachment are frequently used in social work assessments of families, often to the detriment of cultivating an understanding of children's lived experiences and the political and socio-economic contexts of their lives. In the case of a child who has experienced domestic abuse, such framing can lead to misidentifying a coping strategy with maladaptive attachment, thus locating the disorder inside the child rather than seeing that a threatening environment may be making them feel insecure and that their reaction is appropriate (Burman, 2016, p 145). Understanding the child is important when making assessments. On reflection, I appreciate how my own child's attachment to me could have been misconstrued. I remember when my daughter was at pre-school nursery, she would cry every time I collected her. She cried because she loved all the different toys at nursery and didn't want to leave them behind. An onlooker could easily have interpreted that as my daughter's fear of me. Thus, it may be noted that a child has an attachment disorder and blame is placed on the mother, when the child is responding fittingly to what they consider is a hostile environment or situation (Burman, 2016, p 145). Categories developed for the assessment of experimental data and clinical practice, such as attachment styles, do not always translate well in other professional domains, like social work practice, or indeed everyday life.

Contextualisation is also important when considering theories of developmental psychology. Burman criticises developmental psychology for the goals it sets out for 'normal' development for children (Burman, 2016, p 21). She argues that these have been based on a White, middle-class idea of childhood growth, which is not the experience of the majority of children and therefore cannot be seen as 'normal'. They do not take into consideration other social, cultural and economic factors that affect childhood. Critics have argued that developmental psychology's linear growth aim is to make children into 'productive adults'; thus, the aim of the different stages is to mark the move towards productivity (Burman, 2012, 2013, 2016). Here we can see how the ethos and value behind developmental psychology's milestones for children are based on a capitalistic model of production, where the aim of life is production and where the productivity of a child is measured rather than their wellbeing and happiness in the present and in the future (Burman, 2012, 2016; O'Dell et al, 2017). Any deviation from the norm is less about harm caused by abuse to the child but more about harm to the productivity of the future adult. In this way the child continues to be seen as 'becoming' rather than 'being' (Uprichard, 2008; James and Prout, 2015). Thus, we move into the area of prevention, not the prevention of harm but the prevention of deviation (Wastell and White, 2017), for the child that deviates from the 'norm' must be controlled and policed, as discussed in the next section.

The fugitive child

Along with the passive or early years tropes, there is the 'non-child' category, or what I term 'the fugitive child'. The term 'fugitive child' is inspired by sociologist Akwugo Emejula's (2018) talk 'Fugitive Feminism' at the Institute of Contemporary Arts (ICA), London. Emejulu (2018, 2022) argues that humanity has always excluded the 'Other', and she encourages Black women who have not been excluded to inhabit the space of unbelonging, the 'fugitive' space, to work towards their own liberation. Thus, the fugitive child is the child that is neither seen as a child nor awarded the protection and privileges of a child (Meiners, 2016, p 46). Those that fall into this category are children from minoritised groups, for example, children with disabilities, Black children, children who are in the care system and children who have experienced abuse. What we see in the literature is that children who do not fit the idealised trope of the innocent child are dehumanised, othered and pathologised. It is then presented that it is 'they, the othered' who are deviant and need to be 'put right', rather than the injustices that they face being the issue (Meiners, 2016, p 50).

Feminist scholars have long argued how essentialising children means that children who do not fit the White, middle-class hegemonic category are excluded (Castañeda, 2002; Bernstein, 2011; Meiners, 2016). It is the experience of the White, middle-class child that is normalised and protected, while others can be viewed with suspicion and not afforded innocence and protection. Recently, there has been a focus on the number of Black and minoritised children who have been strip-searched by the police. This follows the case of Child Q, who was strip-searched at school during an exam because the teachers thought Child Q smelt of marijuana (Firmin et al, 2022). There was much discussion around 'adultification', whereby Black children are not afforded the protection of children but seen as adults

(Davis and Marsh, 2020; Curtis et al, 2022). This has its origin in colonialism and the dehumanisation of children who do not fit the White, middle-class hegemonic category (which is further explored later in this chapter). This lack of protection of children because they are Black or minoritised is also present in social work interventions. In an overview report, Miller (2015, p 35, cited in Bernard and Harris, 2018) writes of Child M, a missing 14-year-old Black boy, who, rather than being seen as in need of protection, was judged by professionals to be 'a streetwise young man who knew exactly what he was doing'. Professionals falsely thought that Child M was in a gang and was able to protect himself. As Bernard and Harris (2018) note, there was little interest in the everyday lives of children like Child M by any of the professionals involved. Child M was Black and poor, and was already written off at the age of 14. The child was not even given the chance to access an idealised childhood free from discrimination and abuse and was subsequently punished for it.

What we can see here is that the problems Child M faced were individualised; there was no accounting for the other factors outside of his control that affected his life, such as poverty and gang exploitation. In a crude way, it can be seen that Child M had 'failed' to be the 'model' child that would grow up into a 'productive' adult; he had failed to conform to the idealised trope of the child. For the idealised childhood is one based on a narrow understanding of White, middle-class childhood in the post-industrialised countries, and the majority of children of the world, especially those that have experienced abuse, are excluded. Any problems and issues that they face are because they are deficient – instead of being seen to be subjected to risks, they become the risk. They and their families are placed under surveillance and policed (Richie, 2012; Featherstone, 2016; Henry, 2017; Kanyeredzi, 2018). This is particularly pertinent for children from marginalised groups who have also experienced domestic abuse – rather than being supported, they and their families can be seen as a risk and placed under surveillance by social work (Featherstone et al, 2017; Ferguson et al, 2020).

Children with insecure immigration status in the UK can also been seen as 'non-children', where their rights as a child to safety and food are denied due to their immigration status. In their analysis of SCRs, Jolly and Gupta (2024) found that social workers and other professionals were often unaware of how having no recourse to public funds (NRPF) affected the safeguarding of children. For example, they failed to take into account how NRPF increased poverty, homelessness and isolation for families, which had detrimental effects on both children's and parents' wellbeing. With regards to domestic abuse, having no access to financial or statutory support made some women reliant on an abusive partner to the detriment of their and their children's wellbeing and safety.

Unaccompanied child migrants can also have their status and protection as children denied. The figure of the migrant child is related to the fugitive child as it one whose very existence as a child is questioned. This is due to border controls, and in the battle of upholding the fiction of borders, the age of children has been fetishised (Rosen and Khan, 2024, p 46). Here we see how the myth of caring for all children comes into play, as unaccompanied migrant children are placed under racialised age assessments that exclude and deny certain bodies from being a child (Rosen and Khan, 2024, p 47). In their ethnographic study, Rosen and Khan detail how a young boy called Kareem has his body measured and scrutinised in order to ascertain his age. He is measured against what critical childhood scholars call a mythical universal child development chart (Burman, 2008). For there is no universal measurement, only colonial mapping of the body (Dahler, 2020), where Kareem is measured against a Eurocentric ideal of what a child his age should be like. Kareem's knowledge about his own body and age is not believed. He is deemed to be unable to epistemically contribute to the discussion. He is not the deserving child – his knowledge is denied and he is not afforded the protection of childhood.

Thorne (1987) and Hartman (2021) write that children, especially those who are marginalised through race, class, gender and disability, are seen first as a threat before they are seen as needing protection. The obsession with children either being seen as unknowing/innocent or needing to return to a place of innocence in order to be protected enables the children's knowledge to be discounted and reviled. This epistemic injustice enables perpetrators' actions to go unaccounted for, and for children who have been abused to be pathologised and demonised.

Tropes of childhood beyond the social work literature

Using Burman's *Child as method*, I saw how the different tropes/figures of childhood are used to uphold the status quo by consistently returning children to a place of passivity and innocence in order to support them. If the child is deemed too knowing and thus too 'adult-like', they are then not afforded the protection and rights of a child. Another important finding was that children are seen outside of their socio-political environment, which means that any support for children is often depoliticised and decontextualised – as in providing counselling therapy for the child but not also tackling the socio-political environment that is distressing the child in the first place. This was also something that I found in the wider literature in childhood studies with regards to children from marginalised groups globally. Due to limited space in this book, I give only two examples of the tropes of childhood to show how these are mobilised to uphold colonial and patriarchal social order while claiming to 'help' the child.

The figure of the child soldier

The child soldier is the child that is presented as being brutalised by being forced to be active in an army during war time. The figure of the child soldier presents a tension for the empathetic helper – for in order to receive help, the child must be innocent, but how does that fit with a child that has killed or maimed? Maureen Moynah (2011) argues that this is why the child soldier must be seen as being 'forced' to be a child soldier, so their passivity allows the empathetic helper to separate the violence away from the child. The child then can be returned through rehabilitation to the original place of innocence, where they can 'regain' their childhood. Where this narrative fails to protect embodied children who have been, or who are or will be, child soldiers is that they are extracted from their socio-political environment, which obscures the reason why they became child soldiers and/or even why there is a war in the first place that they are pulled in to fight in (Seymour, 2019). Children who are child soldiers are not a homogeneous group, and there are different reasons why children may join an armed conflict.

In her ethnography of child soldiers in the Democratic Republic of Congo, Seymour (2019) questions the child protection claims of the NGOs. During both her time as a child protection officer and as a researcher, she started to question how the focus on 'child soldiers' did little to protect the actual embodied child who had been a soldier. In her research, she interviews Joseph, who had been a child soldier. Joseph had been through the rehabilitation programmes of NGOS but had still struggled. He reflects that it is not the fact of being a child soldier that hinders him but that he has no way to make a living, that the everyday experience of living in poverty and not having a way out was having the most effect on him (Seymour, 2019, p 29). Other former child soldiers lament how when they were part of an army, they at least had food, an income and were looked after, whereas now they were barely surviving poverty (Seymour, 2019, p 31). Seymour does not dismiss or underplay the terrible things her participants experienced as child soldiers; rather, she highlights that it is not the only challenge that they experience and that living in poverty along with ongoing social injustice and inequality were just as important in their everyday lives. Seymour argues that the programmes set up to protect children did very little to actually protect the embodied child because they stopped at 'rehabilitation' and did not tackle the economic and social injustices which left them in poverty.

The figure of the child soldier also fulfils another role – it reinforces the colonial idea of the Global North 'saving' children from being used as soldiers in the 'uncivilised brutal countries'. It is far more palatable for the countries in the Global North to see themselves as the hero 'saving' a child, rather than contributing to the war through the arms trade and both the past and present imperial economic policies that impoverish countries. It also hides the use of child soldiers in the Global North too. In 2019 the Just for Kids Law (JFKL) took the UK Secretary of State for Home Office Department to court for violating the rights of children by their use of children as covert human intelligence (CHIS), essentially using children as spies (Arthur and Kirk, 2023). JFKL argued that the authorising of children to engage in criminal activities, with no criminal liability, in return for information, was not in the best interests of the children and violated their human rights. Here we can see that children who are marginalised can be used in different kinds of war in both the Global North and the Global South.

The figure of the traumatised child

This figure is one of a child so traumatised that they are unable to create knowledge. They are deemed not to have the capacity to create knowledge because they are too vulnerable emotionally, physically and/or psychologically from their traumatic experience. The children are presented as passive recipients of care. The focus is on 'fixing'/'rescuing' children, but the cause of the trauma remains hidden and instead is located inside the child. This figure of a child is usually used by the 'helping' agencies like NGOs, social work or health professionals to justify their intervention in the lives of the children and to promote their transformational interventions (Fassin and Rechtman, 2009; McCarthy, 2021). Images of the children usually focus either on sad and forlorn children who need to be rescued, or very happy children who have been transformed and helped by the agency or intervention (McCarthy, 2021).

Creating knowledge with children about what has caused trauma can disrupt the status quo, because the cause of the trauma may highlight sociopolitical inequalities. This is also relevant in the case of war and genocide, where the cause of the distress in children can remain hidden – so children are said to be suffering from post-traumatic stress disorder (PTSD), but there is no recognition of the ongoing brutality that they are living with and the cause of it. For example, Sheehi and Sheehi (2022) write of psychological intervention for children in Palestine, where the ongoing violence of the Israeli government is not addressed or challenged. This then allows the 'problem' to be located within the child rather than the violent settler colonial state that they are living under. Sheehi and Sheehi (2022, p 102) tell the story of Yoa'd Ghanadry-Hakim, a leading mental health professional at an internationally funded project studying trauma in school children in Palestine. Yoa'd Ghanadry-Hakim found that the pre- and post-research that she conducted did not align with the aims and objectives of the Save the Children Fund (an international aid organisation), which was funding the project. Her research showed that the children's health was worse than before the intervention because the Eurocentric approach of the project did not account for the political and social nuances of the children's everyday lives. Save the Children did not publish the report and Yoa'd Ghanadry-Hakim resigned in protest. Here we see that the knowledge created with the children was dismissed because it did not fit into the narrative of the charity organisation. By discounting or not creating knowledge with children who have experienced trauma, agencies can end up focusing only on the symptoms of trauma and not the causes of it, and unintentionally supporting and upholding the status quo. It can result in the child being pathologised and placed under the spotlight, and not the person or things that cause the trauma.

As a counsellor, I appreciate how one-to-one therapy can enable a space for children to make sense of their experiences. However, if practitioners don't address the injustices that are making children unwell but instead expect them to adjust to the oppression, then as Fanon (2001) writes, we are colluding with the system. Creating knowledge with children can allow us as researchers and practitioners to be attentive to the things that are traumatising them.

Disrupting the Global North/Global South binary

Using *Child as method* to interrogate the different figures of the child present in both the social work literature around children and domestic abuse and the wider literature in childhood studies enabled me to draw parallels with the treatment of marginalised children in both the Global South and the Global North. In effect, the research and practice with children who have experienced domestic abuse in the UK replicated the pattern of research with marginalised children in the Global South, with both predominantly focusing on 'fixing' a problem and not seeing the children beyond the trope of the damaged child. As Twum-Danso Imoh et al (2019, 2024) point out, the majority of the research in the Global South tends to focus on NGOs' concern, and little of the research is actually done with children – much is about measuring children and poverty. Similarly, in the UK, the research with children who have experienced domestic abuse is about the evaluation of services and how to improve policies and practice, but little about or with the children themselves.

This raises two points. Firstly, it is important to recognise that children who are marginalised in the UK are part of global childhoods and have commonalities with marginalised children in the Global South. To not recognise this would continue to embolden the fallacy that all childhoods in the Global North are materially affluent. Thus, it is important, as Twum-Danso Imoh et al (2019, 2024) point out, to dismantle the Global North/Global South binary to be more inclusive of the plurality of children's lives, to acknowledge how global politics and process affects children's lives locally in different ways. The second point is that the dehumanisation of children who are marginalised is a common theme in both research in the Global North and the Global South. Research that focuses on the 'lack' for children can render them passive and unknowing about their lives, whereas they can offer important insight not only into the effects of inequality but also what can support them, and create important knowledge about their personhood and society. Before addressing the epistemic injustice this produces, I will explore the purpose of dehumanisation and the tropes of childhood.

Tropes of childhood and the purpose of dehumanisation

To fully understand the tropes of childhood and its importance in maintaining social order, we must go back to the emergence of modernity and coloniality. Post-industrialised modernity was not only entangled with coloniality, they were co-dependent (Smith, 2012, p 23). Along with theft and violence, colonialism could be viewed as going against the thinking of the premodern world, a project to 'spread' the 'truth' of reason and rationalism, centring 'Man' as conqueror and knower (Cannella and Viruru, 2004, p 25). A key tenet was the idea of 'Man' being created and made in the image of the White man from the colonising/post-industrialised countries. More troubling was that this definition of man became associated with what it meant to be human, and it applied universally (Wynter, 2003). As the post-industrialised countries became powerful by conquering the land of others by force and violence, it not only oppressed others but identified them as not 'man', and therefore not 'human' (McKittrick, 2014, p 54). Not only were the colonised attacked, but they were also deemed by the colonising countries as incapable of producing knowledge and said to lack objectivity (Smith, 1999). In order for this status quo to survive, the culture and belief of society had to enforce it; hence, any challenges to culture had to be repressed. One channel for this repression was through education, with the child being seen as an empty vessel needing to be filled with 'civilising' knowledge (Burman, 2018b, p 26). Burman (2018b, p 39) argues that creating an unknowing and innocent child means instituting a socio-psychic order that enables other forms of unknowing or denial to go undetected. In other words, Burman (2018a argues that adults deceive children to create the reality and the security that they desire. This means children need to be seen as the place of unknowing and innocence in order to keep the status quo and uphold dominant norms and practices. In the case of domestic abuse, this can be clearly seen in the court system, where children's voices are often not heard or not given the same weighting as the perpetrator (usually their father), and where they are often considered to be the one whose opinion needs to change, rather than the behaviour of the perpetrators (Macdonald, 2017).

Burman is not alone in illustrating how the child is used as a political trope to uphold the status quo. Castañeda (2002), in her book *Figuration: Child,*

Bodies, Worlds, interrogates how the figure of the child is used to maintain certain societal values and maintain the status quo. Meiners (2016) argues how the figure of the child is used to support a carceral state that in turn punishes children who do not fall within the remit of White middle class. Barrie Thorne (1987) writes that children have predominantly been thought about through the adult's gaze. Children were either seen as threats to adults, as victims of adults or learners of adult culture (as adults in the making) (Thorne, 1987). As Thorne (1987, p 91) observes, 'it is adults who construct the imagery of children both as quintessential victims and threats to adult society'. Dyer (2020) explores how the cultural expressions of childhood have residues of colonial and imperialist histories and practices. These texts helped to clarify and challenge my thinking about children, but much like the literature on children and domestic abuse, I was left wondering where the child was and, more importantly, what they had to say.

I knew that the core of my confusion was that the children themselves were not being listened to. There was an epistemic injustice (Fricker, 2009). The literature around domestic abuse had been colonised, in that a colonialist ideal of childhood had been utilised to exclude children who had experienced domestic abuse and social work interventions from creating knowledge about their own lives. Not only were they not listened to, but they were also pathologised for not fulfilling the colonialist and imperialist notion of the child, as I explored in the previous sections. While *Child as method* was helpful in analysing the literature on domestic abuse and children, I needed to go beyond theory and produce a space for children to create knowledge about themselves.

Humanising the child and epistemic justice

> Oh, to be erased from your own struggle and knowledge production.
> (Spillers, 2018)

I remember feeling goosebumps when Hortense Spillers uttered these words. I was sitting in the auditorium at the ICA and Spillers was sitting on stage and discussing how Black women, in particular, were excluded from the creation of knowledge about themselves. I felt my heart beat faster, my breathing stopped and I knew that this too was happening to children who had experienced domestic abuse. They were not being allowed to create knowledge about themselves. I knew then that at the core of my unsettledness was the sense that children themselves were not being listened to. There was an epistemic injustice that I felt needed to be addressed (Murris, 2013). The literature around domestic abuse had been colonised, in that a colonialist ideal of childhood had been utilised to exclude children who had experienced domestic abuse and social work interventions from creating knowledge about their own lives. Not only were they not listened to, but they were also pathologised for not fulfilling the colonialist and imperialist notion of the child, as I explored in the previous sections. As Murris (2013) points out, even Fricker (2009), whose work focuses on epistemic justice, does not include children in addressing epistemic injustice. Murris (2013) writes how children are ignored in discussions around philosophy and epistemic justice. They are seen as being unable to create knowledge, or the value and relevance of what they know is often questioned. I returned to the work of Frantz Fanon (2001 [1961], 2017 [1952]) and Burman's (2018b) *Child as method* to try and find a way forward.

Fanon shows a way out of pathologising and blaming survivors of oppression and abuse. He practises and calls for a pedagogy of 'failure' and 'solidarity' (Burman, 2018b, p 140). His pedagogy of failure is illustrated in the way he admits that he doesn't know the answer but is willing to try (Fanon, 2001 [1961], p 204). This is demonstrated in his work with client B, where Fanon (2001 [1961], p 204) admits his own uncertainty. However, this form of 'unknowing' is often rejected within the social work system, resulting in what Cooper (2003) terms a 'risk averse' CP system. By contrast, Fanon, instead of disavowing the fact that he does not know, admits to 'not knowing'. There is no formula or straightforward answer, but Fanon holds the space for exploration. This space then enables his clients/patients to move to their own decisions and creativity. Thus, the pedagogy of failure fosters enough space to develop a pedagogy of solidarity (Burman, 2018b, p 142). This allows the client/patient to be part of their solution to their safety, counteracting the dominant literature in domestic abuse of the 'child' that needs to be saved. Here is a way the child can be part of the safety plan.

In terms of research, the practice of holding the space of 'not knowing and solidarity' is advocated in feminist and Indigenous research, in the work of Chandra Talpade Mohanty (1984, 2003), Linda Tuhiwai Smith (1999) and Eve Tuck (2009). They have consistently called for research into groups who are marginalised within society to be decolonised, for the epistemic violence of ignoring people's knowledge and ways of knowing to be challenged. When embracing children's knowledge, researchers must be open to things that do not fit the damage-focused narrative of domestic abuse. Eve Tuck (2009) has long called for the demise of damage-focused research within her community. Explaining that while the research had once validated their claims of oppression and injustice, to only focus on damage risks pathologising and limiting their community to being defined solely by their oppression (Tuck, 2009, p 413). The call to 'reduce the joy deficit' has also made its way to sociology (Shuster and Westbrook, 2022). For example, Westbrook (2021) and Shuster and Westbrook (2022) argue that the trouble with solely focusing on the hatred towards the transgender community in research is to render their lives as ones of pain and loss, rather than including their sense of liberation and joy too. Similarly, in her research with people who inject drugs, Dennis (2019) challenges the reductive narrative around drug use by exploring pleasure and the body, highlighting the complexity of people's lives, and, in doing so, opens a new way of exploring drug usage. Similarly, if we only focus on the damage done by domestic abuse, we risk defining children solely by the abuse.

I have taken inspiration from these feminist and sociological interventions into the politics of joy and suffering and applied these to children who have experienced domestic abuse. Historically, there has been a trade-off between damage-focused narratives and material gain in the humanitarian and charitable field (Tuck, 2009; Fassin, 2012). Tuck (2009, p 419) writes that marginalised communities have tolerated damage-focused research because there is an explicit and implicit understanding 'that these stories of damage pay off in material, sovereign and political wins'. This is not too dissimilar to how charity groups and organisations have called for research to highlight and measure the impact of domestic abuse so that more material resources could be made available. However, the danger is that this then becomes the only story told about children/families who have experienced domestic abuse. Tuck (2009, p 412) writes that her letter 'Suspending damage: A letter to communities' comes 'from feelings of being over researched yet, ironically, made invisible'. Likewise, while it is important to acknowledge the impact of domestic abuse, to not see children beyond the frame of this abuse is to not see them in their entirety and renders them invisible.

To understand the lives of children who have experienced domestic abuse, we must challenge the imperialistic and colonialist framework which frames the practice of ignoring children's knowledge. This calls for the work and research into domestic abuse to be decolonised, which means research must move away from the myth that children are essentially passive and unknowing (Burman, 2012, 2018a, 2018b). The epistemic discrimination that children are subjected to must be challenged, and children need to be rehumanised and not just used as a political trope (Burman, 2018b). To do this, Fanon (2001 [1961], p 151) calls for the need to go back to the lived experiences of marginalised communities in order to transform knowledge and to challenge injustices. In the literature on domestic abuse, there is very little written about the lived experiences of children and their socio-political world. On the rare occasions when things are written, children are abstracted from their living environment. Fanon (2001 [1961], p 151) writes that the way forward is not through theoretical work alone but through the lived experiences of the most marginalised people, in this case, children who have experienced domestic abuse.

While I have drawn parallels between the colonisation of knowledge of Indigenous communities and other marginalised groups, I also recognise that children can be marginalised within these different groups too because they are not adults. For while childhood studies have called for recognition that childhood is a social construction (James and Prout, 2015), Wells and Montgomery (2014) argue that children are biologically and physically different and we need to account for this. They argue that to not acknowledge this difference makes us blind to the ways in which the precariousness of children's subjecthood and the importance of their social relations for survival makes them more vulnerable. Thus, there is a need to acknowledge how violence and structures of violence are embodied and how children are affected in their everyday lives by different injustices and the search for social recognition (Wells and Montgomery, 2014). As Hunleth (2019) writes, the childhood studies mantra has been that children have agency, and while this is true, there is also a challenging underside to that mantra. For in overemphasising children's power, we can underestimate the constraints and vulnerability of their position in society. Hunleth (2019, p 157) succinctly writes: 'Children are, in fact, agents, but they are not "super agents", we are wise to remember. None of us are.'

Childhood scholars Twum-Danso Imoh and Okyere (2020) argue that we need to move towards a more holistic understanding of child participation that goes beyond voice. Reflecting on their research study with children in both Ghana and Nigeria, Twum-Danso Imoh and Okyere (2020, p 1) write that we need to 'go beyond current dominant understanding and practices of child participation and identify ways of making these more holistic, inclusive and aligned with the meaning that children themselves attach to their everyday lives as well as to the key personal and social relationships they value'. In enabling children to share the way they make meaning in their everyday lives, the children can challenge some of our preconceived ideas about themselves and their lives. Twum-Danso Imoh and Okyere reflect on how they had initially thought that the children did not understand the question of participation, but through photography the children were able to show a more holistic idea of how they participate in public life in their everyday. They were not confined to the narrow definition of participation as 'having their voice heard' but showed how they valued contributing to everyday life in school, home and society. Twum-Danso Imoh and Okyere (2020, p 3) argue that focusing on voice and neglecting the ways that children participate in various contexts can create a standard and deficit models of participation. In their Connectors study, Nolas et al (2018, 2019, 2021) use multimodal ethnography to explore the various ways that children participate in public life. Public participation is not limited to voice but encompasses large and small moments and interactions in the everyday. To broaden children's participation in research and address epistemic injustice, we need to look beyond 'voice' and include the large and the small moments of their everyday.

The case for studying the everyday of children who have experienced domestic abuse

As I argued in the previous section, while existing research on domestic abuse and children is important and highlights the impact of such experience, most studies encapsulate an adult, psychological and social work gaze. There is, as of yet, little research that has been done on the perspectives of children themselves. Child protection, though necessary, is insufficient when it comes to understanding the lived experiences of children who have experienced domestic abuse. In addition to individualising a problem that has long been argued by feminist scholars and others to be social and structural (Mullender et al, 2002; Stanley, 2011; Stanley et al, 2011, 2017; Davies, 2018; Featherstone et al, 2018; Ferguson et al, 2019), it also limits the ways in which we see the individual child – that is, as in need of protection alone. Being attentive to the everyday approach enables us to take a closer look at the entanglements between the society, the family and the child (Hall, 2019). It allows the child's agency and materiality, especially relational agency, to return to the analytical frame, thus broadening our understanding of children who have experienced domestic abuse and reminding us that their lives are not confined, and indeed must not be defined, by these experiences alone. I argue that by exploring the everyday lives of children, we gain a greater appreciation and understanding concerning their lives and desires, which can be shaped but perhaps not delineated by abuse alone.

Families' everyday experiences are important for understanding children's experiences (Ferguson, 2016a; Evans et al, 2019; Hall, 2019). It is this experience of the everyday that is assessed by social workers in order to ascertain whether a child is safe enough (Ferguson, 2016a). The everyday is a space for possibilities, where the individual meets society and relations are made and remade. The everyday is where people and places come together and the tapestries of life are woven (Highmore, 2010; Hall, 2017). It can be a place where the individual's agency may be seen and experienced. In order to explore and learn about the lives of children, I focus on the theoretical concept of the everyday by drawing attention to the routines, rhythms, objects, family practices, places, spaces and relationships that affect children's lives and wellbeing, both in the wider and more intimate spheres. As Les Back (2015, p 820) writes, focusing on the everyday 'brings to the fore how liveable lives are made'.

The interest in studying the everyday has a long history, and much theorising has been done on this subject. The French Marxist philosopher and social theorist Henri Lefebvre (1974) argued in *Critique of Everyday Life* that 'la quotidienne' is made up of repetition, routine and regularity. Using the example of capitalist workplaces, he observed that the structure of everyday life was both cyclical and rhythmical. It had a starting time, break and clocking off. He argued that it divorced people from their true existence, giving them no space and time in which to ponder. Thus, for Lefebvre, the structure of the everyday served as a way for the powerful to continue to regulate and order the lives of those they influenced (Hemmings and Thompson, 2002). Lefebvre (1974) saw the everyday as temporal: it was centred around space, time and habitual living. Michel de Certeau (1984, 1996), a French philosopher, moved away from Lefebvre's focus on the ritual and routine of everyday to explore how people 'do' and 'practice' everyday life. While he recognised that rules, traditions and structures played a role in people's lives, he argued that in the everyday we can also see how people rebel and resist the overriding structures and governance through ways that are adaptive, creative and resilient.

A key challenge to the study of the everyday is defining what it is. De Certeau (1996, p ix) takes the path of the 'science of singularity', by which he means that the particular is studied in the manner by which it contributes to a more general account of the world. This links with feminist and decolonial scholars (Smith, 1999; Mohanty, 2003) who point to the particulars of one's lived experience which, while unique to that person, are able to give a picture of the wider society and power relations. It can be the place where we talk about society and the 'us', that which is common to all. Highmore (2010, p 5) explains that 'even in the most desperate isolation, the ordinary can take hold of what seems exceptional and connect it with other exceptions'. Focusing on the everyday facilitates a way of talking about commonality without intoning the ideology of universality (de Certeau et al, 1996).

Highmore (2010, p 1) writes that 'the everyday' is the accumulation of 'small things' that constitute a more expansive but hard to register 'big thing'. For the everyday opens the way to see how society and governments can police and regulate lives through practice. Highmore (2010) concludes that everyday life is constituted of singular moments held together by overarching power and governance. Despite its focus on the singular, the study of the everyday is vague and no one thing dominates (Highmore, 2011). The everyday holds boredom, routine and familiarity. However, it also comprises accidents, joy and surprise, all parts of everyday life (Highmore, 2002). Much of the everyday cannot be defined neatly into moments of stark contrast, such as pain and joy. The everyday is as much about confusion as it is about clarity, and it is as much about complexity as singular motifs. The everyday does not present a clear and discrete synthesis of life, and it does not aim to provide a grand narrative or totalising account of life (Stewart, 2007, p 1; Back, 2015). Instead, it is about fusing disparate material together, and as Highmore (2011, p 2) writes, 'the ordinary demands a complexity because, at times, nothing is really in the foreground of experience'. This fits well with feminist scholars' writings about domestic abuse, for they have argued against seeing abuse as one-off singular incidents but for it to be viewed as an accumulation and pattern of violence and coercion (Kelly, 1987; Stark, 2009; Katz, 2016; Walby et al, 2016). This does not mean that abuse and violence have no significant effects. Rather, they form part of the ordinary so as to become unrecognised and unremarkable. Normalised and incorporated into the everyday, it is only the extreme violent act that is noted.

The exploration of the everyday is an approach that feminist scholars have long championed. Anne Oakley's (1990, 2019) central work on housework illustrated the ways in which the everyday is gendered and how the study of the domestic sphere is ignored. Nevertheless, the everyday can offer deep insight into how society functions by exploring how power relations at both the micro and macro scale affect everyday living. Significant to feminist thinking (Hall, 2018) is weaving theory into everyday lives. For such an approach provides an understanding of how social difference in lived experiences is ingrained in all levels of the economic, the political and the cultural. Likewise, by looking at the everyday lives of children who have experienced domestic abuse, we can also see how the macro and the micro aspects of political/public life are imprinted on the everyday.

Black feminist scholars have argued that homemaking can also be a form of resistance (Sharpe, 2016; Williamson, 2017). bell hooks (1990, p 48) encourages us to look at the mundaneness of everyday homemaking to find the skills of generations of Black women who have 'essential wisdom to share', and to consider the subversion and resistance of homemaking. Indeed, hooks argues that one of the greatest tactics of the capitalist, patriarchal, White supremacist order is the construction of economic and social structures that deprive people of the means to make a homeplace (hooks, 1990, p 46). hooks (1990, 2016c) writes that the homeplace is where Black women returned the oppressed Black community from being objects to subjects. hooks (1990, p 42) goes on to write: 'One's homeplace was the one site where one could freely confront the issue of humanization, where one could resist. Black women resisted by making homes where all Black people could strive to be subjects, not objects.'

Childhood scholars researching with marginalised children in sub-Saharan Africa have also argued that foregrounding the mundane and everyday existence of children helps to challenge the dominant narrative that the children always come from a place of lack (Twum-Danso Imoh et al, 2022). In a similar way to the argument I set out earlier about children who have experienced domestic abuse, Twum-Danso Imoh et al (2022, p 379) explain that in focusing only on their challenges and difficulties, one paints a one-dimensional picture of children in Africa. Being attentive to the mundane and pedestrian aspect of children's lives allows a plurality of stories to be told and heard rather than a single story of lack (Twum-Danso Imoh et al, 2022, p 4). By moving beyond extremities and difficulties, such an approach allows us to question not only our understanding of the lives of children but our understanding of the world more broadly (Twum-Danso Imoh et al, 2022, p 4). In a similar way I begin by applying the cultural theory of the everyday to the home, a place where children dwell and which is often scrutinised by social workers (Ferguson, 2011).

Conclusion

In this chapter I narrate how I was challenged by the limited research done with children who had experienced domestic abuse and how they were often depicted as passive and damaged. Using Burman's *Child as method* approach, I concluded that there were three dominant tropes of childhood that were present in the social work literature – the passive child, the early years child and the fugitive child. I explored how these tropes of childhood were mobilised to uphold the colonial and patriarchal social norms rather than serving the best interests of the embodied child. Disrupting the binary of the North/South childhoods divide, I illustrated how the tropes of the child soldier and traumatised child were mobilised in similar ways to uphold colonial and patriarchal social norms. Illustrating the parallels between marginalised childhoods in the South and children who have experienced domestic abuse and social work interventions in the UK, I argued that this binary framework must be disrupted to reflect the plurality of children's lives.

Not all children are protected, and some are not even recognised as children and so are not afforded the right to protection. Key to protection is being seen as a passive/innocent child. This figure of the 'passive/innocent child' is not only part of the colonial and patriarchal ideals of child and childhood but a reoccurring figure in the practices and policies of protecting children. I illustrate that in order to be protected, a child must be seen as either passive and/or damaged, while any signs of knowledge or agency are perceived as deviance and the child is not afforded protection. Thus, I argue that even though the practices and policies are presented as being in the best interests of the child, they are rooted in colonial and patriarchal ideas of childhood, which continue to harm and further marginalise certain children. I argue how epistemic injustice is at the core of mobilising these figures of the child, and in order to protect children we need to continuously address this epistemic injustice to enable embodied children to speak back to the figures of the child that dominate their care. I show that we need to go beyond a focus only on 'voice' to create knowledge with children. Drawing from the cultural theories of the everyday, I argue that research must be done with children to create knowledge about their everyday lives. It is in the mundaneness of the everyday that we can create knowledge with children that goes beyond the narrow lens of trauma and abuse. In the next chapter I begin to explore the everyday life of Mystical, a seven-year-old boy.

3

The everyday life of Mystical

Mystical's narrative is emblematic of some of the themes that have run through the stories of all ten children in the research. In this chapter, therefore, I provide a multimodal ethnographic case study of Mystical, and attempt to read his activities, our conversations and his reflections on his everyday life through the conceptual language and preoccupation of 'the everyday'. The following paragraphs describe my conversations and relationship with Mystical. He describes himself as a seven-year-old boy who lives with his mother, Nicole, and two brothers in a flat on a social housing estate in London. My first two visits entailed Mystical and I getting to know each other. My starting point is the beginning of my third in-person visit with him on 6 August 2020 after physical distancing restrictions due to COVID-19 were lifted.

Mystical and I walk out of the lifts and push open the heavy door to the building. We are met with bright sunshine and greenery. The block of flats is one of several on a housing estate with lots of green open space. Each block is separated by a large patch of grass and there are trees surrounding the estate and a playground that has just reopened after being shut during COVID-19 restrictions. Mystical takes his scooter and rides down the path towards the trees. We decide to sit under some trees as we will be shaded from the blistering sun. Although some physical distance restrictions have been lifted, I am still not allowed to meet Mystical inside his home, so I navigate this restriction by meeting him out in the open air.

This is my third outing with Mystical and he appears more energetic and relaxed about our meeting. I had arrived at his home at 11 am, and his mother, Nicole, said that he had been ready and waiting for me for ages. This was a difference from the previous two visits when I had to wait for him to get ready – then he had seemed unsure what he was gaining from my visits but nonetheless was happy to give it a go. I must have passed some sort of test because he is eager and ready for me when I arrive. He had said at the end of the last visit, 'Oh, I thought this was going to be boring, but it was much better' (Field notes, 21 May 2020). To me, this highlighted the importance of participation in the research being fun, relational and interesting for children (Barker and Weller, 2003) and also echoed my research preoccupations of documenting the dreams and joy in the children's lives.

Everyday relations, food and identity

An important aspect of children's everyday lives are their social relations, as discussed in Chapter 6. Building relationships with the children in the study was one way of creating knowledge with them. In Mystical's case, he and I connected through our shared cultural heritage and language, with him dipping in and out of speaking Creole (the language most Mauritians speak to each other) to me. On finding out I was Mauritian in our first meeting, he asked me, 'Do you like *dhal puri*? That's my favourite!' My heart leapt when he mentioned *dhal puri*, as it is indeed one of my favourite foods. It is a popular Mauritian street food that is laborious to make. It is like a flatbread made out of yellow split peas, hence the name '*dhal*', meaning made of lentils, and '*puri*', meaning a type of bread. It is something that every Mauritian knows about, and there is often fierce competition around how best to make it and who makes the best ones. It is also a food that is present in diaspora groups with a history of indentured labourers brought over from India, so it is popular in countries like Trinidad and Mauritius (Cho, 2019, p 155). Through asking me about *dhal puri*, Mystical tells me about his taste in food but also, through this dish, makes a link with our shared family history of slavery and indentured labourers (Cho, 2019, p 155).

Vijay Mishra (1996) identifies *dhal puri* as a site where the history of diaspora and coloniality can be examined. Food rations were identical for Indian indentured labourers throughout the colonies and created a cuisine that has lasted till this day, so according to Mishra (1996, p 430), 'food linked the Indian diaspora from Surinam, to Mauritius to Fiji'. In his autoethnographic documentary *Dal Puri Diaspora* (2012), Richard Fung (a Chinese Trinidadian Canadian) shares the love Mystical and I have for this dish and goes in search of the history of *dhal puri*, travelling from Canada to Trinidad to India. Fung not only focuses on the taste and smell of *dhal puri* but also problematises the link between memory and food (Cho, 2019, p 155). For what Fung shows is that the food that salves a longing for home would not have come into being without slavery/indentured labour – the source of displacement in the first place (Cho, 2019). While Mystical, Fung and I delight in the smell, taste and feel of *dhal puri*, we are not only brought back to a home, we are also connecting through our shared history of indentured labour and displacement. Sociologists and anthropologists have long argued how food is not only about nourishment of the body but also linked to social, political and economic relations (Lévi-Strauss, 1955; Goody, 1982; Douglas, 2003; Caplan, 2006). Here, through food practices at home, Mystical is linked to the history and traditions of his ancestors (Knight et al, 2014).

Food, the nourishment of the body in everyday life, is a way of Mystical showing and nurturing his sense of identity. He and his mother both tell me how he likes a lot of Mauritian food, such as '*bol renversé*' (literally 'upside-down bowl'), another dish that represents Mauritius's ethnically diverse communities. This is an Indo-Chinese dish that is made by layering a fried egg at the bottom of a bowl, followed by stir-fried vegetables and meat/seafood, topped with rice. What makes the dish special is in the theatre of its serving. The bowl is tipped upside down onto a plate and when lifted leaves a dome-shaped food pile, with rice at the bottom, vegetables/meat in the middle and topped with a perfectly fried egg with its runny yolk intact. I am intrigued that Mystical has talked about two dishes that have a strong link to the cultural heritage of Mauritius. The fact that he knows about them illustrates the way in which his mother, Nicole, has through food practices helped to foster his transnational identity (James et al, 2009; Seeberg and Goździak, 2019). Mystical's food choices illustrate his connection to Mauritius while having been born and living in London. Like the majority of children in this study, he is from what Zeitlyn (2012) terms a transnational family, where the links to family and culture cross national and cultural boundaries (Varvantakis et al, 2019).

I wonder whether the dishes not only taste good to him but act as a sensory object that symbolises Mauritius, and thus keeps him connected with his other 'home' (Sutton, 2001, p 74). The sensory aspect of the food is amplified when Mystical shows me the metal cups and bowls (see Figure 3.1) that he likes to eat out of. His mother tells me that he likes

Figure 3.1: Metal cups and bowls (photography by Mystical)

to eat any food that is Mauritian from these bowls, just as people do in Mauritius. Indeed, the metal cups and bowls take me back to my own trips to Mauritius. While metal crockery is used because of its sturdiness and is less likely to break than pottery, it does also have a different sensory feel. Drinking water from a metal tumbler feels different on the mouth than using a glass and immediately transports me to Mauritius, drinking cold drinks to counteract the heat. Mystical tells me the food tastes better in the metal bowls and cups. I wonder if it transports him back to his time in Mauritius: that the use of metal crockery immerses him further through his senses of touch, feel, smell, taste and sound (Sutton, 2001; Klein and Watson, 2019).

Objects can stir our memories. What I find interesting is that while children are often portrayed as being, or becoming, here Mystical illustrates how he also has a past with memories (Moss, 2010). This is similar to other children in the study who recall their memories of holidays, special occasions and other experiences that influence their everyday living (see Chapters 5 and 6), such as Mystical wanting to eat out of the metal dishes.

Mystical's link to Mauritius is kept alive by his mother and his connection with his grandparents, who live there. Nicole, Mystical's mother, having come from Mauritius and married here, has no relatives in the UK. So Mystical has no aunts, uncles, cousins or extended Mauritian family on his mother's side living nearby. He does, however, have a connection with his grandparents in Mauritius, and when he lists the important people in his life, he includes his 'mother with a different name', meaning his maternal grandmother, and his 'other father', meaning his maternal grandfather. For Mystical, digital communication technologies such as WhatsApp, and cheaper flights to Mauritius, have enabled his grandparents to play an important part in his life (Madianou and Miller, 2012; Varvantakis et al, 2019). For him, family relations are created and nurtured over distance, thus stretching relational spaces (Massey, 2004).

Relationships with grandparents vary among the children in the study. Some such as Mystical find this intergenerational relationship nurturing and supportive, while others have lost grandparents or are emotionally distant from them for various reasons. Only one child lived with a grandparent.

Everyday space and safety

When it is time for us to pack up and return home, Mystical turns to me and asks if I can keep his large paper and the art that he has been working on (see Figure 3.2). I ask him if he doesn't want to keep it at home. He shakes his head. He explains that it will get lost in his home as his mother puts his things in his brothers' room and it will disappear in the mess. He is keen for me to keep it.

Figure 3.2: Mystical's artwork (photography by Brenda)

But I have a dilemma: I am making several visits this day and I am worried that his big sheet of paper will get squashed and ruined. I ask him gently if I can ask his mother to keep it somewhere safe in the living room. He looks at me; he's not sure but says we can try. He says that his mother keeps his things in his brothers' room because they are supposed to share it. Mystical tells me that 'the council' (meaning the social worker) wants him to share the room with his siblings, but he doesn't want to.

This short discussion raises several concerns for me. It is clear from my chat with Mystical that he doesn't feel that he has a storage space to keep his things safely. His mother, in trying to help him to make the transition from her bedroom to sharing his brothers', has placed his things there, but Mystical doesn't feel that his things are safe there. There is a link between materials, storage and affect – Mystical feels both himself and his things are unsafe.

Safety, with regards to domestic abuse, is often talked about in relation to the perpetrator, but as Mystical illustrates, safety is an ongoing everyday issue for the wellbeing of children, even when they no longer are living with the perpetrator of domestic abuse (Thiara and Humphreys, 2015). Safety is not just a static state of being but is dynamic, relational and spatial (Alexander et al, 2015; Vera-Gray, 2016). Mystical is navigating his space at home to feel safe. He tries to keep his belongings out of his siblings' bedroom so that he can have more control over keeping his objects safe. He also explains how he does not feel comfortable sharing a room with his siblings. Home is full of affect, and the interaction between people, materials and space can make homes and places feel 'safe' or 'unsafe' (Stewart, 2007; Gottzén and Sandberg, 2019). The affect of a space is drawn from both materiality and sensibilities, so it hinges on the person/body passing though the place (Gottzén and Sandberg, 2019). For Mystical, having no storage container/space for his things and the effect of his siblings' behaviour leaves him feeling unsafe, uncontained and unsettled.

Significantly, he does not passively experience this lack of space and safety. We can see that he tries to create an alternative by asking me to keep his paper and by sleeping in his mother's room and objecting to the 'council's' instructions. This is similar to how children try to create safe spaces while violence and abuse is happening – they may cling to a cuddly toy, listen to loud music or move themselves away from the area of conflict by going to a friend's home. They use their senses, bodies and relations to create a sense of safety for themselves (Alexander et al, 2015; Callaghan et al, 2016a).

This is also an example of Mystical's everyday life being policed – in this case, where he sleeps. I know from my own conversations with his mother that she is being 'criticised' for not having already moved Mystical into his brothers' room. The family live in a two-bedroom flat. His brothers are teenagers and need their own privacy and room. Mystical sleeps in his mother's room. Ideally, they would all have their own bedroom but there is no space for that. A professional decision has been made as to what is best for Mystical, but I am left feeling that his voice, needs and wants are not being heard. This is not the only example – Mystical himself has said that he doesn't want to see his father, but at the time of our meeting there was pressure for him to do so. It makes me reflect on whose voice gets heard (Macdonald, 2017). And which child gets heard, when their stories are very different?

In social work, there has been an emphasis on listening to the child's voice in CP (Featherstone et al, 2018). But the child's voice is not some abstract object (Mizen and Ofosu-Kusi, 2010; Lomax, 2012) – it is relational and must be heard in context. Featherstone et al (2018) argue that CP has followed neoliberal thinking and sees the child as an individual divorced from their environment and social relations. The reification of the child's voice can also be used to reinforce a particular narrative (as discussed in Chapter 2), where a child's voice is taken into consideration if it supports a particular narrative or discarded if it doesn't. Macdonald (2017) found that judges in family courts were more likely to take a child's voice into account if the child wanted to see their father, but if they did not, then some pressure was put on the child to change their point of view. This has given rise to the Women's Aid campaign 'Children First', which draws attention to the fact that children's voices are often overlooked in decisions about contact with fathers when there has been a history of domestic abuse. In Mystical's case I know that his mother is being accused of 'parental alienation' because he does not want to see his father. Parental alienation is a contentious term (Birchall and Choudhry, 2022), and recently the law courts have decided that it must be used with great care. However, it remains, as in Nicole's situation, something that mothers who are separated from fathers who are perpetrators have to navigate (Harman et al, 2019). So even though Mystical is separated from his father, he still has to navigate his way around his father's control and around a patriarchal system that continues to support his father, while holding his mother to account. This is also an issue for some of the other children in the research project, where they continue to navigate their wellbeing, domestic abuse and relationships with their fathers.

Everyday relationships: portrait of a mother

Mystical has a close relationship with his mother. He often refers to her as being 'kind'. He is also very much aware that his mother's parenting is under scrutiny, a discussion that comes about when we are looking at his photos from his camera together. As with the other children in the project, I delivered a small digital toy camera to Mystical before the COVID-19 lockdown. The aim was for him to take photos of things that were interesting or important to him. As he lays out the photos he has taken on the picnic blanket, I ask him what they mean, hoping to create some understanding of what is important to him.

> He replies, 'Oh, I took the photos of the food because my mum told me to – it's because the council think that my mum does not cook food, but she does. I don't know why my brothers say the things they do.'
> (Field notes, 6 August 2020)

Here, I am brought face to face with something important that Mystical is aware of – that the 'council' doesn't think his mother's parenting is 'good enough'. He has an understanding that the intimacy of food sharing and eating is being scrutinised. I know from his mother that he has been questioned about the food he eats at home and whether it is enough. On the

Figure 3.3: From top left to bottom right: food preparations; Nicole preparing food; dinner table; food with a funny face (photography by Mystical)

surface it could be seen that the photos are a ploy by his mother to make her look like she is performing the role of the good mother, but I choose to do what Tina Campt (2017, p 5) advises and try to 'listen to images'. As Berger (2008) writes, there are different ways of seeing and we need to critique the position we are coming from. So I work at setting aside my prejudgements and look at the pictures. What do they tell me? How do I read them?

There are several photographs showing food preparation (see Figures 3.3, top left and 3.3, top right), the dinner table set (see Figure 3.3, bottom left) and food with funny faces (see Figure 3.3, bottom right). In taking photographs of the food, Mystical disrupts the social work gaze and uses the camera as an ally to show the love and care that his mother provides through food. To him, his mother's work and care are not invisible (Federici, 2012) and are made very visible by his photographs. His photographs show the home routine, rituals, rules and relationship that create and nurture care for him (Luttrell, 2020, p 161). Mystical challenges the social work gaze that upholds the narrative that his mother is negligent and doesn't feed him enough. His use of the camera reminds me of Rohde's (1998, p 188) story of the group in Namibia who, having access to disposable cameras, start to explore their own lives, and thus disrupt the narrative of the colonial anthropologists. The camera has a history of being a colonial apparatus, where the colonised are photographed and a particular narrative is told (Mitchell and Reid-Walsh, 2002, p 89). This has often happened to children too, where they have been the subject of photographs and narratives told about them, rather than being considered photographers themselves (Varvantakis et al, 2019). Here, in the hands of Mystical I can see that he has used the camera to challenge what he perceives as the council's idea about his mother's parenting: the camera in his hand has become an ally and a tool of decolonisation (Mitchell and Reid-Walsh, 2002, p 89).

The photographs also show one way in which his identity as a Muslim, much like his identity as a Mauritian, is also nurtured and developed. The photographs were taken during Ramadan and show the food preparation and the celebratory meals created to break the fast. This year (2020), Ramadan fell during the lockdown and most children were at home because of COVID-19 restrictions. This meant that for some Muslim families, it was easier for children to observe the practices of Ramadan than usual, as they could adjust their timetable according to their needs. For example, children were able to be with their adult relatives as they broke their fast later in the day and stayed up with them as they didn't need to get up early for school the next day. It meant that children could take a more active part in Ramadan than usual. This reminds me of the way children have to navigate these differences in a country where their religion and culture are in the minority and how this experience is sometimes different to that of their parents' childhood. This difference is highlighted in Zeitlyn's (2012) ethnography among children with Bangladeshi parents in East London, and Gembus's (2018) work with second-generation Sudanese young people. Mystical occupies what Homi Bhabha (2004) calls a 'third space', where he is creating meaning from both the culture and practices of the country of his birth and the culture from his mother (Seeberg and Goździak, 2019).

What I see in the photos is the intimate celebration of Ramadan between mother and son – the preparing of food, the setting of the table and the breaking of the fast, the everyday family practices and routines where his mother is passing on a tradition and religion. The photographs have an affective quality that I feel strongly (Campt, 2017): I sense the care of a mother and son trying to nurture their relationship and identity (James et al, 2009; Knight et al, 2014). Mystical's Muslim faith is important to him. I can see that it helps him to make sense of the world. For example, when talking about bullies, he refers to God and the fact that he doesn't think God would be mean enough to invent the term 'cry baby' – it must be the bullies who made that word up. For Mystical, God is a benevolent figure.

This sense of fairness and bullies and school is a reoccurring theme in Mystical's everyday life. He tells me that he is bullied at school, by friends and others, because he is small for his age. I find it ironic that his mother is also being scrutinised by the professional team about his size. I wonder whose 'average body' he is being measured against and found to be falling short.

The school nurse uses the body mass index (BMI) to measure whether Mystical is within a 'healthy' range for his height. On seeing that he is on the lower end of healthy, the school nurse says that he looks strong and healthy. However, his BMI score has not increased and this is seen as a concern in a review meeting between his parents and professionals. Medical sociologists have criticised the use of BMI, arguing that the narrative around BMI measurements is upholding a certain societal image of good health, rather than seeing it as part of a story and context (Gutin, 2018). For Mystical, his BMI measurement is not set alongside the fact he is alert, active and healthy, and small in build like his mother, but is used on its own as one of the markers to measure his mother's parenting. His low BMI measurement is then used to uphold a narrative of a 'not good enough' mother (Callaghan, 2015).

A sticker for his mother

As we pack up, Mystical picks up a pack of stickers. He understands that stickers are important because of what they illustrate and reward – he tells me that he doesn't get many stickers but his brothers do. He acknowledges that his brothers are 'good at school' and that he isn't. He tells me of his near miss at getting a silver sticker. When I say to him that he can take some stickers from the art pack I have brought, I am struck with sadness at his response. He immediately asks me if he can take one for his mother. He wants to take one for her because she is kind. He chooses carefully a sticker with the colour red, saying that he thinks she will like it – the sticker says 'well done' with a big thumbs up. I wonder afterwards why I felt so sad. Maybe because I already feel how punitive the child protection (CP) process has felt for his mother and I'm touched by how aware Mystical is of this and he wants to let his mother know. The needs of mother and child are often separated in the discussion in CP, but yet they are very often intertwined (Hughes et al, 2011; Katz, 2014; Stewart, 2020).

Impediments to the good life: being 'good' at school

This is not Mystical's only experience of being categorised and falling short. He has knowledge and understanding of external agencies, such as social work, the school and health care, having a set of criteria that his wellbeing and progress is measured against. For example, with regards to education, he has an understanding that he is not (as he tells me) 'good at school' and tells me about his experience of being on the 'naughty table'. This categorisation by tables is important to Mystical as he repeats to me several times over the course of our meetings how he managed to move tables. He is proud that when he was at school he had moved from the green table to the blue table because of his good work, and then on to the red table, an 'even better' table.

He notices this categorisation, and knows that the green table is the 'bad' table, that the blue table is better and that the yellow table is the 'top' table. He already understands and experiences that to be academically able or to perform academically well is 'much better', that it is valued. Mystical's reflections are not unique and resemble research participants Sam and Chloe's understanding in Jenkins's (2010) study about school, where they explain how the teachers organise the class into 'brainy tables' and tables for those less 'brainy' or 'dumb' (James, 2013, p 145). The tables symbolise the categorisation and hierarchical stratification of academic ability – with the 'brainiest' at the top.

This categorisation and measurement of children's academic capability have been criticised within the literature on education for not accounting for children's individual growth and development, and for not accounting for their different access to resources which can improve their academic performance (Carlile, 2013; Creasy and Corby, 2019, p 108). The effect of social and economic inequality on children's education was placed under the microscope during the COVID-19 pandemic when all schools were closed. The school closure affected the children in this study in different ways, highlighting some of the social and economic inequality among families. For Mystical, home schooling during the lockdown had not been easy. As Chiou and Tucker (2020) show in their study of digital inequality, Mystical's family struggled with accessing his school work via the internet because they did not have a laptop. Instead, one teacher, who lived close by, used to collect the worksheets and deliver them to his home or Mystical's mother used to collect them from her.

Doing the homework was also a struggle. Mystical's assessment of the situation was, 'I never knew homework could be so boring because I had not done it before' (Field notes, 21 May 2020). This captured the strange and difficult times some children were experiencing in adjusting to life in lockdown. Indeed, not only was Mystical finding home schooling difficult, but Mystical's mother and other children and parents across the UK were too (Rosenthal et al, 2020). I too was struggling to get my own children to do any of their schoolwork, and from my fellow school parents' WhatsApp group, it seemed so were many other parents. However, where things differed was that Mystical's lack of work was being monitored and recorded at CP meetings, and his mother was held accountable for the lack of work he was doing.

In one meeting, Nicole, Mystical's mother, was criticised for him being 'too much on the iPad', at which point Nicole reminded everyone that we were in the middle of a pandemic and that it was difficult to keep him occupied all the time. What strikes me about this is the difference in expectation and grace that is afforded to different people. For while my own lack of mothering can be laughed about with my peers and with my children themselves, for Nicole it is yet another mark against her in the assessment of her parenting (Bywaters et al, 2017a; Featherstone et al, 2018). The fact that the family were navigating their way through a pandemic with limited resources was not being considered. Social work academics (Bywaters et al, 2017a; Featherstone et al, 2017, 2018; Gupta, 2017) argue that with the reduction of state support and its infrastructure, it is up to parents to make up for this shortfall, and they are subsequently held accountable if improvements are not made.

The Children Act 1989 was created to enable local authorities to support families, and the Act initially allowed parents to ask for further assistance on behalf of their children (Featherstone et al, 2018). However, over the years we have seen that the Children Act 1989 has been used or thought of as a way of holding parents accountable for supporting and meeting their children's needs (Featherstone et al, 2018). In social work literature, Gupta (2017) writes that poverty is the elephant in the room when determining parents' capacity to meet these needs – this came into play even more so during the pandemic, with the difference between those that were able to access the internet and those that could not becoming even more pronounced. The policing of parents in the lower social economic groups is also an area that has come under scrutiny (Bywaters et al, 2017a). Indeed, the very policies of social work have been criticised for undermining parents and placing children at further risk of harm (Featherstone, 2016; Featherstone et al, 2017). Keddell and Davie (2018) argue that we need to decolonise social work in order to create transformative care with families. In Mystical's life, we see an example of his mother being held to high standards despite having reduced resources during a pandemic. Instead of addressing the economic inequality that is impeding Mystical and his mother from having a good life, we see his mother being held accountable for not providing him with a good enough life.

Mystical's awareness of not living up to the ideal of the good student was demonstrated when I asked him to take a mobile photograph diary of his day, based on the digital methodology used by Plowman and Stevenson (2012). This did not quite go to plan, because instead of him taking pictures of what he was doing, it was his mother taking pictures of Mystical showing what he was doing. At one point during the day, Nicole sent me a picture of him doing his homework. In the text accompanying the image, she had written that he was playing on the iPad but didn't want to be pictured with it, so had quickly sat by his homework and wanted his picture taken there. This disclosure from Nicole demonstrated that she trusted me not to judge her, and it also demonstrated to me how Mystical wanted to be seen by me. I wondered whether he had concluded that to be seen to be doing homework was 'better' than being seen to be on the iPad.

Mystical shows a complex understanding and reflection of the value of what it is to be 'good at school', and that doing schoolwork was more valued than being on the iPad. He is aware of what is going on and understands the value system in existence at the school, though he does not agree with it. One observation that he already makes is that being seen to be 'smarter' does not necessarily correlate with being kinder. He ponders that when he moved up to the blue table, the children were not kind to each other.

For Mystical, kindness is an important value and factor in his life. He often refers to people as either being 'kind' or 'not kind'. All the people he likes are 'kind'. I speculate that he is already showing an understanding about the value of care. He has made a judgement that although the children on the blue table are 'brighter' and hold a higher position in the class hierarchy, they are not as caring in his opinion, so are not 'better children'. He has an understanding that kindness in the everyday makes a good life and is something to work towards. He shows that he has an understanding of the importance of care. He himself performs acts of kindness. He worries that he took the 'new' ruler and should have taken the old one so that he doesn't make his brother feel sad. Children are often portrayed as needing care (James, 2014), but like Mystical, children perform care practices (Hunleth, 2017) which are often overlooked or are pathologised for being carers (García-Sánchez, 2018). Mystical, along with the other children in the study, show how in their everyday lives they are both cared for and practise care too (Luttrell, 2020), thus playing a significant active part in everyday social reproduction (Cairns, 2020). This is further discussed in Chapter 6.

Mystical's appreciation of kindness comes to the fore when he explains to me his idea of what a good school should look like:

> I think that you should have the teacher that is the kindest and the nicest and that teacher stays with you through school, and you wouldn't need to change.
>
> (Field notes, 6 August 2020)

He is perplexed about the constant change, and values kindness. In spending time with him, I observe that he already has a belief that 'care work' matters, and questions why this is not a factor when organising school. Here, he touches on many issues, like stability, relationships and care, as being important for him to thrive in school. He can imagine a better future that does not include constant change, and appreciates care.

Mystical's comment strikes me on two levels, the first being its engagement in what Nolas (2015) describes as 'childhood publics', and the second as a form of speculative fiction in line with cultural anthropology. Nolas (2015), and subsequent research to emerge from the Connectors study, shows how children in their everyday lives make sense of their time in institutions and between institutions. Rather than solely focusing on the narrow definition of participation such as in political campaigns, and in health, education and social work settings (Nolas, 2015), the focus is on examining children's public participation in the everyday, in their humour, idioms, play and behaviour (Nolas et al, 2017; Nolas et al, 2018). Here we can see Mystical interrogating why school is managed the way it is and giving an alternative.

He also imagines a different future reminiscent of the speculative fiction of anthropological and Black feminist works, such as Ursula Le Guin (2002, 2016), Hurston (2010) and Octavia Butler (2019a, 2019b). Mystical's imaginative future places care at its core and is not so different from Tronto (1993), Barnes (2012) and Puig de la Bellacasa (2017). Throughout my time with Mystical, he contemplates and tries to make meaning of public discourse and politics, as well as imagining an alternative future that is based on a different set of values than the ones supporting the status quo. It seems that he has some very good ideas about making a good life possible, but his thoughts are not often sought or validated in the CP arena.

'The voice of Mystical'

The 'voice' of the child is often referred to and reified in social work (Macdonald, 2017; Featherstone et al, 2018). Social workers must be seen to listen to the child, but what does this look like in practice? And what happens when children within one family say different things? Whose voice really counts? During this research, it was Mystical's story that worried me the most. There were several points that made me wonder whether he was being listened to at all.

In writing this section, I wrestled with several ethical dilemmas. The most important issue was whether I had permission to tell the story I am about to tell (Tuck and Yang, 2014). My instinct as a researcher, a practitioner and as a human was that in *not* telling this part of the story, I was doing a great injustice to Mystical and his mother, that I too would be ignoring his story. But did I have their permission? Did Mystical and his mother understand what I was doing with this information? Considering consent to be ongoing and relational rather than a one-time tick box, I decided to visit Mystical and his mother to explore and discuss the use of their story, and whether they gave consent for me to write about it.

It had been five months since the exhibition of the children's photographs (see Chapter 7) and the research project had officially ended. I had been in contact with Mystical via the phone and had visited several times. I knock on the door and he and his mother greet me warmly. They are sitting in the living room, both now fully recovered from COVID-19. We chat about the Christmas break and about the return to school. I ask about Mystical's teacher and how things are going in general. I then speak to Nicole about the research project and how I am at the stage of writing up the ethnography for my thesis. I again reiterate that the purpose of my research is to explore the everyday lives of children who have experienced domestic abuse and social work intervention:

> I begin, 'Nicole, you know how I am writing about children's lives. Well one of the things I wanted to write about was about you and Mystical, about how it was hard for you and Mystical to get the professionals to listen to you both. I wanted to ask whether it was OK for me to write about how when you went through the system and the court that it was difficult to get the professionals to hear you. I won't use your names.' I am nervous and want to make sure that Nicole has understood me fully, so I repeat everything in Mauritian Creole.
> Nicole is clear in her response: 'Yes, it is important that you write about it. People need to know. It might help another family.'
> (Field notes, 31 January 2022)

At that moment I feel my heart become hot. I feel tearful, for despite the difficulties, I am moved by Nicole's generosity and solidarity with other imagined families. She is looking beyond herself and is showing solidarity with strangers, families she does not know and is never likely to meet.

I turn to Mystical, who is playing on his mother's phone, and ask him the same question, whether he gives permission for me to write about getting professionals/grown-ups to listen to him.

> 'Yes ... because grown-ups say that they want to listen but when things are badder [sic] they don't. Like teachers, they keep saying they listen, but when things get bad they don't listen, they just tell you to be quiet,' Mystical explains.
> (Field notes, 31 January 2022)

His point reminds me of a drawing in Lundy's (2007, p 936) article on voice, where a child had drawn an adult saying, 'Shut the hell up because I am always right.' Mystical, similar to other children, has shown that however difficult things are, children do want to have their voices heard. They want to be part of the decisions that are made about their lives. As I discussed in Chapter 2, our anxiety about protecting children and worries about ethical research with children can be so fraught that we in turn fail to listen and take into account their stories. As Callaghan et al (2017a, 2018) ask, what is it exactly that we are protecting children from by not asking them, for they have already experienced and seen some of the worst things humans can do to one another?

It is with this in mind that I continue to tell the story of Nicole and Mystical, and the social work system and court process. I proceed knowing that I 'cannot find the right words, yet silence is also impossible' (Back, 2007, p 4).

Ever since I started the research with Nicole and Mystical, Nicole would often say, 'I wish you were my worker.' I kept reiterating my role as a researcher, but Nicole kept repeating, 'But you listen, you understand me.' I feel this was because we both speak Creole and, through my years as a practitioner, I have become sensitive to the way the system can fail to listen to those it is supposed to support and I try to be empathetic. When I first met Nicole to talk about the project, she had burst into tears with relief saying, 'At last there is someone who can understand me' (Field notes, 2 March 2020). While she could understand and speak English, when it came to the more complex and nuanced patterns of language used in CP, there were many times she was either misunderstood or found it confusing. I had constantly reminded Nicole that she had a right to an interpreter and should get one, but this did not always happen.

I have been privy to hearing about court and CP meetings and reports through Nicole and Mystical, so while I cannot quote from reports because of confidentiality and the uncertain legal status of doing so, I can document their words and experience. Throughout the reports by professionals and the court process, there is a recognition of the difficulties of co-parenting but no reflection on how domestic abuse, especially coercive control, may have a significant effect on this, even though there is an acknowledgement of the children's father's domestic abuse towards Nicole. The violence of the reports and process strikes me hard, because the lack of thought and care employed in some of the professional reports is not proportionate to the important and significant role they will play in affecting the life of Mystical's family. I question whose voice counts and whether the importance given to any of the voices is in proportion to the investment that particular person has in the wellbeing of the family. Who gets to challenge these inaccuracies? In their study of care-experienced young people reading reports about themselves, Shepherd et al (2020) found that the young people often found inaccuracies in their care reports. They argue that these inaccuracies start from when professionals begin to write, without taking into account the multiplicities of children's stories and only choosing the narratives and descriptions that capture 'organisational, subjective, biased or prejudicial perspectives' (Shepherd et al, 2020, p 311).

There is a prevalent narrative in the reports and accounts made by different professionals, some of whom have never met Mystical. The narrative is that Mystical and his siblings are materialistic, that they equate love with money. My head feels heavy as I read the lines. I feel like I am walking through a fog slowly. I can't understand how anyone who knows Mystical can say this. In my time with him, he has shown me the value of care, love and imagination of an alternative future. Did the social worker not see this? It does not relate to what Mystical said about schools and care, or about kindness. My mind twists and turns to try to fathom how you can write those lines about children whose family are living below or just on the poverty line. Is it bad to value material goods? I myself admire a pretty dress and a nice cushion. I appreciate the gifts my family give me, as does Mystical. Does that make us materialistic? Surely it is easier to be ambivalent about material goods when we live with abundance. What does this also say of the other children in the research who have taken photographs of things that they love (which I explore in Chapter 6). Are they materialistic too? Is it even bad to be materialistic in a society that keeps pushing for us to accumulate more and more (Hochschild, 2003; Miller, 2005, 2008, 2010)?

The value judgement on Mystical astounds me. I can see how he gets lost in the myriad of professionals giving voice to his needs. There is little in the CP and court process about the two biggest factors affecting his family and wellbeing – his socio-economic position and the ongoing impact of domestic abuse, especially coercive control. In fact, there are several reports stating that the concern is that he is reluctant to see his father and does not have a strong relationship with him. There is limited exploration with Mystical as to why he may not want to see his father. The emphasis is not on the wellbeing of Mystical but on his father's rights. This line of argument reflects the predominant culture and value of patriarchy that pervades the court and care system when it comes to fathers' rights, contact and children's views, as discussed earlier in this chapter and Chapter 2, and highlighted in the reports by Macdonald (2017) and Morrison et al (2020). In Mystical's case, the most damning evidence of epistemic injustice in the court system was when the judge was reported to have commented on Mystical not wanting to see his father, saying, 'An eight-year-old does not know what he wants. You can't just listen to him' (Field notes, 19 January 2021).

Mystical's voice was further silenced when the professionals accused Nicole of parental alienation. They concluded that Mystical was reluctant to see his father because his mother had turned Mystical against his father. This left Nicole in the difficult position of encouraging Mystical to participate in something he did not want to do (seeing his father) so that it would not be held against her as an example of her bad parenting. Despite the evidence of parental alienation by mothers in cases of domestic abuse being debunked (Birchall and Choudhry, 2022), and numerous research studies about how child contact is used as part of a pattern of coercive control by perpetrators (Holt, 2008; Morrison, 2015; Radford and Hester, 2015; Thiara and Humphreys, 2015), Mystical and Nicole's story shows that there is still a lack of understanding in the social work and court system.

In writing this chapter, it dawns on me that the social worker, then the psychologist, had written into being the narrative they had created. When I was wrestling with how to write, I watched a brilliant talk by the ethnographer Lara Watts (2020). Watts explained that we write into being the reality that we want to see or have imagined. Here I can see that the social worker has created a narrative of a mother who cannot co-parent, a son with no mind of his own who has been influenced by his mother not to see his father, a mother who neglects her children, a mother who cannot control two of her children and has alienated the third child against his father. It is effectively a story about Mystical in which he himself has been erased.

I feel he has been sidelined because he has shown solidarity with his mother, and the system has not. In trying to write in an objective manner, the system/social worker has inadvertently sided with the father. How does one co-parent when there is coercive control? Nowhere in the reports is domestic abuse considered for its impact on the everyday lives of the children.

Living and researching under the shadow of child protection (CP)

Mystical's story affects me throughout the research. I can't sleep. I dream about it. I wake up with fully formed poetry in my head and I am no poet. I begin to understand what Lorde (2020) means when she proclaims how everybody needs poetry. Mystical and Nicole's story has a visceral effect on me – it goes round and round in my head. I feel low and I worry constantly about them. I feel my boundaries as a practitioner, researcher and fellow human blur and stretch. I return to my feminist ethical commitments and look not at what I owe Mystical and his mother but rather how best I can meet my caring responsibilities to Mystical and his mother (Tronto, 1993; Puig de la Bellacasa, 2017; Folkes, 2022).

As a practitioner, I know they are not getting the service that will enhance their safety and allow them to thrive. As a researcher, I am unsure what my role is. I feel like I am doing a dance, but a dance of which I don't know the steps and I am trying not to step on anyone's toes, but constantly feel that my toes are being trodden on. I talk with both Mystical and his mother, together and separately, about my worries about their voice not getting heard. I again talk to Nicole about the importance of having an interpreter at every meeting, so that she can be understood and understand fully what is going on. I tell her that I am worried about her ex-partner's behaviour and how the professionals are not listening to her concerns. She agrees and would like me to take this to the safeguarding lead for the project because 'maybe they will listen to you'. I try to use my position as a researcher to support Nicole and Mystical. I talk to my supervisor and then the safeguarding lead for the project. The safeguarding lead takes our concerns to the social work team. Their answer comes back that domestic abuse has nothing to do with this case – it is in the past. We (the safeguarding lead and I) keep bringing it up, but our concerns keep getting knocked down. I am starting to think that I am imagining things, that I have got it wrong, that what I am feeling and seeing is not real. I write this in my fieldwork diary:

> I feel tearful and powerless. I feel that the mother is not being listened to. I feel angry that the dad is being praised when his past domestic abuse is not being addressed and is not seen to affect Nicole. Family work needs to be done. I know why there is limited ethnographic research with this group – too hard, too heart-breaking. I was ready for the children to break my heart – not mothers.
>
> (Field notes, 27 May 2020)

I know why people may not do this research, but I also know why I can. I feel I am both plastic and robust like a boundary object 'linking entities across different sites' (Burman, 2004, p 371). My experience as a therapist with social services, as a Mauritian, as a mother, as an ethnographer, has given me different ways of knowing and being that have allowed me to occupy the sometimes joyful, fun, vulnerable, confusing and heart-breaking place of researching with families within social work services. I can talk and understand the different languages, but with this comes the vulnerability of negotiating my different roles (Velicu and García-López, 2018).

I know that I don't have all the answers and that family life can be complex, but what strikes me the hardest is how Mystical's voice gets ignored because he is not supporting the prevalent narrative about his mother. How much do we really want to know children, or do we simply like the idea of listening to them? While his opinion is being sought, because it does not fit in with the narrative that the social worker, his father or one of his siblings have, his opinion is discarded. It is too uncomfortable. What is considered to matter is in accordance with social norms rather than with any desire Mystical may have.

Likewise, in CP we can be so wrapped up in its rhetoric that we ignore the actual physical embodied child before us. In his paper 'How children become invisible in child protection work', social work academic Harry Ferguson (2016a) explores how children become invisible even though they are right in front of the social worker. He explores the everyday practice of social workers to get close to children and listen to them, not only to their verbal communication but to their embodied language – to hold, touch, smell and see. Ferguson argues that when this fails to happen, children's abuse can go undetected and, in extreme cases, end in death. In Mystical's case I can see an additional effect: the social worker's lack of closeness to Mystical means that they cannot see or hear the things that make his life liveable. They cannot hear that he feels cared for, safe and loved by his mother. Their lack of closeness has meant he has become invisible, while his siblings have become more visible.

Domestic abuse can affect family dynamics in different ways. Even within the same family, there can be different impacts, affects and stories. I am unable to tell the full story of Mystical because his story is entangled with those of his brothers, and his brothers are not part of the research. These stories are not for me to tell. But what I do observe is that many things work against him being heard, primarily his age and his closeness to his mother.

The frequency of my visits to the family lessen while they go through the court-ordered parental assessment. For the next six months, Mystical's and Nicole's lives are taken up with court meetings and visits from social workers and other professionals, all assessing whether they can stay together. I keep in contact with them and visit when it is convenient for them.

I am surprised how intense the process is, and the fact that it reduces the time and energy they have to sustain family life through everyday practices. They see their friends less and don't go out, with the exception of school and shopping. It is ironic that now that they are going through the most gruelling process, they have less time and energy to engage with the people and things that support them, that give joy to family life. Mystical himself is worried about the visits from the different professionals.

> 'I am a little bit scared of the social workers visiting,' he explains to me.
> 'What scares you about them?' I ask.
> 'I don't like talking to them,' he replies.
> I probe further: 'Do you know why you don't like talking to them?'
> 'I am scared in case they won't let me see my family. I am scared about answering their questions,' he responds.
> 'I can understand it can be scary talking to grown-ups you don't really know. You can only tell them how you feel and what you think. It is not a test like you have in school – where there is a right and a wrong answer – you know what I mean?' I tried to explain, struggling with my own words.
>
> (Field notes, 20 May 2021)

Having your voice heard is more than just saying words aloud. There is an assemblage of things that go on. At our core, both Mystical and I know this. I have not lied to him, but I realise later that I am presenting him with an idealised scenario – where the social workers will take a more nuanced understanding of their family life, will have an understanding of the complexity of domestic abuse, will take into account language, poverty, gender, age, class, physical and mental ability.

Mystical and Nicole are constantly living in the shadow of the past and the future.

Conclusion

It is difficult to conclude this chapter because in many senses it is ongoing. Mystical and his mother, Nicole, are still navigating their way through the social work system and coercive control. But, despite the structural and relational challenges, they have continued to create liveable lives – something that is emblematic of the lives of all the children in the research. Mystical illustrates how children are not listened to when they diverge from the prevalent narrative. In his case, his age and closeness to his mother are held against him and his voice is not heard. Yet he is not a passive and damaged child – during our time together, he shows that he is articulate, wise, kind and creative. In the following chapter, I continue to explore children's everyday lives, and the importance of play and fun.

4

Taking the fun out of play

> 'So, what are we going to play?' asks JoJo Siwa (named after the greatest singer in the world), as she presses her nose up to the mobile telephone screen and slowly backs away, swaying her head.
> (Field notes, 26 March 2020)

In this chapter, I continue to shift attention away from using violence as the only gaze through which to see children's lives and attend, instead, to the way they create, navigate and engage with people, things, spaces and places that bring them joy and fun. 'So, what are we going to play now?' was a question that greeted me each time I telephoned sisters JoJo Siwa (aged six) and Esmeralda (aged eight). The main focus of the phone calls to them was the fun we were going to have and the games we were going to play. This was the case for all the children in the study to varying degrees. Having fun and playing was a key aim of the children's everyday lives. Initially, I felt nervous about writing this chapter because so much of my work as a therapist and activist has been about arguing about the effects of domestic abuse on children – I feared that highlighting the children's love of, and search for, fun and play would take away from the real challenges of injustice and discrimination that they face. Yet searching for fun was an important part of the everyday lives of children in the study and how they made their lives liveable, how they made a good life. It was important for me to reflect and capture this.

As I outlined in Chapter 2, the literature on children who have experienced domestic abuse often portrays them as passive and/or damaged victims of abuse. While it is important to acknowledge the challenges that experiencing abuse creates and the damage it can have, throughout the research the children have shown me that the search for 'fun and play' was an important part of living fulfilling everyday lives. Even doing things they did not like, for example, going to school, had moments that brought them joy and fun, which made the experience bearable. Many of the children were not looking forward to going back to school after lockdown but found the prospect of being with their friends at playtime 'fun and good'.

In this chapter, I want to illustrate the complexity of the children's lives and their very human everyday practice of creating fun and play. In order to broaden my thinking, I drew inspiration from the work of Black feminist scholars, Indigenous scholars, South American and South Asian researchers who have criticised the portrayal by NGOs and other Western scholars of the lives of communities who are marginalised through inequalities and violence. I include the work of feminist social researcher Kirmani (2020), who in researching gender-based violence in India writes about being surprised by 'fun'. It is here that I came across the term *mazaa*, which seemed to capture my struggle with describing/exploring the everyday lives of children. *Mazaa* is a Hindi word for 'pleasure or enjoyment' as defined by the Oxford Hindi–English dictionary (McGregor, 1993). It is known as *maja* in Guajarati and *mojo* in Bangla (Anjaria and Anjaria, 2020). I wonder whether an English-language version would be 'joy' or 'zest for life'; in French it might be 'joie de vivre'; in Mauritian Creole we could say '*belle la vie*'. Drawing from the research work criticising NGOs, I explore how *mazaa* or fun is desired by children and how the creation of *mazaa*/fun is produced through an assemblage of humans and non-humans, social networks and systems.

I draw inspiration from the work of social researchers Khalili (2016) and Kirmani (2020) who criticised North American and European feminist theorists for narrowly focusing their analysis of pleasure on sexual experiences alone when pleasure traverses all parts of life. Drawing from her ethnographic study of Palestinian women refugees in Beirut, Khalili (2016) argues that Ahmed's (2010) critique of happiness is geographically and temporally specific, and that the pursuit of enjoyment is an important opportunity for conviviality in a challenging environment and should be read as political (Khalili, 2016, p 323). In writing about fun and play, it is not my intention to divorce children from painful family dynamics and deny the reality of domestic abuse in their lives. I hope, however, to show that pain can and does coexist alongside joy and pleasure, and that one of the ways that children demonstrate their agency is by creating spaces to seek them out.

This chapter builds upon the work of Pernebo et al (2016), Nolas et al (2018) and Beetham et al (2019). Their research with children who had experienced domestic abuse and their involvement in groups run by social services found that the children valued the fun games and fun food they had during the groups more than the psychoeducation element of the groups. Yet, play has often been co-opted by adults for various educational purposes and therapeutic interventions rather than being valued for the enjoyment it provides. In this chapter, I hope to reclaim play for children as something that is joyous and important for its own sake, and not as a means of production (Oakley, 2005).

Writing this chapter has been difficult but also enlightening. At times I felt that I was wrestling and tussling with an imaginary friend. Someone I felt was there but unseen, like thin air. This is the difficulty of writing about *mazaa* (pleasure and fun) – if we grab it too hard, we end up making it something it is not, for example, a grand theory or a predetermined answer to our research question. To not wrestle with it means to ignore it and label it too frivolous to note. Both ways only reduce the lives of children and their families to a one-dimensional foregone conclusion to fit my predetermined narrative, rather than honouring the complexity of their lives and the fullness of their humanity. In the following paragraphs, I have tried to centre *mazaa* in the lives of the children and tell the story of my own struggle to acknowledge and give space to what brings pleasure (Anjaria and Anjaria, 2020, p 237).

Making sense of fun and play

It was my weekly call to JoJo Siwa and her sister, Esmeralda. COVID-19 physical restrictions had meant that for the moment my interactions with the family were restricted to video calls and doorstep deliveries of art materials. Initially, the weekly calls to JoJo Siwa and Esmeralda had left me confused and questioning my method, wondering about data creation and what on earth it all meant. In this section I explore how I tried to make sense of play.

> 'OK, tell us a joke!' JoJo Siwa's face comes towards the screen.
> 'I know one!' shouts Esmeralda.
> 'No, no … I got one,' JoJo Siwa says as she leans over to Esmeralda and whispers something and both erupt into a loud laughter. 'So why did the chicken cross the road?'
> 'Oh, I don't know. Why did the chicken cross the road?' I ask.
> 'To get to McDonald's,' JoJo Siwa laughs, shaking the phone and rolling around on the bed laughing.
> 'Can we play a game now?' Esmeralda jumps in and asks.
> (Field notes, 26 March 2020)

This was the general pattern of calls to JoJo Siwa and Esmeralda. A combination of jokes, games and laughter. At first, I often left the calls wondering what this 'nothingness' was about. I could not seem to grasp anything – was this even research? My weekly encounters with Esmeralda and JoJo challenged me as a researcher. I was reassured to find that other researchers had also struggled with this. In the Connector study, the researchers in the multimodal, multi-city research project with children at first struggled with the children's playfulness (Varvantakis and Nolas, 2019).

Like Nolas et al (2019), I too often felt out of my depth and 'missing' something. Nothing seemed to fit into the neat categories that I had anticipated my 'findings' to be. In time, I slowly became aware that the significance of our weekly calls was to have fun. It was both as simple and as complicated as that. JoJo Siwa and Esmeralda were showing me what was important in their lives – the art of playing just to have fun.

My relationship with them challenged me in several ways. It taught me that I too, while thinking that I was an all-accepting therapist/researcher, had digested and was regurgitating the predominant thinking that fun was trivial and therefore not important if it was not 'productive'. I had, as Fanon (2017 [1952], p 13) would say, 'missed the mark', and it was within this feeling of 'failure' that I was able to explore and critique some of my grandiose notions about fun and productivity. I had bought into the thinking that there needed to be an outcome, a product to make these encounters of value, that there needed to be another reason for play apart from fun. I was, as Fanon (2017 [1952], p 13) would name, trying to have mastery over play. In this case, I could not see how having fun was going to help my research.

In his article 'What's the point if it can't be fun?', the anthropologist David Graeber (2014) argues that in the world of ethology, the researcher often dismisses the fact that animals have fun because they often can't fathom a reason why. Graeber explains that an analysis of animal behaviour was not considered scientific unless the behaviour could be interpreted as resembling a means/end calculation usually applied to economic transactions. In essence, I too had fallen into the productivity trap besetting ethologists. In this sense, my research joins periodic attempts by scholars in different fields to show that play is not trivial; they do this by taking play seriously in their analysis (Piaget, 2013; Huizinga, 2016; Sahlberg, 2019). Educators have argued about the value of play in the process of learning (Piaget, 2013; Sahlberg, 2019), and social workers have demonstrated how play can help to build relationships with children and can be a way of eliciting information and assessing risk (Luckock et al, 2007; Winter et al, 2017). However, throughout my project, the children have shown that play and fun are important because they are pleasurable on their own terms, and I had to learn to listen harder and more closely to hear what they were saying, as the next sections illustrate.

Bending, changing and breaking rules

Some of the greatest fun that children had was breaking the rules.

> 'So, let's play a number game,' says Esmeralda.
> 'Yes – guess a number between one and ten,' JoJo Siwa joins in.
> 'OK, how about one?' I guess.
> 'NO!' they both reply.
> 'Two?'
> 'No!'
> 'Five?'
> 'No!'
> 'Six?'

'No!'
'Oh, it was between one and ten? Wasn't it?' I query.
'Ha ha … it's 20!' says Esmeralda.
'But …' I protest.
'We cheated!' laughs Esmeralda and JoJo.
(Field notes, 10 December 2020)

Esmeralda and JoJo found much fun in 'tricking' me. Sometimes, Esmeralda would pretend that there was a loss of internet connection and would freeze on screen. Other times, they would simply disappear off screen and return laughing (see Figure 4.1).

The children found fun in the way they could subvert the normal adult–child power relations. This was similar to the first time I started to meet Elsa virtually via WhatsApp video calls. I had met her in person a number of times in her home when I was working with her older brother, Pogi, for the research project. After a couple of meetings with her brother, Elsa's mother and I realised that Elsa wanted to join in the project too. Again, Elsa's mother was unsure how Elsa could contribute to the project in a 'meaningful way' as physical restrictions due to COVID-19 were about to start, but we decided to try it out.

Initially, in my first video call to Elsa, she does not want to speak to me and runs away from the phone. Her mother, Ann, and I continue to chat on the telephone. As we speak, Elsa slowly pokes her head over the phone and I can see her head appearing in the bottom right-hand side of my screen. Elsa's head pops up and out again. This happens for a few minutes, and then her head disappears. Ann and I continue to chat, and a few seconds later, I see a pink spoon thrusted into my screen:

> 'You are a baby; I need to feed you,' says Elsa as she pushes the toy milk bottle towards the screen. 'You need to drink.' As I pretend to drink from the milk bottle, she laughs, then pushes the hair out of her eyes and disappears. Next, she comes back with a hairbrush and starts to 'brush my hair'. 'Good baby,' she giggles and quickly goes away and fetches a bowl and spoon. 'Here, now it is dinner time, baby. Eat!' She laughs at me pretending to be a baby.
> (Field notes, 26 March 2020)

This reversal of roles – her being the one looking after me the baby, instead of me the adult talking to her the child, is fun for Elsa. Maybe it is my presentation of being small and portable via the mobile phone screen that makes it easier to treat me as if I am a baby, but she enjoys it nonetheless. She laughs so hard that soon both Ann and I are laughing too. I find myself caught up in the hilarity of the set-up.

Figure 4.1: A WhatsApp video call (photography by Brenda)

The two scenarios are emblematic of others throughout the research, in which children found much fun and joy in turning the power relations that exist between adults and children upside down. JoJo Siwa and Esmeralda always thought it was great fun to either 'cheat' or win games by making up their own rules for games that I did not know, while Elsa had a lot of fun making me the baby that she needed to look after.

In these instances, for the children, the fun was created by being in charge, by being in control and creating an imaginary world where their rules counted. In essence, the fun was in inverting the rules of society. In his ethnographic work, Geertz (1993 [1972]) analyses the cockfights that he experiences in Bali. He draws on Bentham's (2005 [1908]) theory of 'Deep Play' to help think through what he is seeing. Geertz concludes that while Bentham would ban cockfighting because of its irrationality and harm, the play in cockfighting is more than about money but also about men's position in society, and it is a way of enhancing one's status. The play is fun and exciting because it is telling us about society and our position in it – it plays with our roles. For JoJo Siwa, Elsa and Esmeralda, play is fun because they can create a world where they have more autonomy, but in order to play with me, they need me to surrender some of my autonomy. JoJo Siwa does this by making up a game and then changing the rules; Elsa does this by checking that I will be a baby before continuing to play with me. They both take the chance that I will play. There is a relationality in the play (which I explore later in Chapter 6) and also something revealing about society's concept of rules and fun.

The link between fun and society is highlighted again when I visit Mystical. During the visit, he wants to play a game. I introduce him to 'tic-tac-toe', a game similar to noughts and crosses but each player has three counters that they can move on the grid (see Figure 4.2). The aim of the game, like noughts and crosses, is to get your three counters in a line before your opponent does. Mystical enjoys this game at first. It is new and exciting, but the thrill soon wears off. When he realises that he cannot beat me, he starts to cheat.

> 'You can't do that!' I point out, as Mystical moves one of his counters to the opposite side of the grid.
> 'Why not?' asks Mystical.
> 'It's just the rule of the game,' I explain.
> 'This game is not fair!' cries Mystical.
> 'Oh?' I question.
> 'Because you always win. You know the rules, so I'm going to change it!' decides Mystical. 'I can move two times and you can only move one time when it is your turn.'
>
> (Field notes, 21 December 2020)

We continue the game, and Mystical keeps changing the rules until he can win. We giggle and laugh together about this. It is clear that it is no fun if you cannot ever win. On the bus home, I reflect on this. Mystical is right – there is no fun in playing if you can never win. Psychoanalysts and educators

Figure 4.2: Tic-tac-toe (photography by Mystical)

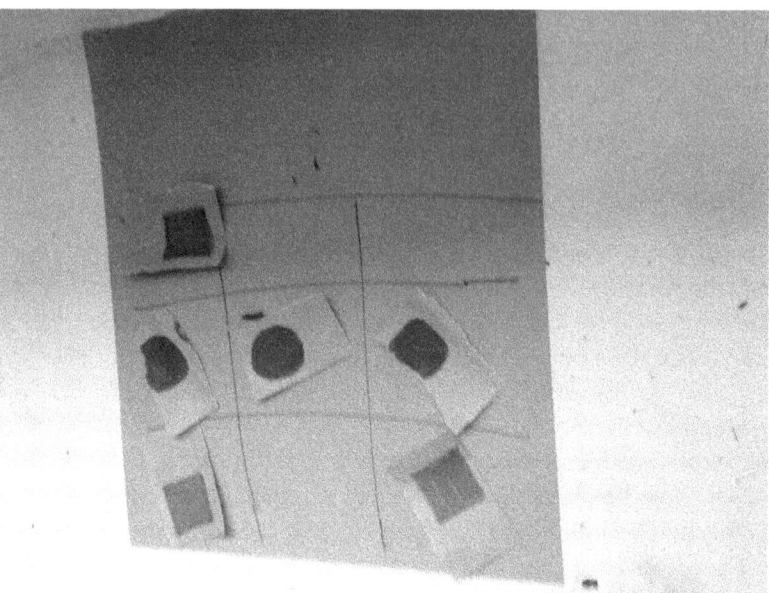

may look at this and argue that the children need to win in order to be in control, perhaps as an effect of their abuse, or that not being able to lose is a sign of immaturity, but what I sense is that Mystical is telling me something more profound about society. The conservative view is that he is breaking the rules of the game in order to win, but an alternative way of looking at it would be to see that he is adjusting the rules so that it becomes fairer – for in fact Mystical starts the game of tic-tac-toe at a disadvantage. He doesn't know the rules; I am older and have years of practice, while he is coming to it as a novice. So instead of accepting the game as it is, he changes the rules to account for his disadvantage and make it fairer, so he can have fun – after all, where is the fun if you can never win?

Esmeralda, JoJo Siwa, Elsa and Mystical created a safe space for play and fun by inverting and bending societal roles and rules. While they had the desire for fun, this was not enough to make fun happen: they needed an assemblage of things to come together (Deleuze and Guattari, 2013a), like me letting go of my own set of rules and roles, the internet working and the materials to make games. Fun and play may appear to be spontaneous, but they often involve an entanglement of things and systems coming together to create the space for fun (as I illustrate later in this chapter).

Elsa, Esmeralda, JoJo Siwa and Mystical's bending and breaking rules reminds me of where feminist Lugones (1987) writes that in order to understand other people, we need to 'playfully' travel to their world.

In her essay, she rejects Huizinga's and Gadamer's definitions of playfulness and play as being ultimately to do with contest and winning, losing and battling (Lugones, 1987, p 15). Rather, she argues, playfulness and play involve a sense of uncertainty, an openness to being a fool, an openness to self-construction, and construction and reconstruction of the world we live in (Lugones, 1987, p 17). Was this not what was happening between Elsa, JoJo Siwa and the other children and myself? Was I not travelling 'playfully' to their world to know them more, and constructing and reconstructing the world together with them? On reflection, my play with the children did change me, how I saw play, how I saw the children and even the focus of the research. The play was not about conquering another's world but about pleasure and through this getting to know one another and seeing one another in our full humanness.

In the case of domestic abuse, Lugones (1987) opens up a way to 'avoid' seeing people only through the eyes of the oppressor or those in power – she does this through her interpretation of play. Lugones writes of her struggle to see her mother beyond the eyes of the Argentinian patriarchy. She sees her mother as only a victim, and she likens it to the slave that Aristotle writes about – we only know the slave through the view of the master. However, when she finally travels to her mother's world, she realises that her mother is not 'foldable and pliable, and exhausted by mainstream Argentinian patriarchal construction of her' but that there are other worlds where her mother 'shines as a creative being' (Lugones, 1987, p 18). Lugones warns against seeing people through the eyes of their oppressors. For children who have experienced domestic abuse, it is important that we do not only see them through the narrative of the abuse, for then we risk only hearing the stories the perpetrators and systems tell us about them. In playfully travelling to the worlds of Elsa, JoJo Siwa, Esmeralda and Mystical, I begin to know them through their worlds, and they do shine as creative beings, and together we make and remake worlds. In doing so, I need to be mindful that I too do not construct the fun out of the children in the research. As Lugones (1987, p 15) writes, 'I am also scared of ending up a serious human, someone with no multi-dimensionality, with no fun for life, someone who has had the fun constructed out of her.'

Playground: an everyday place for fun

As I write this, the charity Save the Children has launched a campaign, 'It's Time to Play', which aims to encourage people to 'make up for those lost lockdown moments' and help children to regain the time and space for play that they lost during COVID-19 (Save the Children Fund, 2021). The call is that children need to play to recover from coronavirus. While I support this approach to play, one of the things this ethnographic study has shown me is that play has been part of children's everyday lives throughout the pandemic. It is part of them navigating relations, creating their identity, getting to know their bodies and potential, taking risks and having copious amounts of fun. The children have not been passive under COVID-19 physical restrictions but have found ways of playing and having fun, of experiencing *mazaa*. Childhood and play researchers Alison Stenning and Wendy Russell (2020) had just started their research into outdoor play when COVID-19 restrictions were introduced. In their initial findings they found that people noticed that more children were playing outside, as there were fewer cars on the road – children were occupying more outdoor spaces in urban places. Their study reinforced their support for the Playing Out Campaign (2021) and the need for the freedom to play outdoors that children have gained through the pandemic not to be lost.

A *Guardian* newspaper headline screams 'Set children free: Are playgrounds a form of incarceration?' (Wainright, 2021). In the article, journalist Oliver Wainwright explores whether playgrounds have been used to imprison children in cities that are not child-friendly in design. He quotes geographer Tim Gill, saying that the lockdown has been brutal for children and 'has been an acceleration of what has been happening to children's lives for the last 50 years, an erosion of their freedom'. In his book *Urban Playground: How Child Friendly Planning Can Save Cities*, Gill (2021) argues that the playground needs to break free from its fenced boundaries and through to the rest of the urban landscape, so that children can play more freely. While there is value in the argument that our cities are not child-friendly, the children in the research project showed that the playground too offers a lot of potential for fun and play. In the playground, they were the masters while the grown-ups were on the periphery. Indeed, as this research shows, playgrounds were a space for conviviality.

The playground has been a friend to the children and me during the pandemic. We have been able to use the space to have fun and get to know each other. For me, the playground can be both a virtual space as well as a physical one. Both types create a space for curiosity, relationship building, knowledge creation and joy (Potter and Cowan, 2020).

'Catch me!' Playground, bodies, risk and fun

My relationship with Rosie and Kyro was nurtured through playing in the playground (see Figure 4.3). It was where we would often meet and play. Every time they would cry out for me to play the game 'it'.

> 'Come on, Brenda – let's play "it"!' Rosie and Kyro cry out.
> 'OK, but who is "it"?' I ask.
> 'No, not me!' Rosie shouts.

Figure 4.3: The playground (photography by Kyro)

'Not me too! I was "it" last time – it's your turn, Rosie!' Kyro shouts back.

'NO! NO! NO!' Rosie is having none of it.

'OK, I will be "it",' I interrupt. 'But where's homie?' I ask. 'Homie' is the safe space where those who are being chased can stay and where the "it" (the chaser) isn't allowed to touch them.

(Field notes, 20 March 2020)

At the beginning of the year, Rosie got frustrated that she could be caught easily. I would make the decision to run slower when chasing her and would make sure I chased Kyro too. It was like a dance that was being performed.

Being caught easily was no fun, but not ever being caught was not fun either – it was the risk, the challenge and the suspense in the chase that were so exciting and fun. As the year progressed, I noticed that the rules changed for 'it' to allow for the growth and changes in all three of our bodies. I noticed that I was running slower (a year in lockdown will do that to your fitness level!) and Rosie and Kyro were beginning to run faster and were stronger. The last time I visited, they immediately said, 'There is no homie for us, but you can rest here.' Despite the bruise to my ego, I was soon glad of the space to rest and catch my breath. I noticed the change in our bodies, as I had to work hard to even have any chance of catching Rosie. She was now a lot faster and more agile than she was a year previously.

Here, both Rosie and Kyro had already assessed the situation and worked out what would be the most fun way to play and give the most joy. For them, there was no fun in never being caught – there was no risk in the game. As for Mystical, earlier in the chapter, who found there was no fun in always losing, there was no fun or thrill if the outcome was already decided.

Risk is a major feature of managing domestic abuse and children. Yet, there is another side to risk – it can be fun. The search and need for risks can be pathologised, but it is a part of everyday play and fun. Without risk, life can be boring and without spark – getting the balance right is an art form, a skill, like a dance. Rosie and Kyro had navigated this with the changing of the rules of 'it' to accommodate their growing bodies and my ageing body.

Gill (2007, p 12) argues that society's fear about risk for children has resulted in what he calls 'the shrinking horizon of childhood'. In his book *No Fear: Growing Up in a Risk Adverse Society*, Gill (2007) explains how some risk is important to children so that they can learn to manage risks as they grow. Satisfying children's desire for risk can lessen the need for them to search for situations that fill that need which can put them in further danger. In addition, children gain benefits over the long term when exposed to activities with a degree of risk, for example, building their confidence and experience in managing difficulties (Gill, 2007, p 16). An important element is that risk and pleasure can be interlinked. In their analysis of safety in public spaces, Indian feminist scholars Phadke et al (2011) argue that pleasure and thrills are entwined and that we can safeguard the fun out of desire. For children in this study, there was very much the desire for risks in their play: risk was fun. Rosie and Kyro loved the chase; Pogi loved going for an adventure in the woods where discarded glass, rubbish and other sharp objects lay. Even when the risk means an injury occurs, it can still seem fun, as Katie showed me.

Sitting on the swings, Katie and I are chatting and chilling (see Figure 4.4). We look around the playground and Katie says:

> 'I hurt myself here once. I had begged my mum to bring me to the playground. She was busy but she still brought me 'cos I begged and begged. I was so happy when we got here … my friend was here. We both went on the see-saw. We both like to be extreme,' Katie giggles, and continues. 'We kept going faster and higher … and then, you know … she had to be more extreme … and she jumped off. I went flying and cut my head open. I had to go to hospital and everything. I got to go in an ambulance; there was a blue flashing light. I remember I was wearing a Mickey Mouse Disney top and there was blood all running down it. Look here,' Katie says, as she points to a line on her forehead. 'See, that is where I cut myself and they had to put stitches.'
>
> (Field notes, 13 February 2021)

Figure 4.4: The swings (photography by Katie)

Katie's eyes widen as she tells me this story, with her voice rising as she delivers the climactic part of being thrown off the see-saw. I can hear the thrill in her voice, as well as the joy in her laughter. Despite the accident, she has kept coming to the playground and using the see-saw. Her story is emblematic of the other children in the study, who all found fun in taking risks, be they physical risks on see-saws and in chase or relationally, like getting to know me and making new friends. The incident had also given her a story, one which she tells with relish. When we reduce the risk in play, we also reduce the stories children can tell. There was fun in taking risks, yet the move over the last two decades has been about reducing children's risks; for example, fewer children walk to school on their own (Creasy and Corby, 2019). Creasy and Corby (2019) argue that this risk management has been less about keeping children safe than 'taming children', which has had long-term effects on children's wellbeing, as it curtails their development and ignores the complexities of their social experience. So rather than working with children in their best interests, restrictions are placed on them (Gill, 2007; Creasy and Corby, 2019). What I learnt from the children in the research is that taking risks can be fun and part of play, so it is important that any safety measures put in place take into consideration children's lived experience and do not restrict their lives so much that their curiosity and 'joie de vivre' are heavily compromised – in effect, risk-assessing the fun out of play. Dennis and Farrugia (2017) write that it is important to consider pleasure when researching and working with managing risks. In their research with people who inject drugs, they make the case for working towards an ethical goal of 'expanding notions of living well' rather than only focusing on harm reduction (Dennis and Farrugia, 2017, p 86). They argue that being attentive to pleasure is a matter of care (Dennis and Farrugia, 2017, p 89). The balancing act between managing risk and fun in play has similarities with the risk management for some of the families experiencing domestic abuse – where the professionals' concerns for avoiding risks can make lives unliveable, as discussed in Chapter 2. The management of risk is not always easy, but it is important to consider pleasure and fun in any safety plan in order to live well.

Desire hiding in plain sight

Risk is not only physical but relational too. Children can be hurt through their interactions with others in the playground, but that does not mean their fun is curtailed, as I find out when I collect Esmeralda and JoJo Siwa from their flat. There are still COVID-19 restrictions in place about meeting inside, so when I arrive at the door, their mother calls out 'Brenda is here!', at which point both appear with their coats on, ready to go out.

> 'Where shall we go?' I ask.
> 'To the playground!' JoJo Siwa shouts excitedly.
> 'The new one, near our house,' Esmeralda suggests.
> 'Which way shall we go?' I ask, as there are two sets of stairways either side of their flat.
> 'This way … that way is smelly,' JoJo Siwa directs.
> (Field notes, 20 October 2020)

The side that she describes as smelly runs alongside the rubbish chute. At the bottom of those stairs is the door to the big rubbish bins. Depending on how near to bin day it is, the stronger the smell of food decomposing and other rubbish of everyday living that has collected there too. So, we descend the opposite stairway.

We skip and walk to the playground. This is a new playground built during the pandemic. On one visit, JoJo Siwa and Esmeralda had chosen a perfect spot on the grass near their home to sit and chat, but soon we had to move because the noise from the builders 'creating' the playground meant we could not hear one another. Esmeralda and JoJo Siwa had seen the playground being built from the beginning, and had to contend with the noise and dust, but now they are happy to finally be able to make use of it. They are excited to give me a guided tour of their new playground and to use my phone to make a video tour of it.

As we approach the playground, the lure of making a video and giving me a tour is usurped by the joy and pleasure of seeing some girls they know gathered in the middle of the playground. They run off ahead to meet the group. There are four girls of primary school age standing there.

JoJo Siwa immediately skips off to play with one of the younger-looking girls. They run across the playground, jump on the slide, laugh and giggle. Esmeralda remains with the other three girls in the centre of the playground. The girls, including Esmeralda, are listening to one of the girls in the centre of the group. They make a circle around her and listen earnestly as she suggests what they should play. They all suggest a game, but options are vetoed by the girl in the middle. Several times during the discussions, the girl in the middle turns to Esmeralda and asks, 'What is your name?' Each time, Esmeralda answers, but it seems the girl in the middle cannot retain the information – I assume it is because Esmeralda's real name is not an 'English'-sounding name. Each time she is asked, Esmeralda steps forward and says her name and retreats.

After much discussion, it is decided that the girls will play 'it'. The top of the slide is 'homie' where you can be safe. Anywhere else is where you can be caught and made 'it' by someone on the opposing team touching you. The teams are split into JoJo Siwa and her friend on one team, and Esmeralda and the three other girls on the other. The girl in the middle instructs JoJo Siwa and her friend that they are going to be 'it', as she makes a dash for the top of the slide, with the rest of her team following her. JoJo Siwa and her friend shrug and start to chase them.

There are screams of excitement at the prospect of being caught or just about escaping, the thrill of nearly being caught illustrated by high-pitched screams and laughter. All the time, the girl in the middle positions herself so that she will be safe enough to not be caught but close enough to the edge to have the thrill of nearly being caught. I watch as Esmeralda and the other two girls tussle for a safe spot on the top of the slide, each taking it in turns to be sacrificed by being dropped off the safe spot called 'homie'. Not once is the girl in the middle caught.

I watch as JoJo Siwa runs and jumps with excitement at being 'it' and then not 'it', and Esmeralda laughing while keeping one eye on the girl in the middle. At times, the girl in the middle still asks Esmeralda for her name and continues telling all of them what to do.

Time passes and it is time for me to return home with the girls. I call out their names, and they both leave the game and skip towards me.

> Their friends ask 'Who is that?' and without missing a beat, JoJo Siwa answers, 'Our art teacher.'

As we walk home, I ask the girls who the other girls in the playground were.

> JoJo Siwa answers, 'It's Makita from my class.'
> I turn to Esmeralda and ask, 'And what about the other girls?'
> 'Oh, they are in my class,' she answers.
> 'What about the girl in the middle?'
> 'Yes, she is too,' answers Esmeralda.
>
> (Field notes, 20 October 2020)

It was at this point that my heart sank and I felt confused. I found the story in my head was different from the story that Esmeralda had expressed. My mind and heart wondered about the barriers she had faced in the playground – the numerous times she said her name, negotiating the space on top of the slide. I remembered the incident when her teacher also got her name wrong (elaborated in Chapter 6). But Esmeralda was happy; she had been pleasantly surprised to see her classmates at the playground and had fun with them. Yes, she had to negotiate the classroom dynamics, but she had fun.

In writing this section, I felt that my practitioner and personal head and heart were in a tussle with the embodiment of *mazaa*/desire in Esmeralda. When I first wrote it, I had focused on how the experience in the playground had reminded me of my father's story – how he was never known by his own name at work but as 'Tony' to make it easier for his colleagues. I also recalled an incident at secondary school, where a group of older girls had asked my friend and I our names, and before I could answer they said 'Oh no, your name is too difficult to pronounce.' Reflecting on the scene described earlier, I had been drawn into thinking solely about the systemic and social barriers that were placed in Esmeralda's way to have fun. How her schoolmate had kept asking for her name but never remembered it. How Esmeralda had to jostle at the top of the slide to keep her place, while her classmate sat firmly and securely. Important as those points are, in my rush to address and acknowledge injustice, I had failed to recognise and acknowledge the embodied joy Esmeralda showed. In some way, in my writing I had belittled that: I had pushed it to the side and focused on injustices and power relations, but in doing so I had done a disservice to Esmeralda. What I had failed to embrace was her desire and fulfilment in experiencing fun and joy.

In her essay 'Suspending damage: A letter to communities', Eve Tuck (2009) calls on her own Indigenous community in Alaska to forgo research that is based on a framework of damage and to move towards a framework of desire. Tuck (2009, p 412) argues that while she respects research that has evidenced the injustices her community has faced, the focus on their 'brokenness' has in turn overshadowed their humanness, and has made their community a site of 'disinvestment and dispossession'. The focus on damage has often separated their struggle from the legacy of racism and colonisation, thus making their struggles vulnerable to pathologisation.

Likewise, a focus on the 'damage' of domestic abuse, divorced from the reality of racism and patriarchy/White supremacy, renders families' struggles open to pathologisation (Richie, 1996, 2012; Ferguson et al, 2020). As a result, children's reaction to abuse and injustices is then open to being pathologised (Callaghan et al, 2017b). In turning towards a framework of desire, Tuck (2009, p 416) explains that they can acknowledge the present and past injustices, as well as 'documenting the wisdom and hope'. In trying to use a desire-focused approach, we can see and begin to appreciate the 'complexity, contradiction and the self determination of lived lives' (Tuck, 2009, p 416). That is to say that even when communities and families/individuals are abused and oppressed/disenfranchised, 'they are so much more than that – so much more that this incomplete story is an act of aggression' (Tuck, 2009, p 416).

Upon reflection, when I return to the scene in the playground, I can see anew what Nolas and Varvantakis (2019, p 137) – drawing from the work of Deleuze and Guattari (2013b) – would call Esmeralda's 'line of desire'. Esmeralda forgoes the video and playground tour and makes a beeline for her classmates in the playground. She skips and runs to join her friends. When the girl in the middle repeatedly asks her name, Esmeralda is not outwardly upset about it; she just answers matter of factly and continues to be part of the circle. She manages the girl's 'bossiness' to join the other girls on the slide. She giggles and laughs, basking in the joy of the thrill of getting caught and chasing. When it is time to go, she skips off with JoJo Siwa and me. Desire, for Guattari and Deleuze (2013a), is not a question of lack but an exponentially growing assemblage, a state of change and flux. It is both embodied and out of the body, relations that challenge the concept of separate and neatly contained subjects. For Esmeralda, her desire was intrinsically linked to her relation to her classmates, the playground and the thrill of everything combined – the chase, being caught. Desire is not the opposite of loss but includes it, for desire is both a longing for a past, 'the not anymore', and a future, 'the not yet' (Tuck, 2010). In this case Esmeralda desires the play with her classmates that has been denied due to COVID-19, and the anticipation of renewed friendship at school. It shows both hope and wisdom, something that was missing in my original writing.

In writing this, I can see how my desire to address injustice ran the risk of overshadowing Esmeralda's joy and painting her as 'victim', but she breaks through that trope. She shows how her desire for play pushes past the limitation of my own imagination and the constraints of the girl in the middle. Esmeralda too, like her sister, JoJo Siwa, and Elsa, had refused to be 'foldable and pliable' (Lugones, 1987, p 18), and by playfully entering her world through the process of writing, I had seen more of her humanness and creativity (Tuck, 2009).

Vouchers for fun: subverting resource for play

In writing about fun, I am not returning to the Enlightenment thinking of equating children's play with innocence. In fact, children's play includes an assemblage of things and can be political and knowing (Rosen, 2017). I agree with Rosen (2017) who argues that while play is not always a political activity, it can at times be political, and being able to create a space for play is entangled in social and political structures, as the following paragraphs illustrate.

In their photographs, the children showed themselves playing in buckets of sand in their kitchen or in paddling pools that were laid out on their balconies, as COVID-19 restrictions limited where they could play. Pogi and his family had used part of their Asda vouchers to buy a packet of sand. They had carried it on the bus, and Pogi had helped to carry it to the lift and to their flat, where Ann (his mother) had emptied a bucket that she usually used for laundry and had created a sand pit. Pogi and his sister had hours of fun getting into the bucket and building sandcastles. On one video call to Mystical, he was keen to show me the paddling pool on his seventh-floor balcony (see Figure 4.5). The phone followed his mother as she placed lukewarm water in a big stock pot and precariously carried it from the kitchen across the living room, through the back door and on to the balcony, and tipped it into the paddling pool. After several trips, the video camera went off as Mystical changed into his scuba suit. It came back on again as he laid back in the paddling pool, enjoying the coolness of the water with the warmth of the sun on his face.

These events helped to remind me that although fun can seem spontaneous and unplanned, there is structural and personal 'work' that goes into creating these moments. Both Pogi's and Mystical's mothers had used their bodies and finances to create a space for fun in the home. Due to COVID-19 restrictions, they were unable to take their children out, so had brought the beach and the pool to their homes, despite the limit on space. Through their and the children's efforts in carrying sand and with other activities, they were able to create a space for fun.

The work of mothers has been framed in sociology in terms of social reproduction (Katz, 2001; Oakley, 2005), meaning how they are implicit in reproducing systems and structures. In the case of domestic abuse, the focus is on child protection and the managing of risks (Radford and Hester, 2006). Here we see the mothers of both Pogi and Mystical prioritising fun and laughter in their care of their children. Pogi's mother uses food vouchers, given by the government to families on low incomes, to buy sand to make a sand pit and creates a beach in their kitchen; Mystical's mother turns the balcony into a mini swimming pool – pushing away the washing line and scooters to make space. There was fun to be had in subverting the normal

Figure 4.5: Pool on the balcony (photography by Brenda)

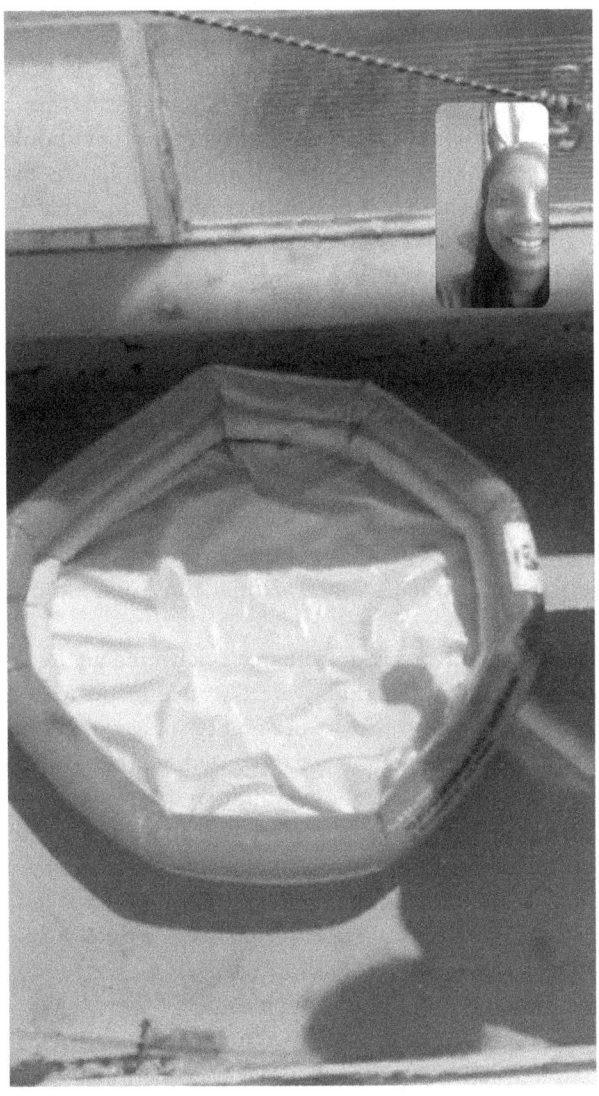

use of a place/space. They both revel in their children's laughter and joy, despite the added tidying up and expense that they have incurred – they have acted through the sheer pleasure of having fun with their children. They both subverted the use of vouchers and place to create a space for fun.

In January 2021, there was much furore and debate about the food parcels that were being delivered to families as they faced another lockdown. While the schools were shut, children who were entitled to free school meals were given either a food parcel or £15 of supermarket vouchers during term time (Barker and Russell, 2020). Such support was not provided in school holidays. But following a campaign by charity groups and Marcus Rashford (the British footballer), the government was forced to make a U-turn and continue to provide free school meals during the holidays for the families. However, when the families began highlighting the meagre food parcels they were receiving, a debate about whether they should be getting food parcels or vouchers was reignited. This debate has its history in the ongoing question of whether the recipients of the aid could be trusted to make the 'right choice' and is linked to the narrative of welfare recipients as reckless and lazy, and more likely to spend it on cigarettes and alcohol (Garthwaite et al, 2015; Treanor, 2020). For example, Ben Bradley, MP for Mansfield, Nottinghamshire, tweeted that free school meal vouchers during summer 2020 effectively ended up in crack dens and brothels in his constituency (Chao-Fong, 2020). The conversation has since been deleted from Twitter. The sense conveyed by Bradley was that any assistance given by the government was to begrudgingly enable basic survival rather than provide any pleasure. This reminds me of Indian feminist scholar Phadke (2020) writing, 'Pleasure which is not linked to consumption has the power to challenge the unspoken notion that only those who can afford it are entitled to pleasure.'

For the families in this study, food parcels delivered at the beginning of the pandemic were helpful as they were not able to go to the shops due to shielding, and in addition there were empty shelves at the supermarket. However, as time went on, vouchers were issued, which meant that families were able to make their own choices about what to purchase. I find it poignant that in Pogi and Elsa's case, their family chose to spend some of it on buying sand. This prioritisation of fun and pleasure illustrates the importance of living a liveable life rather than merely existing, and having the choice to do so. In her interview with Cara Page, pleasure activist Adrienne Maree Brown (2019, p 51) asserts that 'Desire and pleasure are two ways that we assert that there's something worth living for.'

Nurturing pleasure is both an act of care and resistance. Black feminists and Indigenous scholars have long written about how marginalised communities have sought and created joy despite their difficulties (hooks, 1990, 2016c; Smith, 1999; Tuck, 2009, 2010; Williamson, 2017; Hartman, 2021). bell hooks writes that the homeplace can act as a sanctuary from the onslaught of everyday life for families who are marginalised (hooks, 1990, p 47) – a place where we can 'heal our wounds and become whole' (hooks, 1990, p 49). In their acts of subversion of voucher and space, I see how both Ann and Nicole continue that tradition of nurturing the soul of their children through creating a space for *mazaa* – fun and pleasure. Much has been made of home as a place of unsafety or risk for children who have experienced domestic abuse or are under the service of social work, but here we see the conviviality of the home, a place of fun, pleasure and laughter. The families are economically vulnerable, but they still create the resources, space and time to have fun. This was something that was consistently present in my interaction with the children and mothers in the study.

Mothers' delight: a different gaze

One of the surprises for me was the reaction of mothers to the photographs and videos taken by children in the research. After each in-person visit to the children, if the children or I had taken any photographs or videos, I would send them to the mothers via whatever medium they preferred, usually WhatsApp. Their reactions took me aback. Every time, the mothers loved the videos and photographs. Why was I so surprised? I had initially given very little thought to sending the videos and photographs. I had seen it has an act of being ethical and transparent. What I had not anticipated was the alchemy of creating an opportunity for mothers to see their children in a different way to their own lenses, and the lens of the social services. What had often been captured was the children themselves expressing their quest for fun and play. The responses from the mothers were 'gushing'. At times, I was worried that I would take up too much of the data space on their phones, given how long some of the videos shot by children were, but the mothers wanted to see them all.

My reaction reflected my underestimation of how valuable it is for mothers to see the gaze on their children shift from that of an adult to the child themselves. It offered a different way of knowing and being with their children. It was also a way of seeing and knowing their child away from them. For some of the mothers who were under the gaze of child protection, having another 'professional' see their child not through the prism of risk and assessment but the visceral act of playing and making fun was both refreshing and humanising. Summer (mother to Kyro and Rosie) commented how it was brilliant to see someone 'really getting to know the children'.

Loitering with pleasure

In this section I turn my attention to the pleasure children experience with their friends away from adults' gaze. During the process of writing this chapter, I dream about a video Pogi gave me. I wake up with a start and realise that this video is an important part of this chapter and wonder how I can have forgotten it. The video begins with someone saying:

> 'Is it recording now?'
> I hear Pogi say, 'Yes.'
> Another boy then says, 'So we can go now?'
> (Field note, 5 November 2020)

The picture on the screen is of a path. The path is lined on one side with a low brick wall and on the other by a black railing. The camera then shoots up away from the path and on to Pogi and another boy, who I recognise as his friend. Both are in their school clothes, and Pogi's friend is wearing a black hooded jacket. It looks like they are walking home from school. In the background I catch a glimpse of blocks of flats on their housing estate. The camera moves around a lot, as the boy holding the camera laughs. I feel like I am on a ship in rough waters. I feel a little seasick but am taken in by the boys' continuous laughter. Pogi has a stick in his hand, and he is cutting back the moss and weeds shooting out from the cracks in the concrete path and brick wall. The camera then focuses on Pogi's other friend. He is doing a dance, and then comes up to the camera and shows all his teeth. He makes funny faces at the camera, does the peace sign and all three boys laugh and laugh, reminiscent of music videos. They rap and laugh, then the video cuts out.

The next two videos are also short clips taken the same day (5 November 2020) and straight after the first video. They are of Pogi and his friends rapping, laughing and looking for treasures in the overgrown shrubs near their estate. The boys are having fun. They take it in turns to hold the camera. I feel privileged to be offered a glimpse into their private world. I ponder the actions Pogi must have taken to produce this video – he would have decided to take the camera to school, he would have placed the camera in his bag, carried it to school, possibly hoped that it would not get confiscated and then taken it out at the end of the day when he was walking with his friends. As Walkedine and Pini (2021, p 193) write, 'the video diary is always used with an audience in mind', and I am, in this instance, their imagined audience. Pogi has meant for me to see the videos and I feel honoured. Their journey from school to home, where they loiter and have fun. Watching the video makes me understand a little more about Pogi and how important this time with his friends is. He loves it and I see how alive he becomes – full of laughter and joy. This time on the streets is often called loitering, and on so many levels it illustrates the liminal space that Pogi and his friends create and embody.

Pogi and his friends are taking space, both temporal and physical, between the school and home to have fun. It is a space that is under the gaze of neither their teachers nor their parents. They are free to do what they want and explore, and I know Pogi treasures this space and doesn't easily relinquish it. On one occasion, Ann, his mother, had told him to come home for 4 pm as I was visiting. She had offered to wait for him at the school gate when she collected his younger sister Elsa from school, but Pogi had declined her offer and had wanted to walk home with his friends. Little did I know that my visit would clash with this sacred time of walking home with his friends, so as it turned out I waited and waited and waited, till he finally came home at 4.45 pm after spending the time with his friends, feeling no pressure to rush home. Seeing the video, I too would not rush home if I was having this much fun!

The permission to walk home from school without an adult was a milestone in some of the children's lives. Like Pogi, Sagittarius was in year six, and was looking forward to being able to walk home with her friends after school. She was looking forward to having the independence and being seen as a little more grown up. The walk was a rite of passage for both, where they entered the liminal space between childhood and adolescence, between always being under the watchful eye of an adult and being trusted to travel on their own. The anthropologist Victor Turner (2002, p 93) explains that rites of passage exist in all societies and indicate transitions between states. Turner (1995, 2002) describes this liminal space as a possible place for creativity, play and imagination, things that are evident in the video shots of Pogi and his friends after school.

When I look at the video of Pogi and his friends, I see much laughter and fun. Pogi's video exudes a sense of love, belonging, friendship, play and fun. Pogi and his friends have taken ownership of the open space and made it a place for fun. It is a display of agency and desire (Butcher and Velayutham, 2009, p 200). In their book *Why Loiter?*, Phadke et al (2011) argue that it is important that all people have the right and opportunity to loiter without any intent other than for pleasure. Following their three-year study of the use of space on the streets of Mumbai, Phadke et al argue that it is only when loitering is seen as a right for all (to seek pleasure and fun) that safety for women will increase. Phadke et al (2011, p 113) write, 'Most debates on public space are disproportionately focused on danger rather than pleasure ... Pleasure or fun is seen as threatening because it fundamentally questions the idea that women's presence in public space is acceptable only when they have a purpose.' This makes me think as well that if we centred children's pleasure and fun, would this inadvertently make it safer for children too?

In Pogi's video, the boys are enjoying each other's company and just chilling, but I can't keep a sense of sadness and worry at bay. I feel it banging at the back of my head as I look at the pictures. This sadness comes from the knowledge that they as a group of racially marginalised boys will be targeted for extra surveillance and policing, with a greater risk of being viewed as being 'anti-social' and in need of control (Davis and Marsh, 2020, 2022). Statistically, as they grow older, they will not be afforded the luxury of innocence and childhood to protect them from incarceration, harm and exclusion, like in the cases of Child Q and Child M, as discussed in Chapter 2. The latest figures from the Ministry of Justice show that Black children (aged between ten and 17) were four times more likely than White children to be arrested (Robertson and Wainwright, 2020).

I am reminded that as the children in my research grow older, their play and sense of fun will be viewed differently by those in authority, like teachers, police and other adults. Banter and laughs with his friends will become seen as signs of menacing youth. JoJo Siwa and Esmeralda's dances will be construed as sexual. Esmeralda's loudness will be judged negatively as being rough and aggressive. These thoughts go round in my head as I am reminded of Tamir Rice, a 12-year old American Black boy who was killed in the act of playing and having fun. While the main stories have been in America, there is plenty of evidence that Black children in the UK have limited access to freedom of play and are often more likely to be treated as adults (Bernard and Gupta, 2008; Harris, 2016; Hunter, 2019, 2022; Pearce, 2019). In September 2021, Benjamin Olajve, a young Black 13-year-old boy with additional needs, was stopped and searched by police officers looking for a knife. They searched him for 45 minutes and took him to Brixton police station. No weapons were found on him, and he received a black eye and cut wrists from the police's handling of him. He was on his way to McDonald's and was stopped and searched because the police were looking for a Black male with a knife (Krasteva, 2021) – an example of the context that children who are Black or from a marginalised group find themselves in.

Pogi plays with a stick that looks like a dagger, picks up a broken bottle and waves it around. It is done in jest as he acts as a buccaneer and explorer finding treasure. I am reminded that Tamir Rice too was only a boy playing with a toy gun, which later was used to justify his killing – he was not afforded the right to play (Dyer, 2020, p 34). I am hoping this fun and banter will continue but worry about what harm and risks the systemic structures that position the children as in need of order, correction and control will do to them/place them in. But in that moment in the video, they are free, and they are having fun beyond the gaze of the state and of me.

Conclusion

When I look back at how I started my research and why I chose certain methods, I feel that I misunderstood the significance of fun and play. I chose methods and tasks that I hoped the children would enjoy, so that they would participate in the research project. It reflected my perception of fun as a means to an end, a means of production, following the prevalent thinking of seeing 'fun' and 'play' as by-products of the 'real work or findings'. Yet, what I learnt is that the 'trivial' and the 'frivolous' are equally important. In this chapter I move away from the instrumental adult thinking about play as a means to educate or heal from trauma (important as these things are) and focus instead on the 'in-the-moment fun and playing just because we can' feelings that pervaded the research study. I am in agreement with Huizinga (2016, p 2) who said critically of his contemporaries in the 1930s, 'they all start from the assumption that play must serve something which is not play'. Huizinga was criticising an approach that assumes, in the end, that the true cultural meaning and significance of practices of fun are not found in the visceral moment of enjoyment but in some other domain – a domain that often the person having fun is not aware of, and so it is up to the scholar to identify (Anjaria and Anjaria, 2020, p 235). Thus, only looking at fun and play through the eyes of what they mean in terms of abuse and trauma for children continues to replicate the dominant power relations of whose knowledge counts. In not taking what the children say and experience into account but placing more value on my own distant analysis to find a 'hidden meaning' regarding trauma and abuse, I am inadvertently dismissing children's knowledge about their lives. This is a form of 'elitism' that raises questions about whose knowledge counts. Understanding the beauty that the children found in the everyday was also a challenge for me, as I go on to critically describe in the following chapter.

5

The aesthetics of everyday life

As I step out of the car, the rain hits my face. It means my plan for taking Kyro and Rosie to the playground is thwarted. We are still under physical distancing restrictions, so I cannot go into their home. I am used to the weather influencing and disrupting my plans for visits. The weather, like Wi-Fi, is my unofficial co-researcher, throwing me a curve ball every now and again. I had prepared for it, and had packed pens, papers, hand sanitiser and, more importantly, a picnic blanket just in case.

I navigate my way through the intercom and the lift. I walk down the dimly lit corridor. The heat hits me. This building is always hot; Summer (mother to Kyro and Rosie) said that the flat is unbearable during the summer months. The corridor smells of cooked food, hot bodies and air that has stayed still for a long time. After a walk of a hundred metres, I knock on the door of Kyro and Rosie's home. They live on the fourth floor of the large building. Their mother opens the door, and there is a frantic search for socks, shoes and jackets.

I explain that we cannot go out as it is raining, but ask whether we could meet in the corridor (see Figure 5.1) and if they could bring their cameras too. Summer nods. No longer any need for jackets, the search now is for their cameras. Kyro and Rosie rush out the door clutching their cameras, thrusting them at me to show me the photographs they had taken.

Rosie shows me her pictures. There is one striking picture of a knife:

> Rosie points out the green stripes on the knife and I enquire, 'how come you took that picture?'
> 'Because it's beautiful,' says Rosie without missing a beat.
> (Field notes, 20 June 2020)

'Pretty' or 'nice' were the words that often greeted me when I talked to the children in the project about the pictures they had taken. There were numerous photographs of what they thought looked beautiful. This was regardless of their age or gender. It struck me that seeing beauty in the everyday was important in the lives of all the children, and, with their photographs, they wanted to both capture and share the beauty with me. Initially, I had not paid attention to the words 'beautiful' and 'pretty' when the children had explained why they had taken photographs, but as I gathered the photographs from all the children and continued to talk to them about

Figure 5.1: Impromptu activity in the corridor (photography by Brenda)

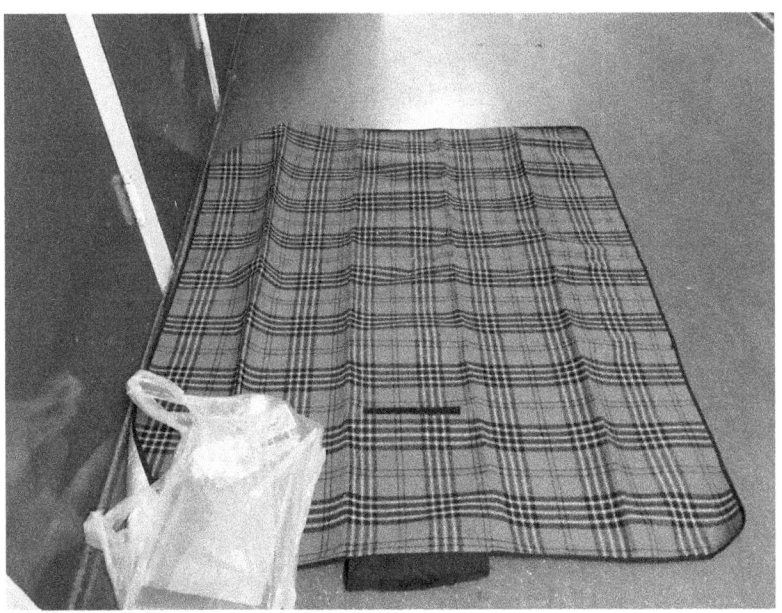

their pictures, 'beautiful' or 'pretty' were common words used. This was an experience shared by geographer David Marshall (2013), who carried out his research with Palestinian refugees in the Balata camp. At first, he too had dismissed 'beauty' as an 'irrelevant filler-word' (Marshall, 2013, p 61), but upon reflection he realised how children had mobilised the word 'beauty' to illustrate their social imaginaries, to describe and make judgements of everyday life. In their multimodal ethnography with children, Varvantakis and Nolas (2021) were also bemused by the photographs that children in Athens took of the Acropolis. Upon closer attention, they too started to think about what the pictures 'are' for the children and what they 'did' for the children, rather than emphasise 'why' they took the pictures (Varvantakis and Nolas, 2021, p 2). Both Marshall (2013) and Varvantakis and Nolas (2021) draw on political, affective and sensory theories to make meaning of the photographs.

In this chapter I draw upon the work of Black feminist scholars (hooks, 1990, 1995; McKittrick, 2014; Campt, 2017), multimodal ethnographers and childhood scholars (Hackett et al, 2017; Lomax, 2020; Luttrell, 2020; Varvantakis and Nolas, 2021), and social science researchers working in the field of NGOs (Fassin and Rechtman, 2009; Fassin, 2012; Marshall, 2013, 2015) to explore how children create, identify and capture beauty in their everyday lives. I argue how, in paying close attention to the everyday practices

Figure 5.2: Knife in the sun (photography by Rosie)

of aesthetics in the lives of children who have experienced domestic abuse, we can see how they 'make meaning of their lives' and how they disrupt the dominant narrative about their lives being primarily about trauma and suffering. We can see how the aesthetics in the home demonstrate care and how children contribute to the practice of aesthetics in the home. Firstly, I argue how children are able to decipher what beauty means to them.

The knife in the sun

> 'Can you see? Look! Look! The sun is shining on the knife. It looks pretty,' explains Rosie, as she points to the picture on her camera of a dinner knife lying on the table with the sun shining on it (see Figure 5.2). 'Can you see how the sun shines on it? Can you see the green line?' Rosie asks.
>
> 'Yes, I can see it. Wow, that is a good picture!' I exclaim as I move nearer to the screen to have a closer look.
>
> 'I think it looks pretty. Now see this one – it's the moth. Remember I showed it to you on the phone?' quizzes Rosie.
>
> 'Yes, I remember.' Indeed, I do recall the moth.
>
> (Field notes, 20 June 2020)

The aesthetics of everyday life

A few weeks before, I had video-called Rosie and her brother Kyro via WhatsApp. While Rosie and I were talking, she spotted a moth. She was fascinated with it and had taken the phone to the wall so that I could have a look. She then dropped the phone (and me) on the floor and disappeared. I was left wondering what had happened and started to call out her name – feeling stranded with a blank screen.

A couple of minutes later, Rosie picked up the phone again and I saw her face.

> 'What happened?' I asked
> 'Oh ... I went and took a picture of the moth because it looked pretty,' Rosie explained nonchalantly, and we continued with our video call.
>
> (Field notes, 11 May 2020)

Now, in the corridor of the block of flats, Rosie is showing me the photo of the moth on her camera (see Figure 5.3). Rosie and Kyro constantly surprised me with their eye for beauty in the everyday. They often used the camera to capture the prettiness of familiar things that we often walk by. On my first walk with them, Kyro took a number of pictures of cars and blossom on trees. His enthusiasm for blossom and trees infiltrated my own thinking, and a few times when I was out walking, I would notice a lovely

Figure 5.3: The moth (photography by Rosie)

tree full of blossom and would take a picture of it on my phone and send it to his mother to show him. Without any planning, we had entered and continued a dialogue about the affect of beauty (Thompson, 2011, p 146; Walton, 2021): the unexplainable warm feelings and joy we experience upon seeing something beautiful (Wohlwill, 1976; Richards, 2001).

My initial dismissal of the words 'beauty' and 'pretty' was a reflection of my want to 'datafy', 'quantify' and 'explain' why the children took the pictures that they did (Mascheroni, 2020). When they simply said, 'Cos it's pretty', this stumped me – for what kind of an explanation was that? What I was missing was that what the children were showing me was that the beauty and prettiness of blossom, moths, cars, trees, animals, people were not easily describable – they were more than emotions that could be succinctly verbalised. In taking the photographs, the children were trying to capture the affect of the beauty of the everyday to show me (Wohlwill, 1976; Richards, 2001; Stewart, 2007). They were showing me a world that was larger than my confined imaginative space, what Maclure et al (2010) call 'mundane realism' – the children were not giving me answers that I could simply codify, compartmentalise and reduce to what is already 'known' about children/reinforce what determines childhood. I had to in effect learn to listen to the photos (Campt, 2017), to learn to see (hooks, 1995), to attune myself to what the children were showing me through their pictures – to be open to disruptions of my preconceived thoughts and narratives. Words alone could not describe all the relational layers and dynamics that were entangled; I had to learn to listen with my whole self (Hordge-Freeman, 2018; Varvantakis and Nolas, 2021).

It called for an embodied/sensory encounter, involving emotional, physical, cognitive and imaginative engagement, which was always relational but involves 'bringing into play memories, images and feelings' (Ansell, 2009, p 200). I had to tune into the children's imaginations (Hackett et al, 2017; Lomax, 2020). In order to do this, I had to also be aware of my own presumptions created and nurtured by my training as a therapist, my background and the dominant narrative around trauma. I had to scrutinise what was shaping my interpretation and attunement (Etherington, 2004). For although affect goes beyond the confines of language, it is, however, still shaped by where we are situated, for instance, our class, race, ethnicity or gender. We are not situated from nowhere (Haraway, 1988). My biased thinking strongly presented itself in my visit to Rosie and Kyro.

Sitting on the rug, Rosie and Kyro start to look through the art materials that I had brought. They touch, fiddle and play with the paper, crayons, felt-tip pens, pencils and boards. 'You can draw something if you want,' I suggest. While Kyro is hesitant to begin with, Rosie picks up a piece of paper and says she is going to draw a tower and a princess. On the blank A4 sheet of paper, she takes the crayons and draws a princess with red hair and a red crown. Next she draws a tower, starting in red, then switching to purple.

> 'I am calling it the Tower Princess,' explains Rosie.
> 'That's a cool name. How come you chose to do this drawing?' I ask.
> 'Cos it looks pretty,' says Rosie.
> (Field notes, 20 June 2020)

I nod in agreement because, indeed, the array of colours does make it look pretty. Looking at the picture, my mind travels to the therapy room at my work. I am struck with guilt at how the narrative around trauma may pathologise children (Callaghan et al, 2017a, 2017b). It makes me ask myself the question as to why children who have experienced domestic abuse are not often seen as 'appreciators' of beauty. Why is what they do and say often only seen through the narrow lens of trauma and domestic abuse?

In his research with Palestinian children in the Balata camp, Marshall (2013) found that there was limited research into their everyday lives, and that there was a significant body of scholarship in the psychological effects of the violence. Thus, the literature often portrays children as 'passive victims or receptors of social norms' (Marshall, 2013, p 54). Undergirding this response is the language of trauma that is utilised. A focus on trauma allows for the telling of the horror of the violence, alleviates some of the psychological distress and also allows NGOs to justify their support (Fassin and Rechtman, 2009), but it denies the fullness of Palestinian children's lives. Likewise, the emphasis on the trauma of domestic abuse can help to highlight the horror of domestic abuse and acknowledge the pain caused, thus justifying support. However, in not seeing children beyond the trauma lens, it reduces them to their trauma and dehumanises them. This was something that I witnessed in my research with Rosie and Kyro. As the family were moved from CIN to CP, I was often asked by their social worker to provide an assessment of their therapeutic needs and whether they needed therapy, and also to write a report about them for the CP conference. Several times I had to reiterate the boundaries of the research and my role as a researcher. I felt the pressure to identify what was 'wrong' with Rosie and Kyro. I declined every time.

What was missing from the questions from the social worker, and what I often overlooked, was not only Rosie and Kyro's appreciation of the beauty in everyday life but also the way the photographs in themselves were beautiful, or what could be described as 'artistic'. I was often moved by their photographs and their ability to bring to my attention the mundane and make it extraordinary. With their cameras, they disrupted the prevalent narrative of trauma: instead of an 'aesthetic of injury', they were showing me the 'affect of beauty' (Thompson, 2011, p 146). With their cameras, they were continuing a conversation with me about what moved them enough to take a photograph, as well as trying to capture the beauty and share its affect with me.

There is one photograph that stirred my heart. At first, I did not notice it, but as I sorted through the photographs to create a photobook for Rosie, I felt drawn to a picture of a lake and a boy standing on the edge of it. Admiring the photograph and paying closer attention, I noticed that I could see a faint reflection of Rosie with her camera taking a photograph. Only on the fourth time of looking did I realise it was a photograph of a picture displayed in the window of a shop (see Figure 5.4). Reflecting in the shop window was the image of Rosie taking the photograph and the high street behind her. I imagine Rosie walking with her mother along the high street with the camera. Stopping to take the picture. Rosie being attracted to the image of the child lost in thought looking at the lake and its surrounding beauty. Both children entranced by the beautiful scenery, but one is physically present by the lake and the other looking from afar. Would Rosie like to swap places with the child in the photograph? Or is it sufficient to see the picture? These are questions that wander into my mind, but there is no straightforward answer. When I asked Rosie about the photograph, she replied, 'It looked nice.' What I find is that the photographs Rosie and others in the project take do not represent the closed and restrictive space offered by the trauma narrative but disrupt and create an open space where there are numerous possibilities and answers.

Figure 5.4: The lake (photography by Rosie)

In the following section I will further explore the different ways that the children, through their photographs, appreciate and acknowledge the aesthetics of everyday life. My first stop is the home, often portrayed as a site of violence, risk and harm, but, portrayed through its aesthetics, a place of care (as further discussed in Chapter 6).

Banners, balloons and waiting for the big day

Katie flicks through the photographs I have brought along with me. She is interested to see how the pictures she has taken with the camera look on paper. She sifts through the pages. We come across a couple of photographs of a skeleton attached to the kitchen door, a spider's cobweb across another door, and bats on the mantelpiece (see Figure 5.5). 'Oh, that was when it was Halloween,' Katie says giggling. 'My mum always decorates the rooms for Halloween. It's fun and we get sweets' (Field notes, 23 December 2020). Halloween was not the only time that the house was decorated. Visiting during Ramadan, there was a table laid out ready for the breaking of the fast at the end of the day. Katie's family was not unusual. In many of the homes that I visited, there was a seasonal aspect to the decor. Homes were being prepared in anticipation for the big day – a celebration of a birthday or Eid, or Christmas or Halloween. It was like the home decor was whispering then slowly building up to the loud roar announcing that celebrations could commence! This was often reflected in the photographs that the children took.

Figure 5.5: Halloween decorations (photography by Katie)

Figure 5.6: (Left) Christmas tree; (right) Christmas table decoration (photography by Mystical)

Speaking to Elsa one day, she takes the phone and scans across the room, giving me a guided tour of her living room. She excitedly tells me about the Christmas tree and the cards and presents underneath – all waiting to be opened on Christmas Day. Mystical too is keen to show me his Christmas tree and presents when I visit (see Figures 5.6, left and 5.6, right). He proudly takes a photograph of a table decoration that he has made at school. He excitedly shows me how the lights on the Christmas tree work and tells me he is allowed to open one small present a day until Christmas Day, when he can open his big presents. It is like there is a countdown.

Reflecting on the home decorations for festivities, I feel there is a rhythm, a temporal flow and a tradition to the home (Lefebvre, 1974; de Certeau, 1984; Pink, 2012). I see how the aesthetics of the home are ones of care, love and celebration (hooks, 1990, p 104; Luttrell, 2020, p 97). The home is often depicted as a place of risk in cases of domestic abuse and social work interventions, but here through my visits (virtual and in person) and through the children's photographs, I can see the care and the work of mothers to make the home a place of celebration and joy (Luttrell, 2020, p 101). I see they use the practice of aesthetics in the home to nurture an affect of tradition, comfort, anticipation and celebration.

The home decor is personalised for birthdays. In Pogi and Elsa's home, there are helium balloons spelling out 'Happy Birthday' and their names stuck to the wall. Not only are there helium balloons but the food too is aesthetically matching the decor, with heart-shaped cakes and themed

Figure 5.7: Heart-shaped cakes (photography by Pogi)

birthday cakes (see Figure 5.7). Like previous years, plans are made about how best to celebrate, but, unlike other years, there are physical distancing rules in place and Ann works hard to meet the wishes of Pogi and Elsa while managing the restrictions.

In Mystical's home, there is a table in the dining room and, in the lead-up to every major festival, Eid, Christmas and birthdays, the table is laid out in preparation for the big day (see Figure 5.8). It acts like a countdown – each day something is added to the table till it is fully prepared for the day. All of the birthdays in the home fall in the same month, but Mystical's mother, Nicole, starts anew for each child and customises the table to their interests. With his camera, Mystical documents the changing of the table decor – like a calendar telling me the season.

Scrolling through the photos on her phone, Mystical's mother shows me pictures from their different birthdays through the years. There is a *Frozen*-themed party and a Minecraft one too. The decorations are for the family to mark each birthday and, like Elsa's mother, she feels it is important to celebrate the life of each family member:

> 'See, these are the ones from before,' Nicole says as she scrolls down her phone. 'Ah, these are when they were very little. I would buy the matching paper plates, cups, party bags and cakes. I even had an entertainer, but I don't have big parties now. I still decorate but

Figure 5.8: Table decorations (photography by Mystical)

I just celebrate amongst ourselves and maybe one or two friends,' Nicole continues.

'Oh, how come you stopped having big birthday parties?' I ask.

'When Mystical was in nursery, I invited all the children in his class. He dressed up as Spiderman and I saved and bought all the matching things. We had serviettes, party bags, cake, everything was Spiderman-themed. I even got a Spiderman entertainer ... see?' says Nicole, as she shows me a photograph of a man dressed up as Spiderman next to Mystical, who was also dressed as Spiderman. 'I did all this preparation and we were excited about the party, but nobody came,' Nicole says sadly.

'Nobody?' I ask, thinking I had misheard.

'Yes, no one came. The weather was bad; it was raining a lot. No one came and they didn't tell me,' Nicole says.

'Oh, I am very sorry. Did they say why?' I explore.

'When we went back to nursery on Monday, some said that their child was sick, or the weather was too bad, and they could not make it. Some did not say anything. Now I do everything, but I only do it for us,' Nicole explains.

(Field notes, 21 December 2020)

Reflecting on Mystical's enthusiasm for showing me the table, and talking me through the different items displayed on it each time I visited near a festivity, showed me how the celebratory decor was not for the eyes of outsiders to the home. Instead, it was an aesthetic of care for those inside the home, and, despite the ambivalence of others, the decor was an important function of caring and celebrating one another in the home.

bell hooks (1990, p 104) writes that 'aesthetic then is more than a philosophy or theory of art and beauty: it is a way of inhabiting a space, a particular location, a way of looking and becoming'. In her chapter on 'Aesthetic of Blackness', hooks (1990, pp 103–13) writes how she had learnt to appreciate aesthetics of the home from her grandma, who in turn learnt from her ancestors. hooks describes this as an 'aesthetic of existence', which meant that coming from the binds of slavery, no lack of material would stop them from looking at the world with a critical eye, or stop them from recognising beauty or using it as a force to enhance inner wellbeing. What I perceive from both Elsa's mother and Mystical's mother is that, despite the abuse they had experienced in the home, the scrutiny of their homemaking and, in Mystical's case, the rejection of others to celebrate with them, the families continued to create in the home, through their aesthetic, a place which nurtured and celebrated life itself. These were not one-off events but part of the ongoing flow of everyday life of caring for each other.

The bedroom

Children's bedrooms are often subjected to scrutiny by social workers (Ferguson, 2011, p 66) as they are places where care is demonstrated through aesthetics. The decor of bedrooms, what is chosen and by whom, can be telling of familial and societal relations and norms. It can also indicate the age of the child. From the Disneyfied characters from children's literature classics often chosen by adults for children, to the posters on the bedroom walls of teenagers, the bedroom is a site for the expressions of relations between individuals and society (Mitchell and Reid-Walsh, 2002, p 130; Highmore, 2014, p 133).

One of the things social workers look for is whether the bedroom is adequately resourced, for example, whether there are sheets on the bed and the room is adequately furnished. However, these material things not only tell of ways parents care, but they can also give an indication of the economic and social constraints the parent is under (Greenstein et al, 2016). For example, a parent may not be able to afford bedroom furnishings, or be able to fix a curtain rail to put up the bedroom curtains. They may not be able to paint a bedroom due to a landlord's restrictions, or they may be in temporary accommodation, and therefore see decorating as pointless if they are to move soon (Moffatt et al, 2016). Here we see how external social, political and economic constraints inevitably influence the child's environment.

For Katie, COVID-19 had an impact on her bedroom space. When I meet her for the first time in person, she has given up her bedroom and is sleeping in the living room. As she gives me a tour of the house, she shows me the sofa where she sleeps. We go upstairs and she quietly taps on the door and then enters a small room. She whispers to me, 'My grandpa is sleeping.' We leave the room and go downstairs. 'My grandpa is sleeping in my room. He's not very well,' Katie elaborates (Field notes, 15 October 2020). At first, I thought it was because Katie's grandpa was ill that he was staying with the family, but a few months later, as I got to know Katie more, I discovered the reason behind his stay.

> As we are playing on the swings, Katie turns to me saying, 'My grandpa has gone back. I don't think my grandpa is ever going to come back to England.'
> 'Why is that?' I ask.
> 'Oh, because when he came last time, he could not go back to Algeria because of COVID-19. He had to stay here till he was allowed back,' she explains.
> (Field notes, 18 January 2021)

After a year of the research, I call Katie – she answers and is very excited. She is in her new bed, in a newly decorated bedroom. She holds the phone and gives me a tour of her room.

Later, I see among the photographs that there is a picture of her newly decorated bedroom (see Figure 5.9). Katie loves her bedroom. I feel that her newly decorated room has filled her with care and joy. She appreciates the effort her mother has made to make her room look 'nice'. At last she has her space back, surrounded with the teddy bears and books that she loves.

A doll that looks like me

A key difference to most ethnography is that the children could see into my own home, since conversations were often held online via WhatsApp video calls. They were intrigued by where I lived and who I lived with. One time, I was in my son's bedroom and Esmeralda wanted to see around

Figure 5.9: Newly decorated room (photography by Katie)

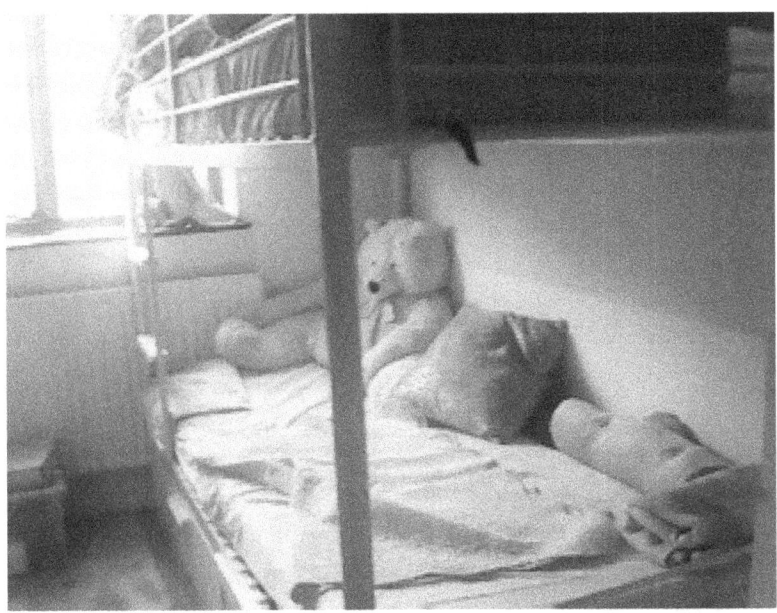

the room. On a separate occasion, I was sitting at my desk with a bookshelf behind me. Esmeralda and I had been playing a game of Pictionary, when she stopped me:

'What's that behind you?' she asks.
  'Behind me? Mmm …' I turn around to look. 'Oh, just books.'
  'No, I see something else,' Esmeralda says. Again, I look but still am puzzled.
  'It's a toy,' she explains. I turn around again and look at the shelf. My eyes go to the top and there I see what she is talking about. I slowly lift the toy and bring it to the phone, so she can see it more closely.
  'It's my doll Jane,' I say (see Figure 5.10).
  'It's important to have something that looks like you,' Esmeralda says.
  'I bought it from a charity shop when I was a grown up. When I was little there weren't many dolls with dark skin,' I explain.
  'Yeah … I want an American doll for my birthday. It's my turn now.' Esmeralda turns to draw on her piece of paper.
(Field notes, 12 November 2020)

I was stunned by Esmeralda's comment. It had touched a 'deep spot' in me, and I knew it was important to her too. On numerous occasions she had told me that she wanted an American Girl doll. I had not heard of this doll,

Figure 5.10: Jane the doll (photography by Brenda)

but with a little research both by talking to Esmeralda and JoJo Siwa and through internet searches, I came across the brand American Girl that made dolls that had different hair and skin colours. There was even a category called 'Truly Me' and 'Create Your Own' where you could choose the skin tone and hair colour and texture to build the doll of your dreams – in Esmeralda's and my case, a doll that looked like us.

I remembered walking into the charity shop and coming across my doll. Even as an adult, my heart leapt as I saw my doll for sale. As a child I had always wanted a doll that looked like me, a doll with dark brown skin and dark hair. The nearest I could find was a Sindy doll with dark hair. So, when Esmeralda had said that it was important to have something that looks like you, it resonated with my own childhood experience. It was not the first time that she had said this to me, so I knew it was important to her.

The culture around dolls touches on aspects of consumer, identity and society (Miller, 2005, 2008). Esmeralda wanted a Black American doll, but like the girls in Chin's (1999) study, she did not have access to it. Looking on the company's website, a doll would cost $100 – not cheap. So, while Black dolls may exist, who actually does have access to them? Despite the cost, there has been an increase in the range of dolls reflecting different skin tones and hair texture over the last couple of decades (Seow, 2019). Some of these dolls have been criticised for reinforcing stereotypes of particular groups, for example, the Bratz dolls for reinforcing a stereotyped sexualised image of Black children/women. However, in her qualitative research with ten Black Caribbean children, Seow (2019) found that the girls saw past the sexualised image of the Bratz dolls and were just happy to have dolls who looked vaguely similar to themselves. The girls had made their own decision, so despite the adult concerns about the over-sexualisation of the dolls, the girls were content to use the dolls for their own purposes. This shows that the children had their own subjectivity and could exert their own agency over the dolls and their meaning despite the constraints, but this is not the narrative that prevails.

Esmeralda challenges the narrative that Black children, because of internalised racism, still prefer White dolls. This narrative follows a well-known study regarding Black dolls and Black children which was done by Clark and Clark (1947), who wrote that even when given the chance, Black children preferred the White doll to the Black doll. Clark and Clark concluded that the Black children had already been affected by the racism in society and had internalised it, and thus preferred the White doll. Even in Seow's (2019) study which showed the girls liking their Bratz dolls, there is one detail about a girl, Sabrina, who had a White American Girl doll. Seow read that the girl had sensed that the White doll was more important than the Black doll.

My own analysis of the girl's response would have been more pragmatic: the girl had taken the White doll because the Black doll was not available. The girl does call the White doll the 'normal'-looking one, but I wonder if this is with reference to what society holds up as normal and not necessarily meaning she preferred it to the Black doll. It is interesting that Tuck (2009, p 414) criticises the Clark study for perpetuating a narrative that Black children were not proud of being Black. Tuck argues that if we were to look at the study long term, we would find that later on both the White children and the Black children preferred the Black doll. Tuck argues that this is not analysed because it does not fit the narrative of the damaged Black child. In this story, Esmeralda is clear she does want a Black doll that looks like her. I can only speculate that a doll that looks like her would symbolise that she is important and valued enough to have a doll that looks like her. The issue of representation is key for Esmeralda: she does not feel that a Black doll would be inferior to a White doll.

Virtual homes

The desire to create an aesthetically pleasing home is not confined to the physical home but is evident online too. When I visit Elsa and Pogi, both are keen to show me the house that they have made online. They have created their own characters that resemble themselves online and have built a home. Elsa proudly shows me around her home, with Pogi pointing out that he started it first and did the hard work, with Elsa only adding a few bits. There are two homes: one is called 'My dream home' and the other 'Me and my sister's home'. Elsa leads me like an estate agent through the two homes. The first is a detached house surrounded by a vast area of very green grass. It has an underground garage, where a sports car is parked. 'There is a car for Pogi. This is one for my dad,' explains Elsa (Field notes, 3 November 2020). Even though the children no longer have contact with their father and Elsa has little memory of him, Pogi has built a car for his father. In their home, they have made a space for him and have provided him with a beautiful car, the virtual home giving them the space to keep their father in mind. In their creation they were able to hold the juxtaposition of knowing they could not see their father but still being able to acknowledge him and create a space for him.

Elsa then walks me through the many bedrooms and bathrooms, and the balcony that overlooks the field. She leaves this home and shows me the home in the 'Me and my sister's home' site (see Figure 5.11). Here, their

Figure 5.11: Virtual home (photography by Elsa)

house is next door to a multistorey hotel. The house is the size of a mansion. We walk around the swimming pool to get to the front door. On pushing the door open, Elsa says, 'These houses don't have keys – you can just walk in' (Field notes, 3 November 2020).

I am intrigued that she points this out. To her, this house seems real apart from the locks on the door. I wonder whether the virtual home's lack of locks represents the freedom and safety to move around. The home is beautifully laid out, with numerous bathrooms and plush bedrooms. Pogi and every member of the family has a room dedicated to themselves. We leave the house and visit the hotel, which has a gym and several floors. The tour is cut short when Elsa tells me she needs to go to the toilet.

I reflect on the two homes – there is so much space in and outside. It is in sharp contrast to the two-bedroom flat in a housing block that they live in. I wonder whether Pogi and Elsa have used the aesthetic on the online game to create a home that 'aesthetically' symbolises space, safety and freedom (Atkinson and Parsayi, 2021). They have used the game to dream and imagine an alternative home that is also part of their actual home (Potter and Cowan, 2020).

Minecraft and curation

While there is much literature and focus on how online games, including Minecraft, have educational properties and foster good habits (Nguyen, 2016; Shapiro, 2020), what I was drawn to was how Tdrommie and others in the study, like Kyro, Pogi and Elsa, created and curated their beautiful online worlds. They took much care over how things looked and what could be included and protected. They were creators and curators of art.

Tdrommie was one of three children who joined the project during COVID-19 physical restrictions. For the first few months, Tdrommie and I communicated via WhatsApp video calls (Watson and Lupton, 2022). At first this was difficult. I was worried about whether I could build a rapport with him. A breakthrough in our relationship came when we started to talk about Minecraft, an online creative game. Tdrommie would often become animated as he described and showed me the beautiful world he had created online. Reflecting on Tdrommie guiding me around his Minecraft world, I am reminded of a proud homeowner showing me around their home, or an art collector showing me around a gallery. I was being shown the things Tdrommie had created, collected and displayed. This was not what I had expected. As someone who is slightly fearful of technology, I had paid little attention to Minecraft and its aesthetics and only acknowledged that it was extremely popular among children. This popularity was reflected in the children in the research, all of whom had either heard of Minecraft or were playing it. It can be played on most consoles, computers and mobile devices like tablets and mobile phones, making it accessible to most children.

As Tdrommie gave me lessons in how to build my own Minecraft world, I learnt that, unlike most video games, there is no linear progression to be made, no opponents to destroy in order to get to the next level and there is no 'game over'. Instead, there are endless possibilities to create (Gu, 2014). As Apperley (2015, p 232) writes, Minecraft is 'an endless cycle of collecting, sorting and sharing'. In essence, it is grounded in the everyday practice of building your world (Gu, 2014, p 134) where you have the opportunity to create your world through different creative tasks. There are two main worlds: Creative and Survival (Cayatte, 2014). In Creative mode, you are free to build with your limitless resources. In Survival mode, the main aim is to ward off hunger and ill health; nonetheless, even if you die you can be 'respawned', which means you come back to life again. So, in essence, the game is never over (Cayatte, 2014, p 207). (There is a third world which is more competitive called Hardcore – which most of the children did not play.) Presented with these endless opportunities to create and build, Tdrommie and the other children build and design elaborate worlds.

Curation is a key part of Minecraft as players not only create but also share their world with others. Tdrommie would often show and share his world with his brother. On YouTube, there are numerous videos of people showing others their Minecraft world. You can be shown around the Minecraft world that looks like the Empire State Building, or an elaborate stately home. Here, the positions of artist and curator are merged, and children themselves become both. I often get called by my son to come and look at what he has built on Minecraft – and I am given a tour of his Minecraft world. Pogi, Elsa and Mystical were also keen to show me around their virtual worlds. As Applerey (2015, p 233) writes, 'the mode of interacting with Minecraft shifts fluidly between play, production and curation'.

As with curation of galleries and museums, there is also an element of plundering and stealing in Minecraft. As Tdrommie shows me around his world, he confesses that he sometimes goes into his brother's world and steals his diamonds because that is what his brother does too sometimes. I also know from eavesdropping on my son's Minecraft escapades with his friends that at times they go into another friend's world and steal some goodies.

Knight (2017) makes the argument that creations on iPads are art. Knight (2017, p 141) argues that art can be created 'no matter what that material is, because the material is always bound by its own eventual parameters'. Like pencils, pens and paper, iPads too are restricted by their medium, but that does not stop children from using them and creating. I would extend Knight's argument to Minecraft and the world that children create with their consoles and mobile devices. While the children are restricted due to the binary coding of their devices among other things, they navigate their way through to create their worlds. The children are driven to create by the sensation of pleasure, an effect of being creative.

Children's creation went beyond the borders of their mobile devices and consoles. For Elsa, the boundaries between the virtual world and the non-virtual world were blurred. She gave me a tour of her house that she built with Pogi and followed it with a tour of her actual physical dollhouse. Some of the children's drawings would reflect characters that were in Minecraft, like creepers and diamonds. A common theme that I pick up from Tdrommie, Pogi and Elsa is that there is pleasure in the art of creation, and a key part of the pleasure is the creation of hope and possibilities. The aesthetics of the video games allow children to create alternative realities and dreams.

Memories and photographs: the aesthetic of remembering, curating and archiving

A key feature of the aesthetics of the home was the telling of the stories. This was illustrated when Katie gave me a tour of her home (Plowman and Stevenson, 2013), and we entered the first bedroom:

> 'This is my brother's room. That's his computer. Yeah … he's got lots of books. He likes to read, like me. Up there are the big books – they are full of memories of when we were young, and things,' Katie says as she points to a stack of photo albums.
>
> (Field notes, 15 October 2020)

Around the house are framed photographs of Katie and her siblings at different ages, in school uniform, on holiday in Algeria. This is similar to other homes that I visit. In Sagittarius's house there is a wall as I enter the living room with photographs of Sagittarius and her sister at different stages of their lives, as well as family members and friends, living and dead, near and across the world. Marta (Sagittarius's mother) talks me through who's who in the photographs. She shows me Sagittarius's favourite uncle and her godfather and talks to me about their travel to Chile to see family. In Mystical's house there are two glass cabinets which display photographs of Mystical and his brothers, as well as souvenirs from Mauritius and Paris. The photographs transport us across different time, space and place to show life past and present, where they have been as well as possible futures – places to visit again, people to meet again.

Looking through the photographs that Katie, Kyro and Rosie have taken, I am surprised to find photographs of photographs. They have taken photographs of framed photographs of themselves and their siblings as babies, in their school uniforms, at their christenings. I look at the pictures and try to listen to what they are saying (Campt, 2017). The photographs of photographs remind me of my own children, and how they love to see photographs of themselves. It informs them of a time that they cannot remember – they cannot believe they were that small. Remembering and documenting the past is important to the children (Hope, 2018; Luttrell, 2020, p 59). The past is often associated with trauma for children who have experienced domestic abuse. I do not want to undermine how painful some past memories can be, but among those memories are feelings of joy, fun and belonging. The photographs are evidence of those memories – in essence, the children are showing me their own archives of photographs. Katie, Kyro, Mystical and others are showing me that the galleries, albums and displays of memories that their mothers have curated are important to them because they form part of their history and identity (Hope, 2018; Luttrell, 2020). The photographs show where they have been, who they have met and who is part of their story.

Outside in

> 'Oh my goodness … oh look,' I can hear Mystical call out, as the camera bobs up and down. He is on the balcony of his flat. On my screen I can see a blanket of snow on all the cars and grass, as far as the eye can see. 'Wow! I've never seen anything like this,' he shouts, as the camera wobbles. 'Eeeeeeeee … I am going to take a picture; I am going to film it,' he continues.
>
> I catch glimpses of the floor of the balcony and the stairs inside his flat as he rushes up to the bedroom window. I see the snow falling through his bedroom window. Then he rushes back downstairs and back outside on to the balcony.
>
> 'Oooh oooh … my feet are cold,' he says as the camera shakes. 'This is amazing! Eeeee … it keeps falling. I've never seen this before,' he gasps.
>
> (Field notes, 21 April 2021)

I am left breathless as the video comes to an end. I am engulfed by Mystical's excitement and awe at the snow. I feel my heart beating faster and I am filled with a sense of joy. The moment he captures is so delightful and beautiful, it is hard to capture in writing. There was a sensory knowingness that seemed to be imparted through the video clip. Mystical was not the only one captured by the snow. Katie, JoJo Siwa and Esmeralda had also taken many photographs of the snow. There were pictures of snow people, snowball fights and snow-covered parks and cars (see Figure 5.12). The excitement of snow was palpable through the images – both moving and still.

For the children, the snow was magical, fun, surprising and beautiful (Sanderud et al, 2020). This practice of seeing things like the weather, trees, plants, animals and water as magical was not new. Early on, on my first ever

Figure 5.12: Snow! (Photography by JoJo Siwa)

walkabout with Esmeralda and JoJo Siwa, they took me on a walk around nearby woods. There, they introduced me to the magic bench (see Figure 5.13). This bench was magical because it was a storytelling bench, it told 'scary stories' and it was in the (what they called) dark woods on an island. They took me to see it. It was the only bench on a green surrounded by trees. To my eye the bench looked lonely. I was intrigued that the bench and the woods had agency in their story (Pacini-Ketchabaw, 2012; Taylor and Pacini-Ketchabaw, 2015; Pacini-Ketchabaw and Blaise, 2021). Sadly, we were not able to get close to the storytelling bench because, as JoJo Siwa explained, it was too scary. So I never got close enough to find out what stories the bench had to tell.

Mystical too had a magical tree that was the best of all the trees on the estate. The tree had maroon-coloured leaves unlike the other green-leafed trees, and that was what made it beautiful and magical. One time when I was out and about with Mystical, we stopped and paused as he took several photographs of the magical tree, all the time trying to capture its essence but never feeling he could get it right. It reminded me of the many times I have been captured by the beauty of a sunset and have tried desperately to record it on my phone, always being disappointed because the photograph was only a glimmer of the magic that was present. There was something about the image on the camera never quite capturing the fullness of the moment, much like some of the children's photographs of the Acropolis of Athens in Varvantakis and Nolas's project (2021).

Figure 5.13: The magical bench (photography by Esmeralda)

Everlasting and shifting shapes

While the children took many photographs of trees, plants, flowers, snow and skies, it was when they talked to me about their photographs that the pictures came alive, and I could see that they were trying to capture the essence of the nature/affect of beauty (Richards, 2001; Walton, 2021). The photograph was only one part of the story, as Katie showed me.

It was my parting gift to them all. I wanted them to have a hard copy of all the lovely photographs they took. I was visiting each child and looking through each photograph to see which ones they wanted in their book.

> 'I think we should call this *everlasting*,' Katie suggests, as she and I flick through her photographs (see Figure 5.14). She is automatically starting to separate her photographs into sections and labelling them. I had come to see her to talk about the book I was producing for each child in the study.
>
> 'Why *everlasting*?' I ask.
>
> 'Because the leaves are always green, and they last forever. I like plants and our garden,' Katie explains. Indeed, there were lots of pictures of plants inside and outside her home.
>
> (Field notes, 16 June 2021)

Figure 5.14: Everlasting (photography by Katie)

It may seem that I am deliberately wanting to paint a romantic picture of children and nature, but these are the stories and descriptions the children themselves gave. What I do find interesting is that they have already attributed magical properties to the trees and greenery (Pacini-Ketchabaw, 2012; Taylor and Pacini-Ketchabaw, 2015; Pacini-Ketchabaw and Blaise, 2021). They see that the trees have a life and a story of their own, that they are more than just trees.

This connection with the trees dispels a prevalent narrative that marginalised and urban children do not appreciate nature or would prefer to stay indoors on their screens (Nxumalo and ross, 2019; Nxumalo, 2020). The children dispute the story of prevailing psychological narratives that they are too damaged or too traumatised to see beyond the pain of their abuse and are somehow lacking. Here they clearly appreciate and connect with their world with a fullness and joy. Kathryn McKittrick (2011, p 950) picks this up in her term 'urbancide'. She (2011, p 953) explores how urban areas which are predominantly inhabited by Black and marginalised communities are often seen as 'lacking' – with the prevailing stories about poverty, trauma and death. Little is written about the joy, beauty and conviviality of the area. McKittrick (2011) likens this prevailing narrative of despair to the plantations, or as Sharpe (2016, p 68) beautifully articulates, the hold of the 'slave ship'. McKittrick argues that it is the story of despair without the contextualisation of social and economic inequality, and without the recognition of the spirit and agency of the inhabitants, that keeps it in the plantations and continues the story of death or urbancide. While Sharpe and McKittrick refer to the story of slavery in the US, the families in the research are all descendants of people/communities that were colonised, be it the Philippines, Mauritius or Chile, all with their history of violence and subjugation. The local area where they live is one where those who are socially and economically marginalised are housed. The stories that prevail are of poverty and despair – the stories are similar to 'urbancide'. But listening to the children, I hear a different story, one of magic and entanglement with beauty and joy and nature. So while I may be guilty at times of absentmindedly flicking through 'another' photograph of trees and greenery (see also Varvantakis and Nolas, 2021), when I look closer, I can hear the story of magic and the blurring of boundaries.

For Mystical and Katie, there is no binary thinking of nature versus technology, indoor versus outdoors: for them, the boundaries are blurred. In the next section the children show me through their pictures that sometimes the outside comes inside, and the inside goes outside.

Shape-shifters

> 'I think we should call these clouds … no … shape-shifters … because they change shapes all the time,' Katie says as she points to numerous pictures of the clouds.
>
> (Field notes, 16 June 2021)

There were several pictures of the sky lit a lovely warm amber by the sunset. Like Katie, Rosie, Kyro and Mystical had also taken pictures of the sky. There were photographs of the sky outside their bedroom window, peeping through the tunnel leading to Asda and photographs of the sky alone. The sky had captured their eye. In her book *Aesthetics of the Familiar*, Saito (2017, p 71) writes how in our busy lives we seldom take note of the celestial phenomena that is the sky, yet here the children in the study have noticed it and taken a picture, making me take note of the familiar. Like the artist Anish Kapoor, the children have made me note the extraordinariness of the sky. In his sculpture named *Cloud Gate* situated outside Chicago's Millennium Park in 2004, Kapoor created a giant stainless-steel structure shaped like a giant bean that reflected the surrounding landscape and emphasised the sky. It was as if, according to Saito (2017, p 75), it was an attempt 'to bring the sky down to earth'. Likewise, I feel that the photographs of the sky were an attempt to draw the outside in, to bring the sky down to earth, to note the extraordinariness of the familiar.

The aesthetics of everyday life

This extraordinariness of the mundane is something that I noticed in a set of pictures by Rosie. In one set I can trace Rosie's walk to the supermarket. There are pictures of the plants near her block of flats (see Figure 5.15, top left), the bus that passes her by (see Figure 5.15, top right), the shops along the road near her home, a wall of graffiti/street art, a sign saying 'Its lovely to have you back', a trolley (see Figure 5.15, bottom right) and, just before she enters the supermarket, there is an array of photographs of the sky (see Figure 5.15, bottom left). A peep of the sky through the tunnel leading to Asda, photographs of just the sky, as well as the sky with the Asda sign peeping through. When asked about the photographs of the sky, both Rosie and Mystical had said 'because it looks nice'.

Through Rosie's photographs I feel I can embody her journey. I feel myself moving with her and feeling the different sounds, smells and sights. I can smell the leaves and hear the leaves rustling, I hear the bus roar past, the ring of the shop door as another customer enters, the clash of trolleys as people try to redeem their pound coin, the warmth of the sun and the feel of a smile that a clear blue sky brings. Varvantakis et al (2019, 2021) and Templeton (2020) write of how children can use photographs to show their use of public spaces. Following Templeton's way of thinking, I can see how Rosie has captured the aesthetics of her neighbourhood through her journey, bringing to life her interaction with her surroundings. I see

Figure 5.15: From top left to bottom right: the trees; the bus; the sky; shopping trolleys (photography by Rosie)

the world from her height – being level with the trolleys, the distance from the sky, looking up at the bus, noticing the leaves coming through the low fence. She shows what geographers Horten et al (2014) write – a detailed knowledge of her area. Horten et al (2014), Templeton (2020) and Varvantakis and Nolas (2021) argue that knowledge about children's use of public spaces and walking are limited, and we need to attend to their everyday to have a better understanding of our environments. Through Rosie's picture I can feel the vibrancy of her neighbourhood and the beauty she sees around her. What could be perceived as a mundane walk to the shops for the weekly groceries was in fact a visual recording of the beauty in her urban neighbourhood.

Conclusion

In this chapter, I explored the different times and ways that the children in the project tried to share with me the beauty they see in their everyday lives. They try to capture through photographs the things they find 'beautiful' or 'pretty'. I was initially dismissive of these descriptions but on reflection became more attuned to how the children were trying to share the affects of beauty with me. Aesthetics played a role in how mothers and children showed care and created joy. Homes would be decorated in the countdown to festivals, like Eid, Christmas and Halloween. The children were excited to show me their virtual worlds too. In their online games and photographs of childhood, I found the children to be curators of memories and beauty. They clearly illustrated that beauty and aesthetics were an important part of their lives, and were attentive to the beauty in public places. In their homes, they created care, joy and love through aesthetics. In the following chapter I examine the love that I experienced in the everyday lives of the children.

6

The art of loving in everyday life

As I flick through the children's photographs and my ethnographic field notes, I get a warm sense of care, tenderness, acceptance, joy, respect and beauty. In essence, I see, feel and hear the act of love in the everyday. Despite the prevalent psychological narrative that children who have experienced domestic abuse score lower on the prosocial scale (Levendosky et al, 2011; Ehrensaft and Cohen, 2012; Taillieu et al, 2016; Callaghan et al, 2017b) or that mothers who have experienced domestic abuse are deemed to lack emotional capacity, rendering their mothering 'not good enough' (Radford and Hester, 2006; Lapierre, 2008, 2010; Callaghan, 2015), the families in the research have shown me the opposite. Through their everyday lives, they have practised acts of care, love and tenderness. In this chapter, I draw on these acts of love in order to 'show' the children's full humanness, which contradicts the prevalent narrative about children and domestic abuse.

The study of love is seen as frivolous in social work (Gatwiri and Ife, 2021), yet it has occupied the minds of some of the reflective thinkers of our time, and is part of the ideologies of some of the major institutional religions, such as Buddhism, Islam, Christianity, Judaism and Hinduism. In their everyday lives, the children and their mothers continue to love and be loved. Through their stories and practices, they illustrate how love is not solely a feeling but a practice, a way of knowing and being in the world (Lorde, 2020, p 56) and a source of energy that transforms their world under a patriarchal society. In this chapter I discuss why love is important. I draw heavily from bell hooks's (2016a, 2016b, 2016c) love trilogy and other Black feminists and writers who have argued that love must be taken seriously.

When domestic abuse is written and spoken about, love is rarely explored, yet as this chapter illustrates, it is important in the everyday lives of the children. Power and control is often cited as key to understanding domestic abuse (Stark, 2009; Katz, 2016; Logan, 2017), but this understanding often falls short in examining the possible reasons undergirding people's quest for this power and control (hooks, 2004). Social work academics (based in Australia) Gatwiri and Ife (2021, p 6) argue that since love is one of the most powerful human emotions, it is amazing that it is omitted from mainstream social work practices. They conclude that this is due to the dominance of 'Western Enlightenment Modernity'. When love is talked about in social work practice, it is often in reference to attachment (Gerhardt, 2015) rather than the more expansive love written about by Lorde (2020, p 51) and hooks (2016a, 2016b, 2016c). hooks (2004, p 17) analyses how love and abuse cannot coexist, and that patriarchy teaches people, especially males, to reject love – both the love of others and the love of self, which can be a key element in domestic abuse. Using ethnographic stories, I explore how the patriarchy and the lack of love can invade the everyday lives of children in the research.

In the chapter I also consider how the children in their different relationships practised love. Nurturing mutuality and solidarity was a key part of their everyday lives; it was something that they both practised and experienced. I explore how they also had to navigate their way through relationships and practices that were not loving. I conclude the chapter with reflections on my own relationship with the children and the love that has sustained this project (Herbert, 2025).

'What's Love Got to Do with It?'

Tina Turner (Lyle and Britten, 1983; Turner, 1984) once sang 'What's love got to do with it? What's love but a second-hand emotion?' Black feminist scholar bell hooks would strongly disagree that love is a second-hand emotion. For hooks (2016a, 2016b, 2016c), love is not only a feeling but a deep knowledge and action that is more than individual romantic relations, as it is often depicted in the post-industrial world. Defying the trivialisation of love to the realm of weakness, sentimentality and individuality, hooks (2016a, p 6) draws on the work of M.S. Peck (2006) and defines love as the 'will to extend one's self for the purpose and nurturing of one's own or another's spiritual growth'. It is this will to extend one's self to another that I saw in the everyday lives of the children. hooks (2016a, p 87) positions love as a powerful political and spiritual force that is capable of transforming all spheres of life: 'politics, religion, the workplace, households and intimate relations'.

hooks is not alone in acknowledging that at the centre of love is a connection with others. The philosophy of love being about one's own and another's spiritual growth has a wide and long story. Philosopher Aristotle wrote of philia, the love that we have for another that extends to us wanting good things for their sake (Torres, 2021). Martin Buber (2020 [1937]) writes that life is meaningless unless we find ourselves in relations with another: when our 'I' meets another's 'thou', we do not objectify them but are in relation with them. This is echoed in the philosophy of ubuntu, which is used in different parts of Africa. Gatwiri (2021, p 67) defines this as seeking 'to affirm and honour the dignity of every human being and [it] seeks to develop and maintain mutually affirming and respectful relationships grounded on deep respect for other people's humanity'. Lorde (2020, p 37) writes that 'recognising the power of the erotic within our lives can give us the energy to pursue genuine change within our world, rather than merely settling for a shift of characters in the same weary drama'. For Lorde (2020, p 32), eros is the personification of love in all its aspects, an energy that brings creativity and harmony. This desire for connection ran throughout my research. Children wanted to know and be known.

Do you want to play? The art of getting to know you, me, us

In order to love we must first know the other, but how do we get to know someone and what does 'getting to know' mean? My interactions with Pogi illustrated the importance of being with and recognising the significance of another person's world, but the beginning was hard.

Geertz (1993 [1972]) writes about how when he first arrived in Bali, he felt invisible, that the Balinese could not relate to him. But then, as if by magic, a moral or metaphysical line would be crossed and the Balinese would consider that he was a real human being and not a cloud or a gust of wind, and would engage warmly with him. In many ways this is how I felt about my relationship with Pogi. While he had agreed to be part of the research, I felt that he was too distant and did not engage with me. I would visit, but it felt hard – not dissimilar to my relationship with Tdrommie that I depicted in the previous chapter. Similarly, when I spoke about play and what games he liked, Pogi's whole body would shift and become full of energy. The first time this happened was when I asked him what game he was playing on his screen:

> 'Do you want to play too?' Pogi asks.
> 'OK, but I don't really know how to. You might have to show me,' I reply. Several minutes pass as he shows me how to hold the controllers and manoeuvre my soldier on the screen.
> 'OK, you got to try and kill me now,' Pogi says as he takes another controller in his hand and starts to move his soldier.
> (Field notes, 10 July 2020)

Several times during this visit, Pogi had to help me. At first, he found it fun sneaking up on my soldier and killing him. He laughed, but as the novelty of having such an easy opponent waned, he tried to make it as easy as he could for me to kill him. As I was leaving after my visit, Pogi kept trying to get his mother to play with him. It was his insistence that made me realise how much he wanted people to enter his world and play his game with him. This desire to share his play became more evident when he enthusiastically took up my offer of going with him to the green wasteland between his block of flats and the golf course, where he and his friends would often go scavenging for treasure.

So, a couple of weeks later, I knock on Pogi's door to go on an adventure. He comes out of his flat and starts to put his shoes on. All shoes are stacked on a rack outside the front door of the flat.

> 'Don't forget to bring your camera,' I say. Pogi goes back in to get the camera. Elsa is pulling at her mum, Ann.
> 'Elsa wants to come too,' says Ann.
> 'Oh OK,' I say. When Pogi returns, I ask if it is OK if Elsa comes.
> 'Yes!' he enthusiastically nods. Ann then asks if she too can come. I ask Pogi, 'Is that OK?'
> Again, Pogi nods enthusiastically 'Yes!'
> While Elsa and Ann go to get their things, I ask Pogi if it is OK if his mother and sister come along. He says that he wants them to as they have never visited his secret place that he goes to with his friends.
> (Field notes, 29 July 2020)

It strikes me how the trip allows Pogi to show things to his family that he has not been able to before; it is an opportunity for him. I wonder if maybe this research is a chance for children to tell their stories not only to others in the community but to their families too. Brant (1994, p 74) writes that we have a desire to be known and felt. That we are in need of being witnessed, for others to know what has passed, what is present and what is to be (Brant, 1994, p 74). This witnessing is an act of love, for witnessing involves being attentive to people and seeing what is meaningful to them (Laura, 2013). In this case it is to acknowledge Pogi's stories and 'to protect their places in the world' (Laura, 2013, p 290).

During the expedition, I am struck with how happy Pogi is to entertain his sister. His sister places her headband on his head while he is putting on his shoes, and he places it correctly on his head so that it fits properly, then she takes it back. There is tenderness and care in his approach to his sister, a reflection of the intimacy between siblings that I discuss later in this chapter.

We talk about the golf balls he has. He is unsure whether he has taken any pictures of them. The golf balls are something that struck me on my second visit to the family. On asking Pogi what interests him and what things are important to him, he showed me a pile of golf balls outside on the balcony. He explained how he goes into the woods with his friend, seeking the golf balls as treasure (see Figure 6.1).

Pogi puts a golf ball into his pocket. Ann and Elsa appear – they are excited to join Pogi and see his place. They go down the stairs first, and I follow at an acceptable COVID-19 physical distance behind. We reach the bottom of the stairs and turn left and walk around the building. We walk towards the wooden fence, which Pogi climbs over, but he says we can walk to the gate. Elsa, Ann and I walk towards the gate and go through it.

Figure 6.1: Treasured golf balls (photography by Pogi)

Pogi then instructs us to find a big stick because that is going to help us on our travels: we will need it to fight the bushes. We follow his lead and look for big sticks. He finds one, then I do, then he finds another one and gives it to his mother and sister. I am affected by his care.

We walk with our big sticks past another grey building and immediately turn right. We are faced with overgrown nettles, plants, bushes and trees. Pogi tells us that we need to skirt the building to work our way around the overgrowth. It has been a while since he has been here, and it has grown immensely. He cuts back the shrubbery with the big stick he is carrying. We step on to a concrete (manhole) square. He then grabs a blue and red crate and positions it further along so we can step on it and walk to the corner. Pogi goes first because he is leading the way. I go second. I walk past Pogi to stand in the corner to make room for him to go back, as his mother and sister are hesitant to come across.

Pogi asks his sister if she wants him to carry her across. She nods. Ann is not sure about this and tells Pogi it might not be a good idea. He says that he can carry Elsa and is strong enough, and lifts his sister up on to his back. He asks his sister to hold on. She looks wonky on him, but he manages to carry her to the crates, where he puts her down. Ann follows them. Pogi seems very proud and wants to show his family this area; he wants to show that he knows what he is doing. Elsa and Ann are unsure about going any further. The decision is taken that Pogi and I will continue the journey. Ann and Elsa do not want to continue and want to keep safe, but Pogi wants to continue to show me his area.

I feel like I am on an adventure. We skirt around the edge of the overgrowth, thrashing away overgrown stinging nettles, branches, leaves, twigs, brambles and grass, and continue (see Figure 6.2). We are met with metal fencing around the corner.

> 'Mmm,' Pogi says. 'It's grown a lot since I was here before with my friends. Oh, look. This is something we found before,' he says as he picks up what looks like a plastic dagger. He uses it to thrash away some more overgrowth. He turns around and says, 'I know another way.'
> (Field notes, 29 July 2020)

He points for us to go back, but this time to cross the overgrowth. More thrashing of nettles, and we reach a wooden and metal fence, but there is a gap. Pogi slips through and over. I am glad that I can still fit through despite three months of quarantine eating. Past the barrier, there are more shrubs, trees and nettles. We continue with Pogi pointing out bits of treasure. He wants me to video it. Exploring this place is very much part of getting to know him, what he is interested in, what moves him, his friendships and his story. He seems happy to show me his secret area, to show me how he

Figure 6.2: An adventure (photography by Pogi)

Figure 6.3: Treasure (photography by Pogi)

and his friends look for treasure and what they consider treasure. Our eyes scan over the sanitary towels, empty food packets and other rubbish left in the shrubs. Glass and golf balls are considered valuable (see Figure 6.3).

In the distance we can hear Elsa calling Pogi's name. I can't tell which direction it is coming from, but Pogi seems to know. We go on searching for treasure. Pogi is keen to point out things he and his friends have found before and which are still in the forest. We continue on our quest, and slowly Pogi shows me the way out. His final advice to the camera is 'never go into the forest without protection'.

He brings me round the building, where we meet his mother and sister, who are relieved to see us. They ask us where we have been because they could not see us. Elsa then says she is hungry. It is time for them to go home. I thank them for the fun, and they head home. Along with the sense of adventure, I am left with a feeling of how important it was for Pogi to show us his secret place and how keen he was to share it with his family. He wanted to be seen, for us to bear witness to his escapade, for us to get to know him. Getting to know Pogi entailed what feminist Maria Lugones (1987) calls 'playfully travelling' to his world, not in a colonialist way to conquer and extricate, but which required (as I explored in the previous chapter) an openness to a new world and to be changed. It required me to be open to change, to be open to reflect on a different view of myself and to recognise and value the humanness of both Pogi and myself. It is this sensual knowledge of mutuality and humanness that is at the centre of love.

Reflecting back on my visits to Pogi, I can sense that he wanted to be known, but he also wanted his mother, sister and me to have fun, to experience for ourselves the joy that he feels when he plays on his PS4 and ventures into the woods. It reminds me of when I discover a recipe that is delicious and works – I am keen for others to try it too. I want them to share in my new discovery, to share in my joy and experience; I want to 'share the love'. Throughout my visits, Pogi works hard at helping me to travel to his world. He teaches me how to use the PS4; he places the crates down so I can step into the woods; he finds wooden sticks for us to fight the bushes; he carries his sister on his back; he is active in building relationships. hooks (2016a, p 13) writes that love is not only a feeling but an action too, and it is not only addressed to a friend, a lover or family but to wider society too. In the following paragraphs I explore how children practise love in different ways.

Sisterly love

The love and solidarity between siblings is one thing that struck me throughout the research. The tenderness shown by Pogi towards his sister Elsa was one moment, but there were many others. At times, I felt like I was intruding on intimate moments between siblings, as well as times of solidarity. This happened the first time I was able to go into the home of Esmeralda and JoJo Siwa.

As I enter the corridor, they squeal and Esmeralda places her hands over her mouth and jumps up and down. After the initial greetings, Stardust (their mother) says they can take me upstairs to their bedroom. Esmeralda and JoJo Siwa share a bedroom. The novelty of having me in their room is exciting, and they are keen to show me their belongings. They show me their bunk beds, doll's house, toys and books. We then settle on the floor and I lay out numerous papers and colouring pens for any artwork they want to do. JoJo Siwa is not interested and takes my phone and starts to make a video recording of their bedroom and to take pictures, while I do some pen and paper artwork with Esmeralda. 'Look!' JoJo Siwa says, thrusting a piece of paper under my nose (Field notes, 24 September 2020). She lays the paper on the floor and takes a picture of it. It is a certificate. The name of whom the certificate is awarded to has been crossed out with a line, with Esmeralda's name written on top.

> 'I don't know how the teacher can say she is proud of Esmeralda and not spell her name right!' JoJo Siwa says, incandescent with rage. She

was so enraged by the misspelling of Esmeralda's name on the certificate that she had crossed out the teacher's writing and had written in large letters the right spelling.

'Yeah, she did not even tell me about it. JoJo Siwa just crossed it out and wrote my name properly,' Esmeralda explains with a shrug.
(Field notes, 24 September 2020)

I admired the outrage and solidarity that JoJo Siwa showed her sibling. For JoJo Siwa, this was a question of justice and recognition of her sister as a person with a name, not any name but her own name.

The solidarity and love between JoJo Siwa and Esmeralda is not something that has magically appeared. As hooks (2016b, p 139) writes, solidarity between sisters is something that is nurtured by an ethic of love. In a world where Black girls can be judged harshly and ignored (Harris, 2016; Essien and Wood, 2020; Halliday, 2021; Curtis et al, 2022), the love shown between the two sisters is practised and builds solidarity, which nurtures their wellbeing and confidence. JoJo Siwa's indignation on behalf of her sister was her demonstrating that the right spelling of Esmeralda's name was important and that Esmeralda had deserved more care and value from the teacher. Reflecting on how important it is to nurture one another, especially in a world that can be hostile, hooks (2016c, p 108) writes, 'For Black girls to have a chance to build healthy self-esteem in an integrated colonizing environment, there must be oppositional strategies and places that promote decolonization.' Here we see that JoJo Siwa does not solely rely on an adult to provide that space of decolonisation, but through her love and care of her sister, she is creating a space where her sister is valued, loved and cared for, where her way of being and knowing is acknowledged and nurtured.

Esmeralda and JoJo Siwa continued to show me that they were active givers of love and care. Later on in the same visit, during an art session, I took out several blank paper figures (see Figure 6.4, left and right). I asked them to draw on, write on or mark the paper with what they thought made a caring person. In my limited imagination, I had expected them to write something about their mother, teachers, social workers or other adults in their lives, but I was surprised when without conferring, both Esmeralda and JoJo Siwa drew and wrote about how they themselves would do 'good'. I could see how school had an influence over their thinking with the referral to the 'golden rule' (a term often used in schools), but in essence they did not focus on the adults in their school but on themselves as doing good.

One of the things that constantly challenged my thinking was that the children saw themselves as active givers of love and care. Katie too wrote

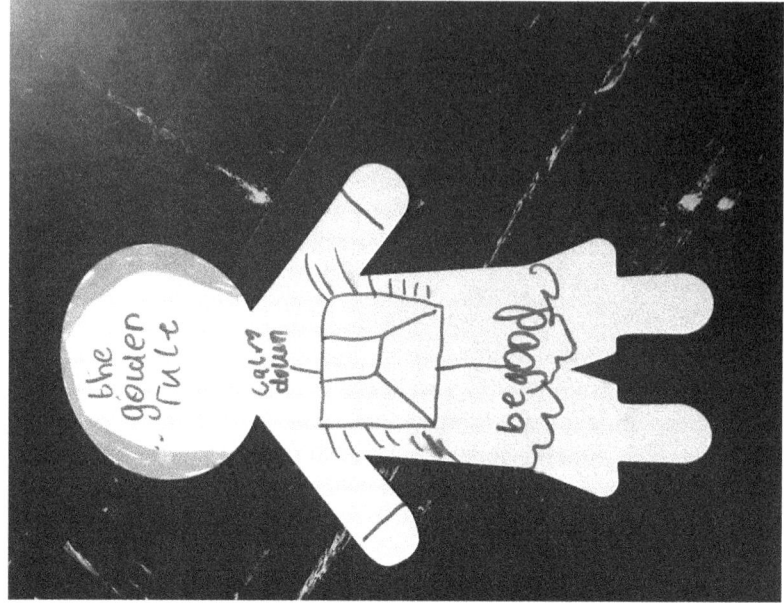
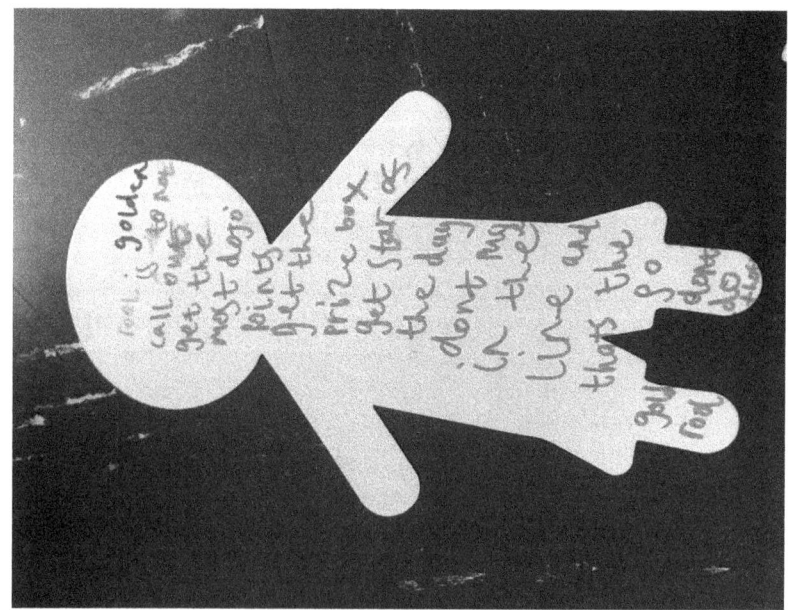

Figure 6.4: (Left) The 'golden rool' (photography by Esmeralda); (right) the 'golden rule' (photography by JoJo Siwa)

about what children could do to take care of others, to act in a loving way (see Figure 6.5, left and right). She had drawn herself and, on the reverse side of the paper, had written about caring for others in the playground. Children did not only see adults as caregivers but themselves too.

During her time in Lusaka, Uganda, anthropologist Jean Hunleth (2017) found that while international health programmes ignored the care work of children, children not only were important in caring for adults with tuberculosis (TB) but they wanted to be 'closer' to the adult, usually a family member, that they cared for. Instead of defining the care work by children as 'bad' or 'good', Hunleth (2017, p 11) encourages us to contextualise children in their everyday lives in order to gain a more nuanced idea of the care given by them. Like the children in Hunleth's study, the children in this study saw themselves as active givers of love and care, and acknowledged their interdependency and relationship with others. There is a complexity around care, for in trying to reduce the exploitation of children, we can reduce them to passive recipients of care rather than see the importance of reciprocity in their relationships (Twum-Danso, 2009a; Twum-Danso Imoh, 2022). We can make the lives of children who need to care due to poverty more precarious when we fail to see how the role of caring is important to their survival and living liveable lives (Evans and Skovdal, 2015). Esmeralda and JoJo Siwa did not see themselves as passive recipients of care but as people capable of giving care too. Katz (2015), in her research with mothers and children who had experienced domestic abuse, found that some children wanted to show care to their mothers, and that this strengthened their relationships and gave them confidence.

Unloving spaces

The support between sisters or females in groups is not always guaranteed and can be fraught with power dynamics that result in bullying and envy. hooks (2016b, p 123) writes how, under a patriarchal society, competition is normalised and we are taught 'only one female can win the day or be chosen' (hooks, 2016c, p 131). Fairytales like *Hansel and Gretel*, *Cinderella*, *Rapunzel* and *Snow White* teach us that only one female can survive, and it is always the younger and/or the prettiest female that wins (Jorgensen, 2019). This was an issue that both Sagittarius and Katie brought up when we talked about their move to secondary school. In September 2020, Sagittarius, Katie and Pogi started year 6 and had already begun to talk about secondary school. It was the time to visit schools and contemplate where they wanted to go, and it often came up in our conversations.

'Have you started looking at schools yet?' I ask Sagittarius.
'Yeah, some.'

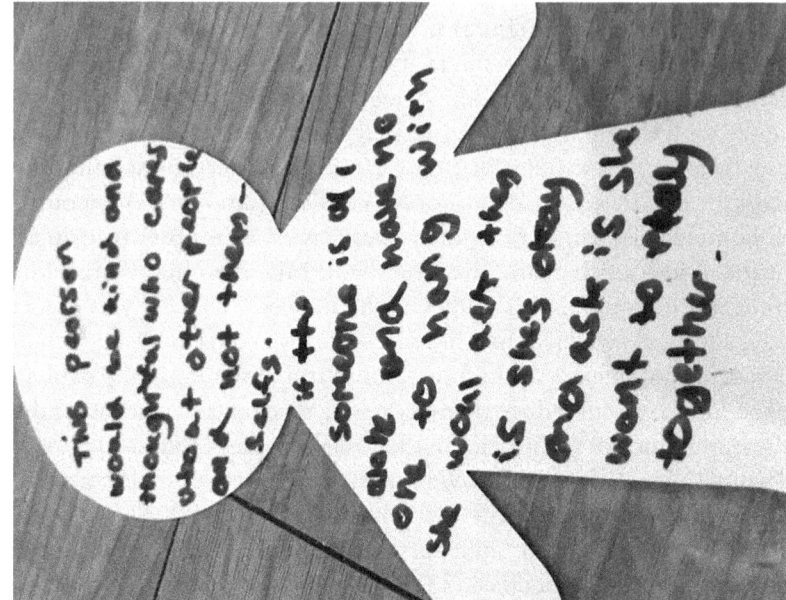

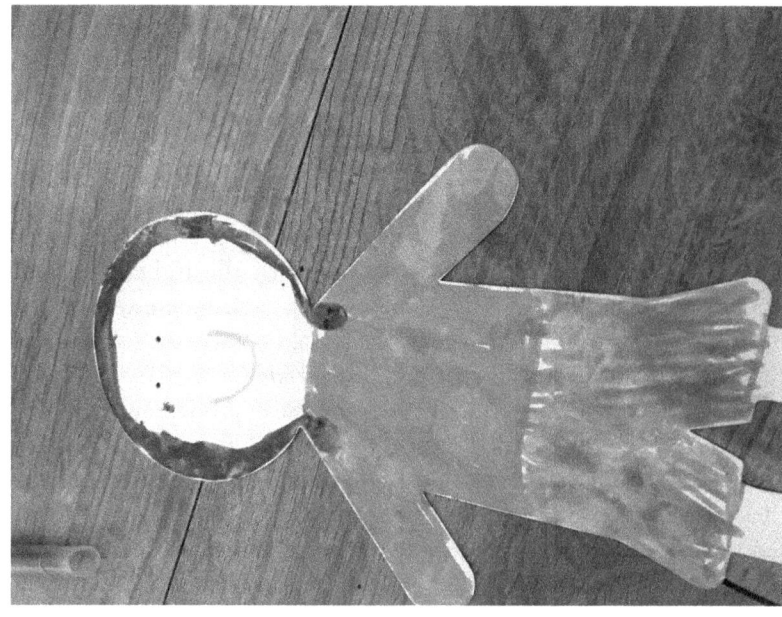

Figure 6.5: (Left) Caring person (photography by Katie); (right) caring actions (photography by Katie)

'Do you have any favourites?'
'I'd like to go to St John's or Southwell.'
'Are there other children from your school that want to go there?'
'Some, some want to go to Ashley but I definitely don't want to go there!'
'Why is that?' I enquire.
'Oh it's an all-girls school; I don't want to go there,' Sagittarius declares. 'My sister went to an all-girls school and she was bullied. Girls can be mean.'
(Field notes, 4 August 2020)

This concern about going to an all-girls school was also something that Katie worried about, as she explained to me:

'Yeah, I want to go to Cranmead but it can be hard to get into. My last choice is St Jude's; I hope I don't get that one. It is just girls and I don't want to go there. You know how girls can be when they are alone together.'
(Field notes, 28 August 2020)

I was intrigued by Katie's and Sagittarius's comments, as both had a close circle of friends who were all girls, but both had a strong belief about all-girls schools. They found the prospect of an all-female space threatening. They recognised that bullying and unkindness were not only to do with boys, and that girls could be unloving too. In their view, all-female/single-sex school spaces were notorious for fostering a threatening space. Like hooks (2016b, p 75), both Katie and Sagittarius questioned the assumption that females were more loving than men. hooks (2016a, p 154) writes, 'Females are encouraged by patriarchal thinking to believe we should be loving, but this does not mean we are any more emotionally equipped to do the work of love than our male counterparts.' Katie and Sagittarius had already concluded that to be a girl or woman did not necessarily make you more loving. As hooks (2016b, p 130) explores, all-female groups do not necessarily mean that values of patriarchy do not thrive, for we all live in a patriarchal society and we need to be reflective to see how these values affect our own behaviour and thoughts. hooks (2016b, p 121) writes that affirming one another as women can be difficult, even for those who claim to be feminists. From childhood, hooks (2016b, p 130) argues, females are taught how to use 'tactics of exclusion, ostracism, and shunning to police one another'. This behaviour is rooted in the knowledge that females 'lack value in the eyes of patriarchy' and can 'gain value only by competing with one another for recognition' (hooks, 2016b, p 131).

Reflecting on Katie's and Sagittarius' views, I observe that what they are concluding is that a single-sex environment does not necessarily create a safe and loving space, and that power dynamics and abuse can continue without due care and attention. Drawing on the history of feminism, hooks writes about how Black women and working-class women were not accepted in the White, middle-class mainstream feminist movement. Indeed, many Black feminist scholars have continued to argue that White feminism has been an exclusive group (hooks, 1987; Hill Collins, 2016; Bhandar and Ziadah, 2020; Vergès, 2021). As I write this section, I am reminded of the current debate around transgender people in the feminist movements, especially with regards to domestic abuse. Leading domestic abuse charities Women's Aid and Nia have struggled with the issue of allowing transgender women to seek shelter or to work in refuges, arguing over whether it compromises a safe space for women fleeing domestic abuse. From my experience in working with refuges, I have encountered abusive behaviour in some single-sex refuges. For Katie and Sagittarius, just having a female-only space does not necessarily create a safe space, and we need to look at dynamics and underlying patriarchal values that continue to thrive and oppress in those spaces.

Patriarchy and love

There were times when I would call Sagittarius and she would be giggling. Often, she would explain that her sister had said something funny. When I visited, I would catch moments of fun, tenderness and care between Sagittarius and her sister through the kitchen window. As I walked past the window to the front door, I would often see them giggling, teasing each other and being tactile with one another. This everyday intimacy was something that came across in Sagittarius's photographs. There is a selection of photographs showing Sagittarius's sister Hope cradling Sagittarius's head, as she applies make-up to Sagittarius's face. The pictures (taken by Marta, their mother) are like scene-by-scene shots of the event. Put together, they appear like a moving image of the intimacy of the sisters. The family are celebrating Halloween. They are sitting on chairs around the dining table. On the table is make-up and cups filled with tea or hot chocolate. The first picture shows Hope smiling and looking at the camera, poised with a lipstick in her hand. We cannot see Sagittarius's face, as she is bending over, head down touching her knees and her hair flowing towards the ground. The next picture shows Hope applying lipstick to Sagittarius's lips, who is squinting and giggling at the same time. Then Sagittarius has her head tilted back and her sister is starting to apply the lipstick.

The end shot is of Sagittarius's head fully tilted and resting on the back of her chair, as Hope, with a look of concentration, applies lipstick to her face. There is a ritual and intimacy to the picture. I can sense the older sister taking on the role of showing the little sister how to apply make-up, the giggles partly because of the awkwardness of trying something new and also because the touch from her sister is tickling. There is a tenderness in Hope holding Sagittarius's head and delicately putting on the lipstick. There is also the ritual and rhythm of getting ready for Halloween, the decor and the dressing up/costumes and sweets that go with it.

This tenderness between siblings is lovely to behold but not always easy to foster. Part of the tactics used by some (not all) of the fathers in this research were to play family members against each other. Often, they would seek to drive a wedge between the family, leaving each member isolated and in the dark. The manipulation of relationships to maintain power in the home is not uncommon in domestic abuse and can continue even after the perpetrator has left the family home (Holt, 2015; Morrison, 2015; Radford and Hester, 2015). With one family in the study, the father had rung the social work department to lodge a complaint about the mother's parenting. As the allegation was serious, an investigation was launched. Fortunately, the family's social worker had an understanding of the family's history of domestic abuse and understood that the allegation was a way for the father to further harass the family and try to break their bond. The social worker was able to advocate for and support the family through the investigation by the Front Door team (a safeguarding team). In this case, unlike Mystical's, the social worker and the family were able to work together for the safety and the nurturing of family life and relationships.

hooks writes that love and abuse cannot coexist (hooks, 2016a, p 6) and that patriarchy stands in the way of love (hooks, 2016a, p xxiv). She explains that while many abusive partners may declare passionately that they love their family, if their action does not nurture their own or their family's spiritual growth, then it is not love. hooks (2016a, p 6) acknowledges that, like in her family, aggressive shaming and abuse often coexist with affection and care, but that is not love. Thus, for hooks, the continuous harassment and policing of mothers by some of the fathers in my study is not love for either the children or their mothers. hooks (2004, 2016a, 2016b, 2016c) concludes that this lack of love is a mark of patriarchy, for patriarchy is the antithesis of love. hooks (2004, p 18) defines patriarchy as 'a political-social system that insists that males are inherently dominating, superior to everything and everyone deemed weak, especially females, and endowed with the right to dominate and rule over the weak and to maintain that dominance through various forms of psychological terrorism and violence'. This urge to dominate runs through not only individuals but systems and groups, including the very systems set up to support families – including in social work.

Systems are made up of people and 'within a culture of domination, shaming others is one way to assert coercive control' (hooks, 2016c, p 82). The CP system can be shaming and coercive, as families have testified

(Hughes et al, 2011; Smithson and Gibson, 2017; Heward-Belle et al, 2018; Stewart, 2020). It can be used as a means of coercing and controlling families in a way that is similar to the abusive fathers (Hughes et al, 2011; Featherstone et al, 2017; Heward-Belle et al, 2018). In the case discussed earlier, the social worker was able to recognise the attempts by the father to manipulate the safeguarding system to break the bonds between the mother and her children and continue his abuse. The social worker was able to demonstrate love by seeing and accepting the family as they were and worked in solidarity with them (hooks, 2016b). As we have seen with Mystical and his family (as discussed in Chapter 3), the system is not always loving to families. However, the children often showed great discernment over what they deemed to be the (un)kindness and (mis)understanding of the professionals in their lives.

'I just nod my head and smile': care without love

Katie and I are sitting on the swings. We are talking about school and her friends.

> 'Yeah, I don't like her,' Katie explains about a teacher. 'She wants to appear nice but she's not really.'
> 'What do you mean?' I ask.
> 'Well, you know my friend Jenny that I talked about? Well, you know her dad isn't well. This teacher told her off the other day and said, "I don't think your parents are doing a good job of bringing you up." That's not a kind thing to say … and she's supposed be the wellbeing teacher and SENCO!' tuts Katie. 'You know she is always trying to pull me aside to have a quiet word to see if I am OK. She thinks she understands but she really doesn't. I just nod my head and smile while she talks,' continues Katie.
>
> (Field notes, 13 February 2021)

In Katie's description and analysis, the teacher has not fostered a level of trust. The teacher had not come to the relationship with a sense of curiosity, of wanting to learn, to get to know her. Katie felt that the teacher thought she already knew the answer, and, together with her treatment of Katie's friend, showed a lack of empathy and understanding – in fact, she had exercised her judgement and authority. In these everyday encounters and practices at school, Katie had assessed that the teacher was not someone she could be vulnerable with.

Katie had, like Fanon (2001 [1961], p 207), arrived at the conclusion that an attitude of 'not knowing' was important for the teacher to build a trusting relationship with her – a relationship that she could be emotionally vulnerable and open in. Katie had felt like a problem to be fixed rather than someone to empathetically engage with. In their paper on teaching about vulnerability and love in social work and drawing from the work of bell hooks, Gatwiri and Ife (2021) explore how unless there is a sense of vulnerability for the teacher, it is impossible to practise teaching with love. Katie's teacher had wanted Katie to be vulnerable with her but had come to the situation as all-knowing – this imbalance of power had made Katie feel anxious. This is understandable, for love relies on a mutuality that creates a safe relational space where it is possible to share, give, receive and show solidarity (hooks, 2016a, 2016b, 2016c). Katie had also seen that the teacher's practice with another student had not been kind; therefore, she had protected herself from further harm and distress. She had used her judgement and wisdom to navigate the situation.

This suspicion of professionals was shared by other children too. On my first walkabout with Mystical, he told me that he thought his social worker was unkind to his mother. He sensed that the social worker didn't believe him or his mother. Pogi too had been so upset by the comments made by a teacher, that his mother was going to go in the next day and talk to a staff member. The lack of loving care was something mothers noted too. Several of them commented on professionals as either 'just doing it as a job' or more positively as 'really caring for the children'. Hearing the children's and mothers' reflections, I wondered what their support had lacked. It seemed that what the children and mothers were reflecting on was the affect of care. At times, they had felt like the professional was ticking a box, doing something that they had to do, as in Katie's case, or not listening or validating their story, like in Mystical's comment. It had left them feeling confused, angry and vulnerable. Something was missing in their care – possibly trust, knowledge, respect – the very essence of love (hooks, 2016a, p 6). hooks (2016a, p 8) writes that 'care is a dimension of love, but simply giving care does not mean that we are loving'. In essence, the children were telling me that their support from different professionals was not loving and this was important to them. Children did not just want to be 'saved' and 'cared for'; they wanted to be met in their whole humanness and to be treated lovingly.

There were professionals who did meet the children where they were at and who were able to build a loving relationship. Pogi and Esmeralda talked briefly about their time with their counsellor at school. The most positive support for a professional was made by Rosie and Kyro.

'Brenda, do you know Claire?' asks Rosie on one visit.
'I know of Claire but I have never met her,' I answer.
'Claire is our social worker. You should meet her. You two could become best friends!' advises Rosie.
(Field notes, 7 December 2020)

Rosie and Kyro would try several times to match me with Claire. Claire had made them feel valued and important. She was also fun to be with, and they felt she wanted the best for them. Summer, their mother, commented that 'Claire really cared for the children, not like some of the other social workers I have known'. It was obvious that they liked Claire but also that they thought having a friend was important. I would often joke with Summer that Rosie and Kyro must think that I am lonely as I kept turning up alone to play.

Philia: love of a friend

Friendship was a key aspect of children's everyday lives. While there were ups and downs and conflict, it was in their friendships that children found much solace, fun, support, love and joy. This was clearly illustrated by Katie when I asked her to mark the important events in her life on a river I had drawn on a piece of paper. I called it the 'river of life'. Quickly and without pause, Katie took the pens and marked the important events that came to her mind straight away (see Figure 6.6).

> 'The first one is the nursery, when my friend left for another school,' Katie says, as she starts to explain her marks along the river. 'Then we had a pool party – everyone at nursery came. Then in reception I met Zoe, my best friend. Then I went to Zoe's party. She had a joint party with Tina. She was our best friend too. It was a cinema party.'
> (Field notes, 1 October 2020)

It was clear from our conversation that relationships were important to her. She continued to mark the paper with the birth of her siblings, school trips and her holiday to Algeria to see her grandma. She was similar to the other children in the study, who were keen to tell me about their friends and people they liked. hooks (2016a, p 134) writes, 'many of us learn as children that friendship should never be seen as just as important as family ties. However, friendship is the place in which a majority of us have our first glimpse of redemptive love and community.' Friendship played a key role in building the children's community.

Proximity was a factor in whether someone became a friend. All of the children had friends that lived nearby or went to their school, and the friends that lived further away were the children of their mothers' friends. Due to restrictions on their movements (for example, most children still had to be accompanied by an adult anywhere), the younger children were dependent on their mothers being able to host their friends in the home, or being invited to their friends' houses. As they grew older, some, like Pogi, were able to spend time with their friends outside of their home without adult supervision.

Figure 6.6: River of life (photography by Katie)

Due to the pandemic, the friendships continued to be nurtured online, via WhatsApp, online games, text messages and phone calls. On one of our walks together, Sagittarius started talking about feelings and her friend Maya:

'It is important for children not to keep their feelings inside or they might get mental illness. I can speak to my mum, sister and my friend Maya. It is all OK with my dad now. I did speak to Maya, it was a secret, but she already knew because her mum spoke to my mum. Maya listened – she told me it was going to be OK. I told her when I was sad, what was happening, what it was like. I listen to Maya too,' explains Sagittarius.

(Field notes, 4 August 2020)

Here, Sagittarius is describing how she found support in her friend Maya, and had confided in her about the difficulties at home. In their research with children who had experienced domestic abuse, Callaghan et al (2016b, 2017b) found that children searched for and found support from their friends. Some would go to their friend's house or invite their friends over to protect themselves from their father's abuse. However, what is often missing from research is how children are supportive towards their friends too. In Sagittarius's case, the relationship was not one way only but mutually supportive, as she ends by saying, 'I listen to Maya too' (Field notes, 4 August 2020). Katie also talks about supporting her friend Jenny whose father is unwell. The videos of Pogi and his friend show him jesting and playing with his friends. Like for others in the research, there was a mutuality and interdependence in their relationships.

The children saw their relations in a wider context than just their immediate friends and would discuss topics regarding their community and wider society with me. When asked what adults should ask children about, Sagittarius had said that they should ask about what children know, about their feelings and about climate change too (see Figure 6.7a). Katie too had written that adults should ask children about climate change, pollution, cutting trees and farming animals (see Figure 6.7b). Their worlds were not only confined to themselves but expanded to caring for the wider society.

Mystical also turned his gaze outward when I asked him if he wanted to draw a 'river of life' to plot the most important things that had happened to him since he was born. He quickly took the paper from me and said, 'No, I am going to draw a rainbow' (Field notes, 24 September 2020). He then proceeded to draw two rainbows (see Figures 6.8a and 6.8b).

> 'I am going to draw a lucky rainbow and an unlucky rainbow, in only one colour, red! Oh and don't worry, I am only missing one prayer, but it is OK, my mum is praying,' Mystical explains.
> (Field notes, 24 September 2020)

Mystical's mother had left the room to go and pray. He wanted to reassure me that it was OK and I had not disturbed him too much. He suggested that his mother's prayer would cover him:

> 'I'm going to change it to brown,' Mystical says, as he continues to draw and colour his unlucky rainbow. After a few minutes, he looks at me, showing great concern, and says, 'I think you got scammed just with the brown. I am going to do a lucky rainbow with gold coins and an unlucky rainbow with chocolate coins. The unlucky rainbow is not really unlucky because if you get it, you get infinite chocolate.'
> (Field notes, 24 September 2020)

There were several things that struck me as loving in my interactions with Mystical. He had an understanding that his mother's prayers would include him, that God would accept his mother's prayers on his behalf. He was concerned for me – when the brown felt-tip pen stopped working, he was worried that I had been robbed. In his drawing of the two rainbows, he had created a world where everyone won something. He didn't leave anyone out, although one seems to get a better prize than another, but the difference being that one was more lucky than the other. There was no meritocracy for Mystical – it was down to luck – but even if you were unlucky, you received something.

Figure 6.7a: What grown-ups should know (photography by Sagittarius)

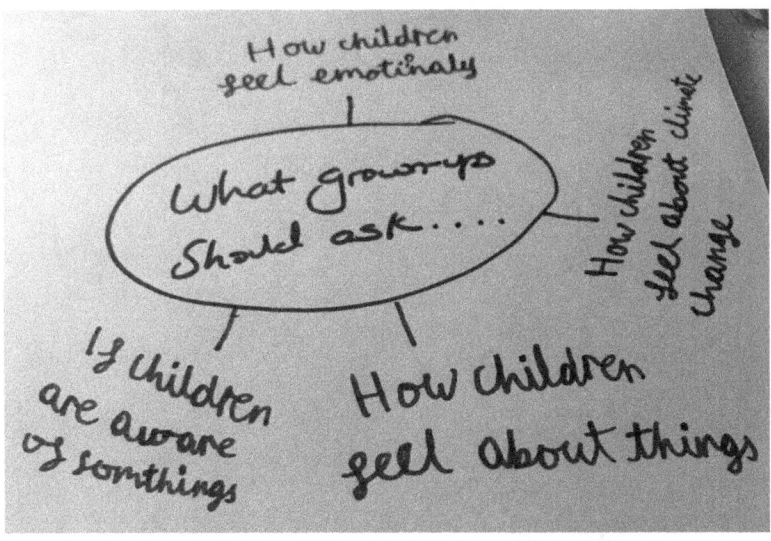

Figure 6.7b: What I wish grown-ups would ask (photography by Katie)

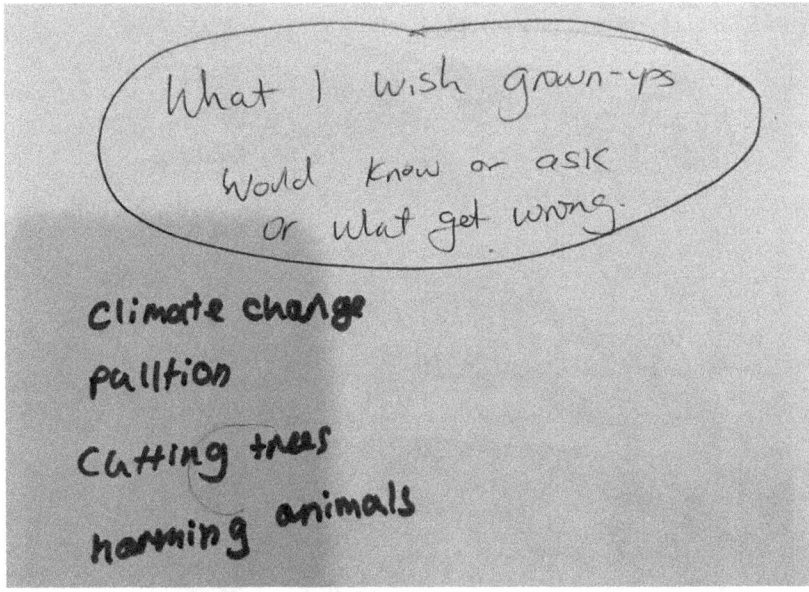

Figure 6.8a: Unlucky rainbow (photography by Mystical)

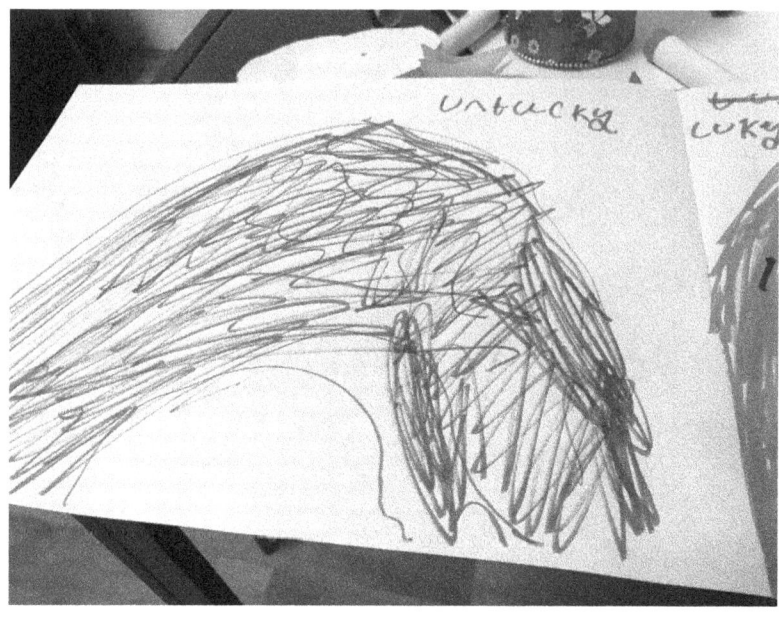

Figure 6.8b: Lucky rainbow (photography by Mystical)

Mystical and Sagittarius reminded me that children are interested in building community by taking care of others. For Sagittarius, it was about recognising the interdependency we have with each other and the world; for Mystical, it was about everybody having something. In their three-year ethnographic study, Nolas et al (2015, 2017) found that children were very active in everyday public life. They had thoughts and feelings, which they expressed in different ways. Mystical, Sagittarius and the other children showed that they were interested in the wider world and were not limited to only thinking of surviving domestic abuse. There was far more to them than that.

Multi-species love

For Elsa, Pogi, Sagittarius, Tdrommie, JoJo Siwa and Esmeralda, their dogs, cat and rabbit were an integral part of their families. Their pets were loved ones with whom they shared much joy, love, frustration, freedom, care and companionship. The animals occupied emotional and physical space in the home (Jalongo, 2021; Stearns, 2022). For the children in the study, pets were important in their everyday lives in creating spaces of safety and love, as Sagittarius showed me.

Eight months into the ethnography, Sagittarius introduced me to her tiny new kitten, named Tabitha (see Figure 6.9). Her mother and sister had given Tabitha to her as a gift, making Sagittarius very happy. The family already had a dog, Lola, but Sagittarius felt that Lola belonged to her sister more, so she was happy to have a pet of her own. Marta (Sagittarius's mother) explained to me the reason behind Sagittarius's feelings:

> 'We got Lola for Sagittarius's sister. A friend said it would help with her health. So Lola was always close to Sagittarius's sister. We never could have a pet before. Their father wouldn't allow it. So, when he left, we got Lola. We were free to get Lola and she has been so good for us.'
> (Field notes, 28 September 2020)

Getting a pet after the perpetrator of abuse is no longer in the home was a recurring theme. In the case of Sagittarius and her family, they were not allowed to get a pet while their father was in the home. For others, like Esmeralda, their pet was stolen from their old home (when they lived with their father) – so once they were settled, they got a dog called Sky. The pets were a symbol of freedom and choice, as the children's mothers Marta and Stardust explained to me. In part, the families and their pets/ dogs were, in Donna Haraway's (2008) phrase, 'worlding' – literally making worlds together. For Sagittarius and her sister, they were creating a new world, a new relationship of safety, love and care with Lola and Tabitha. As I watched Sagittarius play with Tabitha, I could sense the warmth and care as she stroked and tickled Tabitha, and Tabitha moved her head and paws in reaction to the loving touch. There was a connection that lifted them both. This went along with the mundaneness and mess of everyday relations, for as I sat watching them, Lola was peeing in my shoes, which I had left at the front door! A case of imagined possibilities mixed with everyday mess (Haraway, 2003, p 35). In *The Common Worlds of Children and Animals*, Affrica Taylor and Veronica Pacini-Ketchabaw (2020) explore the entangled lives of children and animals. Like Haraway, they move beyond the romanticised notion that children are innocent and thus will inevitably get on with animals. Rather, they argue that lives with animals are fleshy, messy and not always happy (Taylor and Pacini-Ketchabaw, 2017) but that the relationality between children and animals can give us insight into how we make our worlds (Taylor and Pacini-Ketchabaw, 2020).

Haraway (2003, p 25) explains that in exploring the relations between humans and dogs, she is able to think through the concept of 'living well'. Instead of reducing the relationship to only similarities, she (2003, p 34) explores the difference – what she calls the relation to the 'significant otherness'. In doing this, Haraway (2003, p 35) respects the love that can exist between humans and animals – for instead of romanticising the relationship, we can note the societal, political, environmental, historic and biological mediating forces of the relationship. In the situation with Sagittarius and her family, the relationship between them and Lola and Tabitha was entwined in their own new freedom in their home – it was both symbolic and fleshy. There was Lola and Tabitha taking space on their bed, on the sofa and in the living room, needing to be fed, walked and cuddled. Like Haraway, Sagittarius does not reduce Tabitha and Lola to passive recipients of care and affection. She talks about Lola choosing her sister and not her, of Lola looking at Tabitha as if Tabitha is her baby. Later in the year when I visit Sagittarius, she regales me with tales of Tabitha teasing Lola, and Lola feeling jealous of Tabitha.

Marta's sentiment that the pets added so much to family life was echoed by Pogi and Elsa's mother Ann. On one visit after the first lockdown, I was introduced to Hops, a grey furry rabbit. Hops was hiding under the mini trampoline in the living room, and Elsa was trying to coax him out. My subsequent visits would always include an update on how he was settling in. There were numerous photographs of Hops participating in the everyday lives of Elsa and Pogi. There were pictures of him on the bed next to a sleeping Pogi, in his hutch in the kitchen, on the balcony and under the mini trampoline in the living room (see Figure 6.10). He was part of the everyday lives of the family. When he had been living with the family for a year, they took him to church to celebrate the anniversary and to give thanks, with Ann saying, 'I never knew Hops would be so good for us. He is like another child in the family' (Field notes, 3 November 2020).

Figure 6.9: Tabitha (photography by Sagittarius)

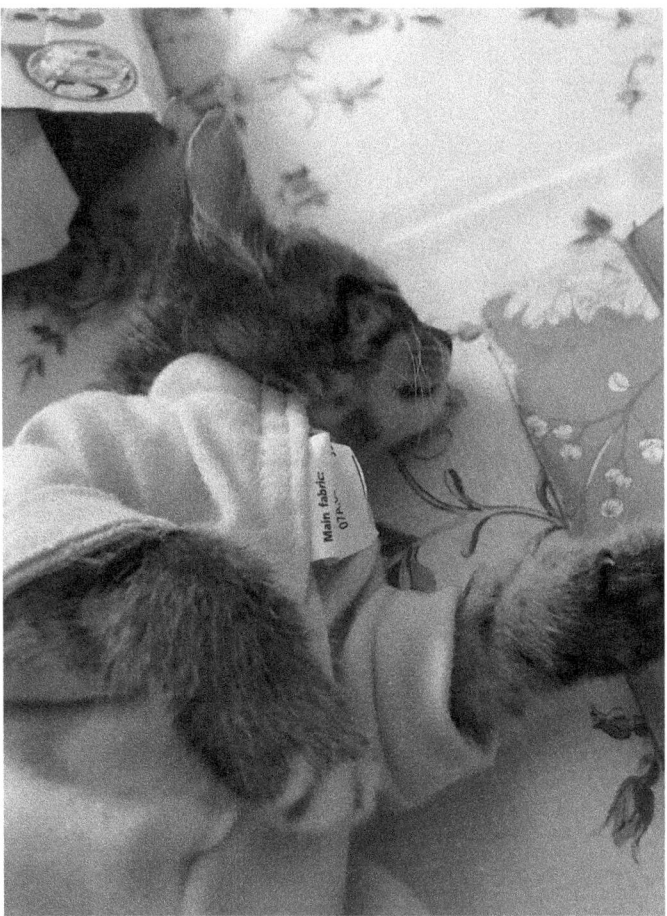

There is a relationality between animals and children, a crossing of boundaries of intimacies – space, relations and place (Gabb, 2010, p 80). As Haraway (2003, p 11) writes, the relation between pets and humans is part of a 'queer family of companion species', but she cautions against seeing animals as a 'substitute family'. She argues that we need to find different words to describe this kin making, and not to make animals into humans but recognise their difference in both flesh and idea. Otherwise, we risk disparaging the relationship and reducing it to a fictitious 'unconditional love' (Haraway, 2003, p 33).

While acknowledging the children's love of animals and their pets, I don't want to give the impression that it is 'natural' to love animals and pets, but I recognise the cultural aspects which nurture that love. This was brought home to me when Mystical talked about how his mother did not like dogs and that in Mauritius dogs were not allowed in the home. This was something that reminded me of my parents too. Both my parents had grown up with dogs in Mauritius but often would tell of their shock at finding out that dogs lived in the homes of English people. Not feeling comfortable with living with an animal inside the home does not necessarily signify a lack of love for animals, for both my parents loved their dogs growing up. It is also important not to fall into the trap of thinking a love for, and ease with, animals is 'natural', and to not be comfortable with animals is somehow 'devious' behaviour. This came to light in the parental assessment of Nicole (Mystical's mother). One time I called her, and she was very upset. The social worker carrying out the assessment had repeatedly asked her if she would get Mystical a dog if he wanted one. Several times, Nicole had tried to explain her rationale for refusing to do so. She had explained that there was no space in the home, and how she grew up understanding that dogs should live outside. However, she felt that her refusal was viewed as demonstrating that she was an uncaring mother who was not being child-centred. Nicole was often left feeling like a 'not-good-enough' mother after these meetings.

Mothers' love

A chapter about love would not be complete without writing about the love expressed, felt and practised between the children and their mothers. The children took numerous photographs of their mothers. I am also keenly aware that the children's participation in the project would not have been possible without their mothers' consent and facilitation. All the mothers had agreed for their children to participate in the project because they thought they would enjoy it and 'get something out of it'.

In June Jordan's (2012) beautiful and powerful poem '1977: Poem for Mrs. Fannie Lou Hamer', Jordan writes of the homemaking of Mrs Hamer who, despite the violence in her neighbourhood, practises care and love that welcomes Jordan. It is the last couple of lines 'in a homemade field of love' that I feel captures the essence of the children's pictures and expression of their mothers' care and love. For despite the past and ongoing abuse, economic struggles, racial marginalisation and patriarchal system, the mothers practised care and love. They had, in what hooks (1990, p 49) writes, created a space where 'we return for renewal and self-recovery, where we can heal our wounds and become whole'.

Throughout Chapters 3, 4 and 5, there are examples of practices of care and love. Mystical's photographs of his mother's food preparation, Elsa and Pogi's mother creating a beach in the kitchen, Sagittarius's mother getting her a kitten. The mothers have worked to create a loving home. In their

Figure 6.10: Hops (photography by Elsa)

photographs, the children show this solidarity and love for their mothers in different ways, as I will explore in this section.

The children took many photographs of their mothers on the move. The photographs were often blurry, depicting them in the midst of doing something or going somewhere. There is an abundance of photographs of their mothers walking to the shops, on public transport, making blackberry jam, setting the table for dinner, rotating the roundabout in the playground, strolling in the park, walking the dog, washing, cooking and chopping. These movements are what Luttrell (2020, p 86) calls 'geographies of care', because they involve a constellation of resources, people, schedules, feelings and intimacies. In photographing their mothers' movements, the children made visible the work that their mothers do.

It was not only their mothers in action that the children 'captured' to show care and love – they also took photographs of the material things that demonstrated their love. Sagittarius took a picture of the hot chocolate that her mother made for her while she was studying at home. Esmeralda had a picture of the pineapple upside-down cake that her mother made and that she loved. Mystical recorded the table decorations and food preparations that his mother did awaiting celebrations. The acts and materiality of care and love are not lost on the children, and their solidarity is not lost on me.

At times, I wondered whether the children were aware of the scrutiny that their mothers were under, and were showing solidarity with their mothers. In her slow study with children from an area of Massachusetts, education scholar Wendy Luttrell (2020, p 86) wonders whether the children are attuned to anxiety or stigma around their upbringing, and whether what they hear is laced with moral messages of 'good' and 'bad' mothering and care. It may be that the children are doing what Hochschild (2003, p 172) describes – attuning their ears like 'tuning forks to gauge the emotional terror of adult talk'.

The children do not only capture their mothers at work. I am struck by the intimacy and the quiet moments that the children photograph their mothers in. Rosie captures her mother sitting on the washing machine, swinging her legs as she talks on the phone. There are several pictures of their mothers' faces – a collection of smiles and surprised looks. Elsa has a close-up of her mother wearing a mask while sitting on the bus; Katie has a picture of her mother entering the bedroom; Kyro has taken pictures of old photographs of his mother kissing him when he was younger; Elsa has a picture of her mother checking her phone; Rosie insists on taking a photograph of her mother with me. The children present their mothers as human beings – not just as providers of care and love. They are valued for being who they are.

Reflecting on the children and their mothers, I think back to bell hooks's (2016c, p 115) praise for single mothers, when she wrote, 'there is so much evidence to document that this group, more than any other, against the odds has created a space of love within the home'. From this research, I would add that the children and their mothers have created a safe space for love. Their creation of a loving space is built despite the challenges of domestic abuse, social work scrutiny, racism, sexism and other social and economic disadvantages.

My 'other family': researcher's love

There is a joke in my family (but like all jokes, there may be an element of truth in it). My children and my partner say that I have two families – them and my 'other family', the children in this research study. Whenever I would go to a quieter room to WhatsApp video call, my son would say that I was going to talk to my 'other children'. My visits were to see my 'other family' too. While we laughed and joked about this, my children had picked up on my care and love for the participants in the research.

I think of them often. I wonder how Sagittarius, Katie and Pogi are settling into their new school. What is the latest game that Mystical and Tdrommie are interested in? Whether Esmeralda and JoJo Siwa have any new jokes. How Elsa is finding her new teacher, and whether Rosie and Kyro have settled into their new home. I wish them all the very best for their futures and hope they flourish and thrive. Through this research I have come to wrestle with, then understand and accept, that love is an important element of the research relationship (Herbert, 2025). Love is an important aspect of decolonial research methods. It is not about fluffy feelings but about justice, acceptance and care (hooks, 2016a). It is about seeing and accepting the children as they are and wanting the very best for them (hooks, 2016a, p 6). It means playing to their strengths and knowing that together knowledge is created. As hooks (2016c, p 73) writes, 'Decolonization is the necessary groundwork for the development of self-love.' In this research it means that until we accept that children are able to contribute to knowledge creation, we cannot say that we value, care and respect them. hooks (2016c, p 73) writes, 'The heart of decolonization is the recognition of equality among humans, coupled with the understanding that racial categories which negatively stigmatize Blackness were created as a political tool of imperialist white domination.' As I have argued in Chapter 2, this is similar to the stigmatised category of being a child who has experienced domestic abuse also being used to uphold a White patriarchal system.

It is this relationality that enabled the children and myself to develop a space where we could create knowledge, yet I find myself nervous writing about the love I felt for the children and their families. For I have been taught that love is not important or appropriate. As Yassine (2021, p 93) writes, 'In mainstream social work, love is not only deemed irrelevant, but also deemed as dangerous.' Drawing from the work of bell hooks, Yassine (2021) writes about how working from a love ethic is a radical act of care but is often pulled up as being unprofessional. Yassine (2021) cites the work of her fellow Indigenous social workers working with families from the Indigenous community in Australia, who would often do home visits after hours and spend a lot of time with families in order to work effectively and support them. Often, the social workers would be pulled up for a 'lack of professional' boundaries. Thus, argues Yassine (2021), boundaries are cultural and, in this case, 'white and western'.

Here, it is important to note that working from a love ethic does not mean ignoring power inequalities in relationships. Key to love is acknowledgement, discernment and management of the power dynamics within relationships – in this case between me the researcher and the children. Love calls for a self-awareness, a reflexivity, which realises my strengths, weaknesses, bias, attitudes and position that can hinder my relationship with the children. As hooks (2016a, p 157) writes, 'listening does not simply mean we hear other voices when they speak but that we also learn to listen to the voice of our own heart as well as inner voices'. If we fail to really listen, we will not be changed by our research, which means we are not truly working from a love ethic. Listening to children is more than listening to voice. As Nolas et al (2018, p 4) argue, it is a 'social practice existing in affective, cultural, embodied, relational, temporal and spatial configuration', and if listening does not involve our whole selves and those of the children, can we really say we are listening to children and paying adequate attention (Nolas and Varvantakis, 2021)? Writer James Baldwin (2017, p 82) explains this in terms of the White man who, 'armed with spiritual traveller's checks, visits surreptitiously after dark'. He is referring to the White man who visits the Black neighbourhood for cultural voyeurism and illicit activities. Baldwin criticises the White visitor for objectifying and exoticising the people he encounters. He writes that if he remains unchanged, it is not a loving exchange, it is an 'I–It' relationship, which Martin Buber (2020 [1937]) alludes to. Baldwin (2017, p 81) writes that:

> love takes off the mask that we fear we cannot live without and know we cannot live within. I use the word 'love' here not merely in the personal sense but as a state of being, or a state of grace – not in the infantile American sense of being made happy but in the tough and universal sense of the quest and daring and growth.

Researching with love required me to respect the humanness of both myself and the children. It involved both seeing and respecting individuals' worth, uniqueness, human rights and the sacredness of their humanity (Chigangaidze, 2021, p 152). When we practise this, we create a relational space that can foster an environment for learning together. Audre Lorde (2020, p 33) wrote that love is a nurturer of knowledge: 'The erotic is the nurturer or nursemaid of all our deepest knowledge. The erotic functions for me in several ways, and the first is in providing the power which comes from sharing deeply any pursuit with another person.'

Conclusion

The children and their mothers demonstrated how they created a space to practise love. While the literature on domestic abuse and children often centres around fear in the home, the children illustrated through their photographs and my visits that they valued and practised love. They were active in creating loving spaces, as well being critical of care that was not loving. hooks (2016c, p 92) concluded that there should be more scholarly work and popular material focusing on Black self-love. I would argue that there needs to be more work showing how children and mothers who have experienced domestic abuse continue to practise love, challenging the prevalent literature that they are lacking in emotional competency (Callaghan et al, 2017b). The children have shown me how their homes are places of resistance, where they create spaces for self-love. They have created the homeplace as a site where love flourishes in the everyday despite the obstacles. They continue to challenge the tropes of the passive, early years and fugitive child.

7

Conclusion: Floating Matters

It was an exhibition that prompted my research journey, and it was an exhibition that closed the multimodal ethnographic project with the children. Before I conclude this book, I start with an ethnographic vignette of the exhibition I curated to celebrate the end of the research project.

> I am sitting in the office. My legs are swinging as I sit on the chair and my hands keep reaching for my phone and checking the time. I am nervous, like I have organised a birthday party and am waiting for the guests to arrive. It is the morning of the first day of the exhibition (see Figures 7.1a and 7.1b), and I am waiting for the first family (the guests) to arrive.
>
> To be COVID-19 safe, each family has their own viewing slot. I feel my heart beating a little faster – my mind asks the questions of whether they will like it and, more importantly, whether they will come. I had phoned, texted and sent an invite, but I suspect some invites had not arrived. This exhibition is the fulfilment of a promise to the children. I had promised them an exhibition of their work when I first talked about the research project. Little did I know that so much of the project had to change for COVID-19 reasons, but this, the exhibition, we managed to do. Will they come?
>
> The buzzer of the intercom rings – I jump off my chair and head straight to the intercom on the wall with a screen showing the face of Mystical's mum. I excitedly pick up the telephone and say 'Come in!', and press the button to let her through.
>
> I skip down the stairs and open the door. They are here – the first family is here! I greet them at the front door. They say 'hello' and sanitise their hands and write their names down on the register.
>
> 'We both dressed in red today,' Nicole explains, showing the effort they had made with their appearance. They do look smart – my heart flutters at the thought that they care.
>
> I eagerly usher them up the stairs and into the room where the exhibition is. As he enters the room, Mystical exclaims, 'Wow!' He races around trying to find his pictures. At first, he is lost: the photographs hanging down from a string all look the same – just a mass of floating rectangular-shaped paper.
>
> (Field notes, 5 August 2021)

Conclusion

Figure 7.1a: Floating Matters exhibition (photography by Brenda)

Figure 7.1b: Floating Matters exhibition close up (photography by Brenda)

The team at the children's centre had suggested that I hang each photograph with string running from one end of the room to the other – a bit like a washing line, which is ironic as the study was about the everyday lives of children and their homes. The washing line reminded me of the one Mystical had on his balcony. He was very proud to tell me that it was a gift from his grandparents in Mauritius. I also remember visiting Sagittarius and her family when it was laundry day, arriving to find her mother folding clothes into neat piles on the sofa. Here on the 'washing line' hung the photographs the children had taken of their everyday lives. They were floating pieces of imagination, of love, beauty and joy.

There were five lines, and I made sure that on each line there were photographs from each of the children. Each line had an unwritten theme in my head – home, pets, food, play and beauty. These themes had come up when I visited each child to discuss their photo book. It was sitting on the bus on the way to planning the exhibition that I thought of the title 'Floating Matters'. It was a play on words, for the pictures were floating and they were 'matter' – something that had mass and occupied space – but they also 'mattered'; they were of significance. I wanted to show the children that they really did matter and so did the knowledge they created.

It is not lost on me that an exhibition prompted me to start the PhD project, and an exhibition ended the research project. The content and photographers for the two exhibitions were very different. One I felt was about impoverishment and passivity; the other was children telling their own stories through photographs. On reflection, I can see clearly how my own childhood has guided my choice of research topic and methodology. But as I come to the end of the book, I ask myself whether I did anything different – did I allow a different story about children who have experienced domestic abuse and social work intervention to be told? In this final chapter, I discuss and reflect on what and how knowledge has been created and what meaning the children made of their everyday lives. I commence by revisiting the literature on children who have experienced domestic abuse and social work intervention.

Who gets to tell the story?

In Chapter 2, I narrated my journey reviewing the research about children who have experienced domestic abuse and social work intervention, and my realisation that children were essentially missing from creating knowledge about their own lives (Spillers, 2018). There was an epistemic injustice where their ability to create knowledge and the relevance of their knowledge were questioned. We knew little about them and their lives beyond the lens of trauma and abuse. In my research with Mystical, Tdrommie, Kyro, Rosie, Sagittarius, Esmeralda, JoJo Siwa, Pogi, Elsa and Katie, and using the cultural theories of the everyday, I was able to explore the meanings they made of their lives.

The children in the book disrupted the political tropes of the passive, early years and fugitive child that were prevalent in the social work literature on children and domestic abuse. They showed themselves in their full humanness, challenging predominant narratives of children who have experienced domestic abuse and social care intervention of being passive and damaged (Callaghan et al, 2017a). This is not to deny that domestic abuse has had a negative impact on their lives but that the children were more than their experiences of abuse and trauma (Tuck, 2009). Being attentive to the everyday lives of Pogi, Elsa, Tdrommie, Mystical, Katie, Kyro, Rosie, Sagittarius, JoJo Siwa and Esmeralda challenged me to see them beyond the narrow lens of domestic abuse and trauma.

In Chapter 3 we can see how Mystical challenges the trope of the passive, unknowing child. While the social workers and courts try to mobilise his age and his close relationship with his mother to show that he is unknowing, my interactions with him show that he is articulate and knowing. His knowledge is dismissed because it does not sit with the prevalent narrative on social discourse. Mystical's knowledge is discounted, a form of what Fricker (2009) calls epistemic injustice that is used to uphold a patriarchal social order, while claiming to 'protect' him.

The children continued to challenge the tropes of passivity and unknowingness throughout the book. Esmeralda and JoJo Siwa considered themselves as active carers (Chapter 6), and Katie questioned the quality of care given by the safeguarding lead at her school (Chapter 6). Even the manner in which the children chose to engage or not to engage with me illustrated their agency and knowingness, with Pogi choosing to stay out and play with his friends rather than meet with me (Chapter 4), and Tdrommie not wanting to do any art or take pictures (Chapter 4).

Throughout the book the children have illustrated that they are more than their experience of abuse and trauma. Rosie taking pictures of something because 'it's beautiful' (Chapter 5), and Esmeralda, JoJo Siwa and Elsa having fun by teasing me during our WhatsApp video calls (Chapter 4). The children have shown their search for fun, beauty and love in the everyday. They disrupted the literature around domestic abuse and children that portrays them as passive, damaged and fugitive children.

In their photographs and stories of the everyday, the children show their mothers doing their best. They challenge the thinking that their mothers are 'failing to protect' and show the numerous ways that their mothers, despite economic austerity and COVID-19, are imaginative and creative not only in feeding them and caring for them but in creating practices of fun and play. Examples included exchanging vouchers for sand (Chapter 4), putting paddling pools on the balcony (Chapter 4) and decorating their homes for special occasions (Chapter 5). The children show that their lives are not only ones of despair and fear but are filled with joy, love and beauty too. Like hooks (1990, p 42) writes, their mothers used the home as a place to nurture and love them, making them subjects despite a hostile outside environment.

The book highlights a way of engaging children in research that disrupts the colonialist tropes of childhood. Clearly, children can create knowledge, but how this can be facilitated warrants thought and care, which a multimodal ethnography provided. In the next section I argue that a multimodal ethnography enabled me to decolonise the literature and research methods around domestic abuse and children.

Decolonising the figure of the child through multimodality

Using multimodal methods gave the children the ability to choose which medium they wanted to communicate through and did not limit them to one only. They were able to choose as many or as few as they wanted. There was not only one way to communicate. When I initially put together the art packs for the children in the project, I did so with the premise that they were free to use whatever they wanted in the pack, to record and create what they wanted, if they wanted to use it at all. I knew that not all children would use the packs, but the option was there. There was no prescription about what they should use or even how, although I provided some simply written instructions if they wanted any guidance. My main driving force was the desire to connect with the children, and to hold that connection through COVID-19 physical restrictions. I definitely felt like I was stepping into the unknown, something research should be about. I also gave the children the choice to mix media and use different modes to communicate (Clark, 2011, 2017). It was a move away from text and verbal communication (Lomax, 2012; Nolas et al, 2018; Varvantakis and Nolas, 2019). Despite being a reluctant ethnographer, I have become increasingly drawn to the works of multimodal ethnographers, in anthropology and sociology alike, throughout the research process. Rather than seeing multimodality as a way only of critiquing, translating or explaining, multimodal anthropologists and ethnographers look to multimodal methods as a way of 'being with', creating, collaborating and inventing with their interlocutors (Nolas et al, 2018; Dattatreyan and Marrero-Guillamón, 2019; Varvantakis and Nolas, 2019; Welcome and Thomas, 2021; Johnson, 2022).

During the research I began to understand multimodal ethnography as a way of working past binaries and categories that limit understanding and participation (Varvantakis and Nolas, 2019; Welcome and Thomas, 2021; Johnson, 2022). It challenged my preconceived categories and perception that try to codify and sort data. While this felt unsettling for me at times, it enabled me to practise what Fanon (2017 [1952], p 13) calls a pedagogy of 'failure', a pedagogy of 'not knowing' – a way of listening without knowing the answer, of not seeking mastery. Yasmin Gunaratnam (2013, p 106) writes of the potential to create knowledge which can arise when we are receptive, vulnerable and open to 'not knowing in advance' how to respond to 'unpredictable demands' of those we do not know well. This calls for courage to be a vulnerable listener, as written by anthropologist Ruth Behar (2022). Behar (2022, p 6) writes that we can often use methods as a way of controlling our anxieties and that there is no easy route to confront the 'self that observes'.

What the multimodal ethnographers helped me to think through was a move away from my need to translate children's wishes, urges and communications, forcing them through a normative discourse. Ethnographer Saba Mahmood (2012, p 199) labels it epistemic violence when we try to 'assimilate the Other to a language of translatability' through a hegemonic discourse. Throughout this book I tell of my own struggle to avoid taming and controlling children's stories and actions to make them familiar and comprehensible, thus limiting myself and the children to what is already known. Instead, I have tried to disrupt, expand and break what is known, this way avoiding producing knowledge in advance of time, and remaining open to alternative narratives and ways of being in the world (Gunaratnam, 2013).

This unknowing is pioneered by feminist decolonial scholars like Chandra Talpade Mohanty (1984, 2003) and Linda Tuhiwai Smith (1999). In her classic article 'Under Western eyes: Feminist scholarship and colonial discourses', Mohanty (1984) challenges researchers of post-industrialised communities working with marginalised communities. Mohanty criticises the practice of reducing the 'Other' to make them more translatable without ever reducing the researcher, thus always presenting the researcher as always knowing more than the researched. This, Mohanty (2003, p 501) argues, erases specificity and flattens forms of experience and subjectivities. Mohanty (2003, p 501) is attentive to the local as well as the macro. Recently, anthropologists Leniqueca A. Welcome and Deborah A. Thomas (2021) argue that multimodal methods can assist in challenging what is known and honouring the local and linking it to the macro. In their work with collage, the participants not only show their community in a different light but also highlight the macro politics which oppress and destroy, and keep them socially and economically marginalised.

Multimodality can also disrupt the temporal flow of knowledge and challenge the simplistic form of causal effects. Linda Tuhiwai Smith (1999) and Eve Tuck (2009, 2014) have warned that using research of localised marginalised communities, linking it to macro levels and then going back to solving the problem of the community can risk portraying the community as always in want. We risk not seeing beyond this field of vison, of not knowing what we are missing or that we are missing it altogether.

Lather (2001, p 217) summarises this risk when she writes 'recognition that we often do not know what we are seeing, how much we are missing, what we are understanding, or even how to locate these lacks'. This was best represented in my (mis)understanding of play (as written about in Chapter 4). Initially, I was pulled towards only seeing play through the eyes/lens of educators, of play therapy and play scholars, rather than from the perspective of the children themselves. Slowly, I started to make sense of the material not in isolation but in relation to the children and myself. I neither took the children away from their environment or relationships nor took myself away from mine.

It takes time

The use of creative and visual methods to research with children has been de rigeur for a number of years (Lomax, 2020), but that does not make it necessarily child-friendly, child-focused or decolonial. Key to research being child-focused or decolonial is an awareness of power relations – it asks whose knowledge counts and whose story gets heard, and who gets to tell the story.

Culture and its effect on values can have a significant impact on how adults hear children and take on board what they say (Twum-Danso, 2009b, p 380). With regards to domestic abuse and social work interventions, children have rarely been viewed outside the area of protection. I had to constantly reflect on my own beliefs about children, childhood and participation, so that I did not view them only through the narrow lens of trauma and abuse that I was accustomed to working in as a professional counsellor. One way I found to address this risk was to spend significant time with the children in order to build a relationship and create knowledge together.

While there have been debates as to whether ethnography and multimodality go together (Dicks et al, 2011), for this project I have seen how they can work together and enhance the creativity of knowledge for the children and the researcher. At times, I brought creative activities for the children to do, and several times I was surprised by what the children used the activities for. For example, the way Mystical used the paper I brought to draw a rainbow (Chapter 6), or how Esmeralda and JoJo Siwa labelled their practice of care (see Chapter 6); in both cases the children's responses surprised me out of my complacency and assumptions. This creation of knowledge was possible because we, the children and I, had built a trusting relationship through the practice of ethnography. I am not sure, in this project, whether a one-off interaction would have nurtured the mutual vulnerability that fostered a space for knowledge creativity. I may not have been so open to what the children were saying. Over time, through my ears, eyes and senses, I had attuned myself to the children. I knew from our interactions together that they too attuned their bodies to what adults were saying and chose who to trust and who to be suspicious of; they were navigating these relations all the time, as Katie and her reaction to her teacher showed in Chapter 6. Thus, multimodal ethnography alone was not enough to build a relationship with children; it needed to include what decolonial and feminist scholars have continuously advocated – an ethic of care and love.

It was in writing this concluding chapter that I realised the importance of Mystical's name. Every child had chosen their pseudonyms. At first, Mystical had chosen Pro, then later he changed it to Brave Lion, and finally he chose Mystical. Initially, I had not realised the significance of the names and how they correlated with what was happening in his life. I first got to know Mystical through video calls because of the physical restrictions due to COVID-19. He had chosen Pro because of Roblox, and when we had talked about names, he had chosen a username that he had seen while on the game. He then later wanted to change his name to Brave Lion. When I look back at my field notes, I realise that he had changed his name to Brave Lion during the time there was much turbulence in his life and the family were going through court proceedings. It was at the end of the project, when I returned to ask specific permission to write about their experience, that Mystical had changed his name to Mystical. At first, both Nicole, his mother, and I did not hear him correctly and thought he had said 'Mr Tickle'.

> 'Mr Tickle?' I query.
> 'Are you sure you want Mr Tickle as a name?' asks Nicole.
> 'No! Not Mr Tickle! It's MYSTICAL!' Mystical shouts. 'Like magical because I am magical!'
> (Field notes, 31 January 2021)

Mystical is indeed magical – a mystical force that it has been my pleasure to travel and learn with. I am left wondering whether as things had calmed down after the court proceedings that he felt like he was magical because he had weathered the storm. I would not have noticed this change if I had not carried out an ethnography for 18 months. It reminds me that people and things are not static – we are constantly shifting, turning, moving and sometimes still. In going for the 'rolling film' of their lives rather than a limited 'snapshot' (Ferguson et al, 2020), we created a different way of knowing.

'Blah blah blah': creating with children

The children were not always interested in the analysis of the research. They were happy to create and participate but often ambivalent about talking about their photographs any further. This was evident when I visited them to create their photo book. I had a strong urge to place the children's photographs in a book for them – a sort of souvenir of our time together. They were keeping the cameras with the pictures in them, but I wanted something tangible that they could hold and touch, and flick through to see their photographs. I wanted them to have something solid to hold. Maybe I wanted to capture our time together – to curate and archive memories in a book for them. The children had taken lots of photographs and it was not feasible to put them all into a book, so I visited each of the children to go through their pictures to see what they wanted in their book. There were a variety of responses. Tdrommie was adamant that he didn't want a book. He had not really used the art materials and had preferred for me to visit and talk about his games and PS4. This was something that he was set on from the beginning of the research project and had been consistent. Others were interested in looking at their photographs but wanted me to choose. On one visit, Kyro, after the initial excitement of seeing his photographs printed on paper, turned and asked me when we were going to the playground, as 'You always take us to the playground. Can we go now? Can we play now?'

I have tried to return to the children often to let them know about what I said about the research, but I have yet to find a way that they find interesting. As much as possible I have returned to the children to ask whether what I have thought or written does justice to their experiences and what they told me. For any talks that I have given about the research, I have given the children a summary of my points. Most of the time, the children have wanted to play or talk about what they were up to at school and have brushed away talk about the research as being in the past or even boring. This was clearly demonstrated when I went to visit Esmeralda and JoJo Siwa after I had given a talk about the research for an online session about ethnography in social work research:

> 'So, I gave a talk about the project,' I say to Esmeralda and JoJo Siwa.
> 'Oh,' comments Esmeralda.
> 'Yes, I talked about how we talked on the phone, how we played games and went for walks,' I describe. 'It is on YouTube.'
> 'YouTube! Can we see it?' shouts JoJo Siwa.
> 'Oh OK – let me get it on my phone,' I say as I search for my phone. Esmeralda and JoJo Siwa gather around me. 'Here it is,' I say, as I press play. I forward it to the part where I am talking with the PowerPoint taking up most of the screen. Esmeralda and JoJo Siwa look closely at the scene.
> 'Mmm … oh … it's just grown-ups going blah, blah, blah.' Esmeralda shakes her head, as they both move away from the screen. 'Let's play a game!'
>
> (Field notes, 14 October 2021)

While the children enjoyed being part of the research, looking at their printed pictures and seeing their photographs displayed in the exhibition, they were less interested in reading or listening to what I had written or spoken about for the research. This is something that I need to work on; I need to make the research more accessible and engaging for the children in the study. I have contemplated turning the book into a comic, something which would entail more time and dedicated funding. The children are interested in the research but are disappointed that I have written a book for adults. However, they are interested that other people want to hear about the project, and that other people are taking their stories seriously. They want to be known and want their stories heard.

What will you do with my story?

The research with the children allowed us a space to create together. This not only allowed them to express themselves but also allowed others to listen better. With the children's photographs, I was able to create a photo book and curate an exhibition. The photo book was seen not only by the director and assistant director of the local authority but Ofsted inspectors too. The head of the social work service also came to the exhibition and was curious about the everyday lives of the children. The children were able to show their mothers, friends and relatives their photographs in their book and the exhibition, and to show what was important to them to these significant others in their lives. The photographs allowed the children to return the gaze; they were not the subject of the gaze but the ones doing the gazing. This format encourages others to become more alert and attentive to the way they see their everyday world.

Too often, children's views are sought but little is done to act upon them. This was particularly pertinent in a session that took place in the Scottish Assembly, where an adult was asking the children to 'speak louder' but one girl had written on her card 'listen louder' (Houghton, 2006, p 86). This shows that while much emphasis is placed on hearing the 'voice' of the child, the bigger question is whether we listen to it and what we do with it.

It is important that we do not see children who have experienced domestic abuse only through the lens of trauma and abuse; otherwise, we risk hearing only the stories the perpetrators tell us about them. Through this research, Pogi, Elsa, Tdrommie, Sagittarius, Mystical, Katie, Esmeralda, JoJo Siwa, Rosie and Kyro have all showed their humanness and difference. They have disrupted the narrative of damage and passivity, thus disrupting the colonialist trope of the unknowing child. They have shown they are more than competent in contributing to creating knowledge about their own lives. It is important that we continue through research with children to challenge the tropes of childhood in the field of domestic abuse. As I have argued in Chapter 2, these tropes are mobilised both in the Global North and the Global South to enforce a colonialist and patriarchal social view that upholds the status quo and further marginalises the children and their families in the name of protection.

While it is good to continue to interrogate how tropes of childhood are used politically, it is also important that the lives of children are not ignored but brought into the discussion, lest we repeat the pattern of ignoring the embodied child.

More than that!

As I come to the end of the book, I remember my role (in my professional capacity at work) as a facilitator of groups for children affected by domestic abuse. I remember we asked every group of children to complete an evaluation survey for the group they had participated in. Each time, the three major things they enjoyed about the groups were 'meeting other children who are like me', 'free time at the end' and 'the food and snacks'. As group facilitators, we struggled with these comments, as they were not something we could boast about to funders or those who commissioned the groups. Our existence as support for the children was always precariously funded. We knew the children loved the groups, but that was not enough to warrant further funding. Our evaluation had to show how the groups could 'help children recover from domestic abuse' in a more concrete way. Then and now, when I listen more carefully, I hear the children say what they value, what they want. They didn't want to be othered; they wanted to break the isolation of being othered, and importantly, they wanted the space and care to have fun. Nolas et al (2018) and Beetham et al (2019) both show this in their research of these same community groups of children and their mothers: children wanted a space to have fun.

'But they look so ordinary' was a common phrase that practitioners, including social workers, would say as they walked through the exhibition. Since finishing the project, I have tried to disseminate the research as much as I can, so have given talks to practitioners at several local authorities. They were struck by what Campt (2012, p 100) calls the 'fugitivite domesticity', in that the children's pictures were so ordinary and mundane that they challenged their ideas of the child who has experienced abuse. The pictures were beyond the spectacle of violence that they had expected. Several times after a talk, therapists or social workers would come up to me and ask, 'But what did they say about their trauma?' I had to reply that the children didn't speak about it, and they wanted to show me other aspects of their lives that went beyond the abuse. I asked myself, why was it that some practitioners wanted to keep children in the place of injury? On reflecting on Luke Willis Thompson's (2017) *autoportrait* of Diamond Reynolds, Campt (2023, p 170) asks why we want Reynolds to recount the murder of her partner Philando Castile. Campt reflects on why Thompson decided on doing a silent film of Reynolds. This made me ponder too why children are kept in the place of injury in research and practice. Why did the therapists who questioned me want to just hear about the abuse and trauma? What right do we have to demand that children show us their injuries all the time?

Campt writes that the most challenging thing about a fugitive child is not that they are different but that they are very similar to the 'normal' child. When we recognise that the fugitive child, the child that is othered, is similar, then it disrupts the hierarchy of childhoods; it disrupts the colonial and patriarchal social norms. The children in this book showed how they created beauty, love and fun in the everyday; they went beyond the place of injury. It reminds me of June Jordan's letter in defence of the children she worked with in a Saturday workshop. Jordan is incensed that a supporter of the workshop is questioning the children's work:

> Will I accept that a Black child can write 'creatively' and 'honestly' and yet *not* write about incest, filth, violence, and degradations of every sort? … That Black people are only the products of racist, white America and that, therefore, we can be and we can express only what racist white America has forced us to experience, namely: mutilation, despisal, ignorance, and horror.
>
> (Jordan, 1989, p 13)

I love Jordan's defence of the children and knowledge that they were more than the racist world they lived in, that they could live and see beyond the despair. The children in this research showed how they are much more than their experience of abuse and trauma and that they care about fun, beauty and love in the everyday. Shalhoub-Kevorkian (2024) also talks about the importance of humanising children and to be attentive to the way that they live, love and play, and warns us against dehumanising them by only holding them in the position of death and dying. The dehumanisation of people has long been part of the colonial way of justifying their death (hooks, 2016c, p xix). I am aware of the high number of children who have been killed in Gaza, Sudan and the Democratic Republic of Congo. Where their deaths are seen as not only inevitable but justified (Shalhoub-Kevorkian, 2023). The dehumanisation is important in order to justify the continuous violence against marginalised children both in the Global North and the Global South. Therefore, it is important that research and practice need to be challenged into thinking beyond keeping children in a place of injury only.

On reflection, I see that, as a practitioner and researcher in this field, so much of the focus is on the damage of domestic abuse and trauma. Yet perhaps we should be supporting children more to break down the barriers and create opportunities for fun, beauty and love. Do we ever ask children what makes for good fun and joy in their lives? While the children search for fun and gravitate towards it, the opportunity for fun is also constructed through social and systemic relations and resources. Esmeralda navigates her way through the playground politics to play and have fun; she is not devoid of having fun, but it is hard when you are the new kid on the block and struggle with the hierarchy of the school relationship ladder. Maybe we should be making it easier for her to have fun.

While not wanting to diminish the challenges and negative effects of experiencing domestic abuse, I was struck by how the narrative in the literature and in practice reduced children to their abuse alone. I struggled throughout this research with the epistemic grip that trauma and abuse hold over the scholarship on domestic abuse. I often felt like I was practising a form of heresy to expand the knowledge of children's personhood beyond trauma and abuse, but Mystical, Sagittarius, Katie, Elsa, Pogi, Tdrommie, Esmeralda, JoJo Siwa, Rosie and Kyro showed me that they were more than their experience of domestic abuse. Throughout the 18-month ethnography, there were times when they did experience the challenges of domestic abuse, especially when dealing with coercive control, but that was not the only challenge in their lives. When we focus on trauma alone, we often miss the social and economic factors, like poverty, racism and misogyny, that can impact on children's lives. There is a danger that in focusing on the tropes of the passive, early years and fugitive child, we make their environments more unsafe; because if we see children as passive and unknowing, then we don't use their knowledge to make them feel safe and cared for, as in the case of Mystical in Chapter 3 and Katie in Chapter 6. We also miss the way that children navigate their way through these constraints and make meaning of their lives (Callaghan et al, 2017b).

The figure of the child that is born out of this research is one that is alive and knowing, actively searching for fun, beauty and love. They are wise to the actions of others but at times are constrained by the unloving behaviour of others, so they navigate it as best they can. They are learning and growing, never static. The children are also different from one another and show there is no 'one size fits all' in practice and in theories about children. This figure of the child challenges the damage-focused narrative of domestic abuse and children; it refutes the one-dimensional, essentialised tropes of the passive, early years and fugitive child. It challenges us to look at the wider political landscape and the patriarchal and colonial social order that these tropes uphold. The children of this research have burst through these tropes. They also illustrate why a focus on protection and safety is not enough. We need to look beyond and focus on fun, beauty and love in order to support them to flourish and to address inequality.

As I reflect back on how I started this project, wanting to right the wrongs of the system in misinterpreting children, I am reminded of Les Back's (2015, p 834) words:

> there is nothing better for a sociologist full of righteous desire to say something worth listening to than be the bearer of bad news. Tales of social damage, hopelessness and injustice always make for a good sociological story. But the cost is that we too often look past or don't listen to the moments of the repair and hope which a liveable life is made possible.

While it is important to address domestic abuse and its impact, there is much to be gained from moving away from damage-focused research with children who have experienced domestic abuse and social work interventions. For one, it grants them visibility and opens up a space of possibility for their full humanity to emerge (Tuck, 2009), and, as Back (2015, p 834) reminds us, 'public issues are alive in the mundane aspects of everyday life'.

This book is anchored in being attentive to the everyday lives of children. Saidiyah Hartman (2021, p 21) writes in *Wayward Lives* that the notes from welfare do-gooders and social workers portrayed the lives of the 'poor' in a specific way to garner support or punishment. I find that NGOs, practitioners and researchers in both the Global North and the Global South can do something similar – they can capture pictures to show how 'bad' something is. But in trying to capture the lives to be uplifted or chastised, we can miss the lives being lived right before our eyes. In this book I often wondered how much of our 'good intentions' are embedded in notions that dehumanise and (un)intentionally uphold the status quo. What would happen if we shifted our gaze? What could joy-led, rather than damage-led, research mean globally for children who are marginalised? How would child protection look if we focused beyond the bare minimum of safety and towards the right to fun, beauty and love for children? Maybe there would be less, to use Esmeralda's words, 'blah, blah, blah' from adults and more of a resounding 'Yes!' when Kyro and Rosie ask, 'Can we play now?'

APPENDIX

Methods

In line with the thinking that children express themselves in different ways as well as the restrictions of physical distancing due to COVID-19, the following methods were used. As each child was different and had different preferences and abilities, I experimented with the different methods so that each child had the opportunity to choose what worked for them (Clark, 2011). There are no methods that are particularly child-friendly; what makes something child-friendly is whether a child feels comfortable in using it (Barker and Weller, 2003). Relationships are key in using methods (Smith, 1999; Hall, 2009, 2019); thus, a key element of the methodology is its focus on relationality and a belief that knowledge is built in relation to others.

Art packs

Just before the COVID-19 physical restrictions were imposed on 23 March 2020, I created an art pack which I delivered to all the children who were interested in the project, with instructions to guide them. They were free to use any material in the pack to tell me about their everyday lives, homes and dreams. The guide was just a prompt. Inside the art pack were paper, glue-stick pens, pencils, modelling clay, pipe cleaners, lolly sticks and a small toy digital camera (see Figures A.1a and A.1b).

The aim of the art packs was to enable the children to be creative with the art materials to express their thoughts and feelings while in lockdown.

Video calls, telephone calls and home visits

As I was unable to do in-person home visits at the beginning of the project, mothers and children agreed that I could video call them once a week to continue the research. In essence, I was doing home visits using digital technologies, such as WhatsApp and FaceTime (Pink et al, 2016; Watson and Lupton, 2022).

Telephone and video calls were used to connect and build relationships with mothers and children and to get to know them more and the rhythms and routines of their everyday lives (Pink, 2012; Pink et al, 2016).

I visited, digitally or in person, the majority of children once a week for 18 months.

Appendix

Figure A.1a: Assembling the art pack (photography by Brenda)

Figure A.1b: Art pack (photography by Brenda)

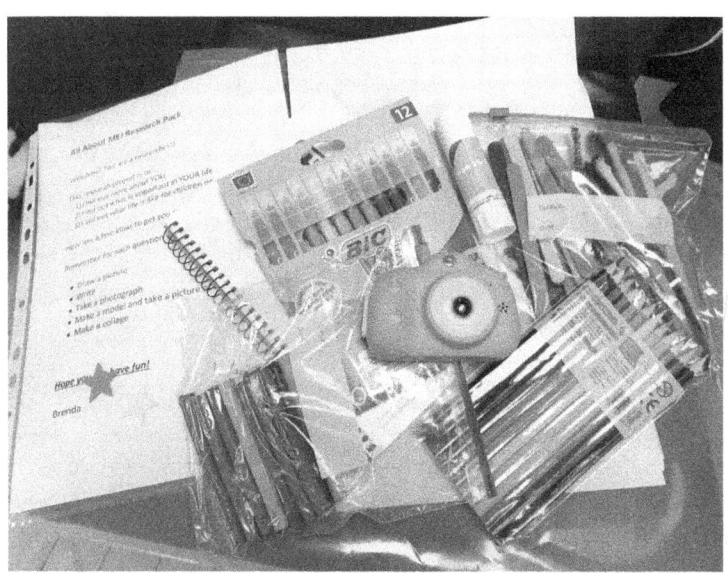

Prompted photography/videos

Following Plowman and Stevenson's (2012) idea, I agreed on a day with both the children and their mothers of when they would document their day through pictures. I asked them to send me throughout the day one picture and one sentence via their mobile phone, when prompted to do so by my text message. The aim was to capture their routines and practices as they unfolded.

I played with this method to capture their everyday routines of family life with varying degrees of success. Some children wanted to take part, while others didn't or forgot to take pictures even when prompted.

Gaming (Minecraft/Roblox)

Playing video and computer games was popular with some of the children, especially Minecraft and Roblox (Nguyen, 2016). Through the telephone calls and art packs, children explored their favourite games. I was also able to play with them so we experienced a game together (Pink, 2013). Gaming was a feature of some of the children's lives during COVID-19, and I explored its meaning with them (Coward-Gibbs, 2022).

Video and computer games were also very important for children's social lives and something they talked about often. I explored through play how children made sense of their use of the games (Plowman et al, 2010; Lupton and Watson, 2020).

Use of internet (YouTube)

YouTube was something that featured in the children's lives (Neumann and Herodotou, 2020; Vanwesenbeeck et al, 2020). A way of exploring this was through conversations with them but also watching YouTube programmes with them to experience and make sense of the programmes. There have been evaluations and analyses of what children watch (Neumann and Herodotou, 2020; Vanwesenbeeck et al, 2020) but all done from an adult's gaze. I spent time with the children watching their programmes with them, and they also took photographs of their favourite shows.

Object stories

In order to explore what objects were important to them, I gave each child a bag to decorate and fill with symbols or actual objects that meant something to them (Holmes, 2020). This created the opportunity to talk about material objects and their meaning for them (Bell and Spikins, 2018).

Photography

The children were given a small, inexpensive digital camera to take pictures of whatever interested them. I encouraged them to take pictures both inside and outside their homes. Children are often subjects of photographs (Varvantakis et al, 2019), but here I hoped to use the photographs to elicit what was important to them and what they found interesting (Lomax, 2020; Luttrell, 2020).

Walking (physically distanced)

Walking or ethnography on the move has become increasingly popular and can be used in a variety of ways (Horton et al, 2014; Lamb et al, 2019; Rose, 2020). As lockdown restrictions lifted, I went on walks with the children and asked them to lead me to their favourite places or places that interested them. This allowed me to learn more about their sense of place, space, time and relations as they guided me through their neighbourhoods.

Exhibition

At the end of the 18-month ethnography, I curated an exhibition of the children's photographs. Each family was able to view the exhibition at an allotted time to comply with COVID-19 regulations. I had originally wanted to use the photo storyboard method (Varvantakis et al, 2019; Luttrell, 2020) to curate the exhibition – where children could come together and discuss which photographs to exhibit – but I was unable to due to COVID-19 physical restrictions. The exhibition was held at a children's centre in the local borough. One child did not want his photographs to be part of the exhibition.

Photo book

As a way of thanking the children for participating in the research and celebrating their work, I collated and created individual photo books for each child using their photographs. I gave each child a personal hardback photo book and a certificate congratulating them on being a great researcher. For each child, I gave them a printed canvas photograph of them that I had taken during the research process. I wanted to thank and celebrate the children.

References

Ahmed, S. (2010) *The promise of happiness*. Duke University Press. https://doi.org/10.1515/9780822392781.

Alexander, J.H., Callaghan, J.E.M., Sixsmith, J. and Fellin, L. (2015) 'Children's corporeal agency and use of space in situations of domestic violence', in B. Evans, J. Horton and T. Skelton (eds), *Play, recreation, health and well being* (pp 1–21). Springer Singapore. https://doi.org/10.1007/978-981-4585-96-5_23-1.

Al-Mohammad, H. and Peluso, D. (2012) 'Ethics and the "rough ground" of the everyday: The overlappings of life in postinvasion Iraq', *HAU: Journal of Ethnographic Theory*, 2(2), 42–58. https://doi.org/10.14318/hau.2.2.004.

Anjaria, J.S. and Anjaria, U. (2020) '*Mazaa*: Rethinking fun, pleasure and play in South Asia', *South Asia: Journal of South Asian Studies*, 43(2), 232–42. https://doi.org/10.1080/00856401.2020.1725718.

Ansell, N. (2009) 'Childhood and the politics of scale: Descaling children's geographies?', *Progress in Human Geography*, 33(2), 190–209. https://doi.org/10.1177/0309132508090980.

Apperley, T. (2015) 'Glitch sorting: Minecraft, curation and the postdigital', in D.M. Berry and M. Dieter (eds), *Postdigital aesthetics* (pp 232–44). Palgrave Macmillan. https://doi.org/10.1057/9781137437204_18.

Arthur, R. and Kirk, T. (2023) 'Children as covert human intelligence sources: Spies first, children second', *Youth Justice*, 23(3), 372–87. https://doi.org/10.1177/14732254231154160.

Atkinson, P. and Parsayi, F. (2021) 'Video games and aesthetic contemplation', *Games and Culture*, 16(5), 519–37. https://doi.org/10.1177/1555412020914726.

Bannerji, H. (ed) (1993) *Returning the gaze: Essays on racism, feminism, and politics*. Sister Vision.

Back, L. (2007) *The art of listening* (English edn). Berg.

Back, L. (2012) 'Live sociology: Social research and its futures', *Sociological Review*, 60(supplement 1), 18–39. https://doi.org/10.1111/j.1467-954X.2012.02115.x.

Back, L. (2015) 'Why everyday life matters: Class, community and making life livable', *Sociology*, 49(5), 820–36. https://doi.org/10.1177/0038038515589292.

Bair-Merritt, M.H., Blackstone, M. and Feudtner, C. (2006) 'Physical health outcomes of childhood exposure to intimate partner violence: A systematic review', *Pediatrics*, 117(2), e278–90. https://doi.org/10.1542/peds.2005-1473.

Baldwin, J. (2017) *The fire next time*. Penguin Books.

References

Barker, J. and Weller, S. (2003) '"Is it fun?" Developing children centred research methods', *International Journal of Sociology and Social Policy*, 23(1/2), 33–58. https://doi.org/10.1108/01443330310790435.

Barker, M. and Russell, J. (2020) 'Feeding the food insecure in Britain: Learning from the 2020 COVID-19 crisis', *Food Security*, 12(4), 865–70. https://doi.org/10.1007/s12571-020-01080-5.

Barnes, M. (2012) *Care in everyday life: An ethic of care in practice*. Policy Press.

Bassel, L. and Emejulu, A. (2017) *Minority women and austerity: Survival and resistance in France and Britain*. Policy Press.

Beetham, T., Gabriel, L. and James, H. (2019) 'Young children's narrations of relational recovery: A school-based group for children who have experienced domestic violence', *Journal of Family Violence*, 34(6), 565–75. https://doi.org/10.1007/s10896018-0028-7.

Behar, R. (2022) *The vulnerable observer: Anthropology that breaks your heart*. Beacon Press.

Bell, T. and Spikins, P. (2018) 'The object of my affection: Attachment security and material culture', *Time and Mind*, 11(1), 23–39. https://doi.org/10.1080/1751696X.2018.1433355.

Bell, V. (2014) 'Photo-image', in C. Lury and N. Wakeford (eds), *Inventive methods: The happening of the social* (pp 147–62). Routledge.

Bentham, J., Dumont, E. and Hildreth, R. (2005 [1908]) *Theory of legislation*. Elibron Classics.

Berger, J. (2008) *Ways of seeing*. Penguin Books.

Bernard, C. and Gupta, A. (2008) 'Black African children and the child protection system', *British Journal of Social Work*, 38(3), 476–92. https://doi.org/10.1093/bjsw/bcl370.

Bernard, C. and Harris, P. (2018) 'Serious case reviews: The lived experience of Black children', *Child & Family Social Work*, 24(2), 256–63. https://doi.org/10.1111/cfs.12610.

Bernstein, R. (2011) *Racial innocence: Performing American childhood from slavery to civil rights*. New York University Press.

Bhabha, H.K. (2004) *The location of culture*. Routledge.

Bhandar, B. and Ziadah, R. (eds) (2020) *Revolutionary feminisms: Conversations on collective action and radical thought*. Verso Books.

Birchall, J. and Choudhry, S. (2022) '"I was punished for telling the truth": How allegations of parental alienation are used to silence, sideline and disempower survivors of domestic abuse in family law proceedings', *Journal of Gender-Based Violence*, 6(1), 115–31. https://doi.org/10.1332/239868021X16287966471815.

Black, D.S., Sussman, S. and Unger, J.B. (2010) 'A further look at the intergenerational transmission of violence: Witnessing interparental violence in emerging adulthood', *Journal of Interpersonal Violence*, 25(6), 1022–42. https://doi.org/10.1177/0886260509340539.

Bogat, G.A., DeJonghe, E., Levendosky, A.A., Davidson, W.S. and von Eye, A. (2006) 'Trauma symptoms among infants exposed to intimate partner violence', *Child Abuse & Neglect*, 30(2), 109–25.

Brandon, M. (2008) 'Analysing child deaths and serious injury through abuse and neglect: What can we learn? A biennial analysis of serious case reviews 2003–2005'. Available at: http://dera.ioe.ac.uk/7190/1/dcsf-rr023.pdf. (Accessed: 24 May 2017).

Brant, B. (1994) *Writing as witness: Essay and talk*. Women's Press.

Brown, A.M. (2019) *Pleasure activism: The politics of feeling good*. AK Press.

Buber, M. (2020 [1937]) *I and thou*. Translated by R.G. Smith. Martino Publishing.

Bunting, L., Davidson, G., McCarten, C., Hanratty, J., Bywaters, P., Mason, W. and Steils, N. (2018) 'The association between child maltreatment and adult poverty: A systematic review of longitudinal research', *Child Abuse & Neglect*, 77, 121–33. https://doi.org/10.1016/j.chiabu.2017.12.022.

Burman, E. (2004) 'Boundary objects and group analysis: Between psychoanalysis and social theory', *Group Analysis*, 37(3), 361–79. https://doi.org/10.1177/533316404045525.

Burman, E. (2008) *Developments: Child, image, nation*. Routledge.

Burman, E. (2012) 'Deconstructing neoliberal childhood: Towards a feminist antipsychological approach', *Childhood*, 19(4), 423–38. https://doi.org/10.1177/0907568211430767.

Burman, E. (2013) 'Desiring development? Psychoanalytic contributions to antidevelopmental psychology', *International Journal of Qualitative Studies in Education*, 26(1), 56–74. https://doi.org/10.1080/09518398.2011.604650.

Burman, E. (2016) *Deconstructing developmental psychology* (3rd edn). Routledge.

Burman, E. (2018a) 'Brexit, "child as method," and the pedagogy of failure: How discourses of childhood structure the resistance of racist discourse to analysis', *Review of Education, Pedagogy, and Cultural Studies*, 40(2), 119–43. https://doi.org/10.1080/10714413.2018.1442082.

Burman, E. (2018b) *Fanon, education, action: Child as Method* (1st edn). Routledge.

Burman, E. and Millei, Z. (2022) 'Post-socialist geopolitical uncertainties: Researching memories of childhood with "child as method"', *Children & Society*, 36(5), 993–1009. https://doi.org/10.1111/chso.12551.

Butcher, M. and Velayutham, S. (eds) (2009) *Dissent and cultural resistance in Asia's cities*. Routledge.

Butler, O.E. (2019a) *Parable of the sower*. Headline.

Butler, O.E. (2019b) *The parable of the talents*. Headline.

Byrne, M.D. and Taylor, B. (2007) 'Children at risk from domestic violence and their educational attainment: Perspectives of education welfare officers, social workers and teachers', *Child Care in Practice*, 13(3), 185–201. https://doi.org/10.1080/13575270701353465.

Bywaters, P., Brady, G., Bunting, L., Daniel, B., Featherstone, B., Jones, C., Morris, K., Scourfield, J., Sparks, T. and Webb, C. (2017a) 'Inequalities in English child protection practice under austerity: A universal challenge?', *Child & Family Social Work*, 23(1), 53–61. https://doi.org/10.1111/cfs.12383.

Bywaters, P., Kwhali, J., Brady, G., Sparks, T. and Bos, E. (2017b) 'Out of sight, out of mind: Ethnic inequalities in child protection and out-of-home care intervention rates', *British Journal of Social Work*, 47(7), 1884–902. https://doi.org/10.1093/bjsw/bcw165.

Cairns, I. and Callander, I. (2022) '"Gold standard" legislation for adults only: Reconceptualising children as "adjoined victims" under the Domestic Abuse (Scotland) Act 2018', *Social & Legal Studies*, 31(6), 914–40. https://doi.org/10.1177/09646639221089252.

Cairns, K. (2020) 'Children, reproductive labor, and intergenerational solidarity', *Focaal*, 2020(86), 121–4. https://doi.org/10.3167/fcl.2020.860110.

Callaghan, J.E.M. (2015) 'Mothers and children? Representations of mothers in research on children's outcomes in domestic violence', *Psychology of Women Section Review*, 17, 13–20.

Callaghan, J.E.M., Alexander, J.H. and Fellin, L.C. (2016a) 'Children's embodied experience of living with domestic violence: "I'd go into my panic, and shake, really bad"', *Subjectivity*, 9(4), 399–419. https://doi.org/10.1057/s41286-016-0011-9.

Callaghan, J.E.M., Fellin, L.C. and Alexander, J.H. (2017a) 'Children's experiences of domestic violence: A teaching and training challenge', in C. Newnes and L. Golding (eds), *Teaching critical psychology* (pp 219–37). Routledge.

Callaghan, J.E.M., Fellin, L.C. and Alexander, J.H. (2018) 'Beyond vulnerability: Working with children who have experienced domestic violence', in L. O'Dell, C. Brownlow and H. Bertilsdotter Rosqvist (eds), *Different childhoods: Non/normative development and transgressive trajectories* (pp 85–101). Routledge.

Callaghan, J.E.M., Alexander, J.H., Sixsmith, J. and Fellin, L.C. (2015) Beyond "witnessing": Children's experiences of coercive control in domestic violence and abuse. *Journal of Interpersonal Violence*, 33(10), 1551–81. https://doi.org/10.1177/0886260515618946.

Callaghan, J.E.M., Alexander, J.H., Sixsmith, J. and Fellin, L.C. (2016b) 'Children's experiences of domestic violence and abuse: Siblings' accounts of relational coping', *Clinical Child Psychology and Psychiatry*, 21(4), 649–68. https://doi.org/10.1177/1359104515620250.

Callaghan, J.E.M., Fellin, L.C., Alexander, J.H., Mavrou, S. and Papathanasiou, M. (2017b) 'Children and domestic violence: Emotional competencies in embodied and relational contexts', *Psychology of Violence*, 7(3), 333. https://doi.org/10.1037/vio0000108.

Campt, T. (2012) *Image matters: Archive, photography, and the African diaspora in Europe*. Duke University Press.

Campt, T. (2017) *Listening to images*. Duke University Press.

Campt, T. (2023) *A black gaze: Artists changing how we see* (1st paperback edn). MIT Press.

Cannella, G.S. and Viruru, R. (2004) *Childhood and postcolonization: Power, education, and contemporary practice*. RoutledgeFalmer.

Caplan, P. (2006) '"Is it real food?" Who benefits from globalisation in Tanzania and India?', *Sociological Research Online*, 11(4), 81–93. https://doi.org/10.5153/sro.1472.

Carlile, A. (2013) *Permanent exclusion from school and institutional prejudice: Creating change through critical bureaucracy*. Sense.

Cassal, L.C.B. (2024) *Age, nation, and development: Child as method and legal gender recognition in the UK* (unpublished doctoral dissertation). University of Manchester.

Castañeda, C. (2002) *Figurations: Child, bodies, worlds*. Duke University Press.

Cater, Å. and Øverlien, C. (2014) 'Children exposed to domestic violence: A discussion about research ethics and researchers' responsibilities', *Nordic Social Work Research*, 4(1), 67–79. https://doi.org/10.1080/2156857X.2013.801878.

Cayatte, R. (2014) 'Where game, play and art collide', in N. Garrelts (ed), *Understanding Minecraft: Essays on play, community and possibilities* (pp 203–14). McFarland & Company, Inc.

Chao-Fong, L. (2020) 'Tory MP suggests free school meals "effectively" go to crack dens and brothels', *Huffington Post*, 23 October. Available at: www.huffingtonpost.co.uk/entry/tory-mp-suggests-free-school-meals-vouchers-effectively-go-to-crack-dens-and-brothels_uk_5f931b2bc5b6481d48fd2961. (Accessed: 28 October 2022).

Chen, K.-H. (2010) *Asia as method: Toward deimperialization*. Duke University Press.

Cheney, K.E. (2017) *Crying for our elders: African orphanhood in the age of HIV and AIDS*. University of Chicago Press.

Chigangaidze, R.K. (2021) 'An exposition of humanistic-existential social work in light of ubuntu philosophy: Towards theorizing ubuntu in social work practice', *Journal of Religion & Spirituality in Social Work: Social Thought*, 40(2), 146–65. https://doi.org/10.1080/15426432.2020.1859431.

Children Act 1989. Available at: www.legislation.gov.uk/ukpga/1989/41/contents. (Accessed: 14 December 2022).

References

Children Act 2004. Available at: www.legislation.gov.uk/ukpga/2004/31/contents. (Accessed: 2 December 2022).

Chin, E. (1999) 'Ethnically correct dolls: Toying with the race industry', *American Anthropologist*, 101(2), 305–21. https://doi.org/10.1525/aa.1999.101.2.305.

Chiou, L. and Tucker, C. (2020) *Social distancing, internet access and inequality* (p w26982). National Bureau of Economic Research. https://doi.org/10.3386/w26982.

Cho, L. (2019) 'Diasporic intimacy: Chinese-Canadian documentary and the poetics of relation', in Cho, L., *The Oxford Handbook of Canadian Cinema* (J. Marchessault and W. Straw (eds), pp 146–64). Oxford University Press. https://doi.org/10.1093/oxfordhb/9780190229108.013.9.

Christinaki, A. (2025) 'Age assessment and migration control: "Child as method"', *Global Studies of Childhood*. https://doi.org/10.1177/20436106251319471.

Clark, A. (2011) 'Multimodal map making with young children: Exploring ethnographic and participatory methods', *Qualitative Research*, 11(3), 311–30. https://doi.org/10.1177/1468794111400532.

Clark, A. (2017) *Listening to young children: A guide to understanding and using the mosaic approach* (expanded 3rd edn). Jessica Kingsley Publishers.

Clark, K. and Clark, M. (1947) 'Racial identification and preference in Negro children', in T.M. Newcomb and E.L. Harley (eds), *Reading in social psychology* (pp 169–78). Holt Rinehart and Winston.

Conkbayir, M. (2014) *Early childhood theories and contemporary issues*. Bloomsbury.

Cooper, A., Hetherington, R. and Katz, I. (2003) *The risk factor: Making the child protection system work for children*. Demos.

Coward-Gibbs, M. (2022) 'Why don't we play pandemic? Analog gaming communities in lockdown', in B. Lashua, C.W. Johnson and D.C. Parry (eds), *Leisure in the time of coronavirus* (pp 157–63). Routledge.

Creasy, R. and Corby, F. (2019) *Taming childhood?* Springer Berlin Heidelberg.

Crossley, S. (2018) *Troublemakers: The construction of 'troubled families' as a social problem*. Policy Press.

Crowley, A. (2015) 'Is anyone listening? The impact of children's participation on public policy', *International Journal of Children's Rights*, 23(3), 602–21. https://doi.org/10.1163/15718182-02303005.

Curtis, M.G., Karlsen, A.S. and Anderson, L.A. (2022) 'Transmuting girls into women: Examining the adultification of Black female sexual assault survivors through Twitter feedback', *Violence against Women*, 29(2), 321–46. https://doi.org/10.1177/10778012221083334.

Dal Puri Diaspora (documentary) (2012) Directed by R. Fung. Vtape.

Dattatreyan, E.G. and Marrero-Guillamón, I. (2019) 'Introduction: Multimodal anthropology and the politics of invention', *American Anthropologist*, 121(1), 220–8. https://doi.org/10.1111/aman.13183.

Dahler, N. (2020) 'Biometrics as imperialism: Age assessments of young asylum seekers in Denmark', *Race & Class*, 62(1), 24–45. https://doi.org/10.1177/0306396820925648.

Davies, P. (2018) 'Tackling domestic abuse locally: Paradigms, ideologies and the political tensions of multi-agency working', *Journal of Gender-Based Violence*, 2(3), 429–46. https://doi.org/info:doi/10.1332/239868018X15392672654573.

Davis, J. and Marsh, N. (2020) 'Boys to men: The cost of "adultification" in safeguarding responses to Black boys', *Critical and Radical Social Work*, 8(2), 255–9. https://doi.org/10.1332/204986020X15945756023543.

Davis, J. and Marsh, N. (2022) 'The myth of the universal child', in D. Holmes (ed), *Safeguarding young people: Risk, rights, resilience and relationships* (pp 111–28). Jessica Kingsley Publishers.

de Certeau, M. (1984) *The practice of everyday life*. University of Chicago Press.

de Certeau, M., Giard, L. and Mayol, P. (1996) *The practice of everyday life (Volume 2: Living and cooking)* (new revised and augmented edn). University of Minnesota Press.

Deleuze, G. and Guattari, F. (2013a) *A thousand plateaus: Capitalism and schizophrenia* (1st paperback edn). Bloomsbury.

Deleuze, G. and Guattari, F. (2013b) *Anti-Oedipus: Capitalism and schizophrenia*, R. Hurley, M. Seem and H.R. Lane (trans). Bloomsbury.

Dennis, F. (2019) *Injecting bodies in more-than-human worlds* (1st edn). Routledge.

Dennis, F. and Farrugia, A. (2017) 'Materialising drugged pleasures: Practice, politics, care', *International Journal of Drug Policy*, 49, 86–91. https://doi.org/10.1016/j.drugpo.2017.10.001.

Department for Education (DfE) (2018) 'Working together to safeguard children: A guide to inter-agency working to safeguard and promote the welfare of children'. Available at: www.gov.uk/guidance/case-management-guidance/definitions. (Accessed: 26 November 2021).

Department of Education (2021) *Characteristics of children in need: 2020 to 2021*. Available at: www.gov.uk/government/statistics/characteristics-of-children-in-need-2020-to2021. (Accessed: 2 December 2022).

Devaney, J. (2008) 'Chronic child abuse and domestic violence: Children and families with long-term and complex needs', *Child & Family Social Work*, 13(4), 443–53. https://doi.org/10.1111/j.1365-2206.2008.00559.x.

Dicks, B. (2014) 'Action, experience, communication: Three methodological paradigms for researching multimodal and multisensory settings', *Qualitative Research*, 14(6), 656–74. https://doi.org/10.1177/1468794113501687.

Dicks, B., Flewitt, R., Lancaster, L. and Pahl, K. (2011). 'Multimodality and ethnography: Working at the intersection', *Qualitative Research*, 11(3), 227–37. https://doi.org/10.1177/1468794111400682.

References

Di Napoli Pastore, M. (2022) 'Play, create, transform: A pluriverse of children and childhoods from southern Mozambique', *Journal of the British Academy*, 10s2, 111–32. https://doi.org/10.5871/jba/010s2.111.

Domestic Abuse Act 2021. Available at: www.legislation.gov.uk/ukpga/2021/17/contents/enacted. (Accessed: 2 December 2022).

Douglas, M. (2003) *Purity and danger*. Routledge. https://doi.org/10.4324/9780203361832.

Dyer, H. (2020) *The queer aesthetics of childhood: Asymmetries of innocence and the cultural politics of child development*. Rutgers University Press.

Edleson, J.L. (1999) 'Children's witnessing of adult domestic violence', *Journal of Interpersonal Violence*, 14(8), 839–70. https://doi.org/10.1177/088626099014008004.

Ehrensaft, M.K. (2008) 'Intimate partner violence: Persistence of myths and implications for intervention', *Children and Youth Services Review*, 30(3), 276–86. https://doi.org/10.1016/j.childyouth.2007.10.005.

Ehrensaft, M.K. and Cohen, P. (2012) 'Contribution of family violence to the intergenerational transmission of externalizing behavior', *Prevention Science*, 13(4), 370–83. https://doi.org/10.1007/s11121-011-0223-8.

Ellis, K. (2018) 'Contested vulnerability: A case study of girls in secure care', *Children and Youth Services Review*, 88, 156–63. https://doi.org/10.1016/j.childyouth.2018.02.047.

Emejulu, A. (2018) 'Towards a fugitive feminism' (lecture). Fugitive Feminism, Institute of Contemporary Arts, 19 July.

Emejulu, A. (2022) *Fugitive Feminism*. Silver Press.

Emejulu, A. and Bassel, L. (2018) 'Austerity and the politics of becoming', *Journal of Common Market Studies*, 56, 109. https://doi.org/10.1111/jcms.12774.

Emejulu, A. and Sobande, F. (eds) (2019) *To exist is to resist: Black feminism in Europe*. Pluto Press.

Enlow, M.B., Egeland, B., Blood, E.A., Wright, R.O. and Wright, R.J. (2012) 'Interpersonal trauma exposure and cognitive development in children to age 8 years: A longitudinal study', *Journal of Epidemiology and Community Health*, 66(11), 1005–10. https://doi.org/10.1136/jech-2011200727.

Eriksson, M., Hester, M., Keskinen, S. and Pringle, K. (2005) *Tackling men's violence in families: Nordic issues and dilemmas*. Policy Press. Available at: http://gup.ub.gu.se/publication/33388-tackling-mens-violence-in-families-nordic-issues-anddilemmas. (Accessed: 8 January 2017).

Essien, I. and Wood, J.L. (2020) 'I love my hair: The weaponizing of Black girls' hair by educators in early childhood education', *Early Childhood Education Journal*, 49, 401–12. https://doi.org/10.1007/s10643-020-01081-1.

Etherington, K. (2004) *Becoming a reflexive researcher: Using our selves in research* (illustrated edn). Jessica Kingsley Publishers.

Etherington, N. and Baker, L. (2018) 'From "buzzword" to best practice: Applying intersectionality to children exposed to intimate partner violence', *Trauma, Violence, & Abuse*, 19(1), 58–75. https://doi.org/10.1177/1524838016631128.

Evans, R. and Skovdal, M. (2015) 'Defining children's rights to work and care in subSaharan Africa: Tensions and challenges in policy and practice', in K. Kallio, S. Mills and T. Skelton (eds), *Politics, citizenship and rights* (pp 1–14). Springer Singapore. https://doi.org/10.1007/978-981-4585-94-1_12-1.

Evans, R., Bowlby, S., Gottzén, L. and Ribbens McCarthy, J. (2019) 'Unpacking "family troubles", care and relationality across time and space', *Children's Geographies*, 17(5), 501–13. https://doi.org/10.1080/14733285.2019.1655139.

Evans, S.E., Davies, C. and DiLillo, D. (2008) 'Exposure to domestic violence: A metaanalysis of child and adolescent outcomes', *Aggression and Violent Behavior*, 13(2), 131–40. https://doi.org/10.1016/j.avb.2008.02.005.

Fahmy, E. and Williamson, E. (2018) 'Poverty and domestic violence and abuse (DVA) in the UK', *Journal of Gender-Based Violence*, 2(3), 481–501. https://doi.org/info:doi/10.1332/239868018X15263881184558.

Fanon, F. (1988 [1964]) *Toward the African revolution: Political essays* (New Evergreen edn). Grove Press.

Fanon, F. (2001 [1961]) *The wretched of the earth*. Penguin Books.

Fanon, F. (2007 [1959]) *A dying colonialism*. H. Chevalier (trans). Grove Press.

Fanon, F. (2017 [1952]) *Black skin, white masks* (new edition). C.L. Markmann (trans). PlutoPress.

Fassin, D. (2012) *Humanitarian reason: A moral history of the present times*. University of California Press.

Fassin, D. and Rechtman, R. (2009) *The empire of trauma: An inquiry into the condition of victimhood*. Princeton University Press.

Featherstone, B. (2016) 'Poverty matters: Protecting children in tough times in England', *Families, Relationships and Societies*, 5(1), 145–6. https://doi.org/10.1332/204674316X14540714620120.

Featherstone, B., Morris, K. and White, S. (2014) 'A marriage made in hell: Early intervention meets child protection', *British Journal of Social Work*, 44(7), 1735–49. https://doi.org/10.1093/bjsw/bct052.

Featherstone, B., Gupta, A., Morris, K. and White, S. (2018) *Protecting children: A social model*. Policy Press.

Featherstone, B., Morris, K., Daniel, B., Bywaters, P., Brady, G., Bunting, L., Mason, W. and Mirza, N. (2017) 'Poverty, inequality, child abuse and neglect: Changing the conversation across the UK in child protection?', *Children and Youth Services Review*, 97, 127–33. https://doi.org/10.1016/j.childyouth.2017.06.009.

References

Federici, S. (2012) *Revolution at point zero: Housework, reproduction, and feminist struggle*. PM Press.

Fellin, L.C., Callaghan, J.E.M., Alexander, J.H., Harrison-Breed, C., Mavrou, S. and Papathanasiou, M. (2018) 'Empowering young people who experienced domestic violence and abuse: The development of a group therapy intervention', *Clinical Child Psychology and Psychiatry*, 24(1), 170–89. https://doi.org/10.1177/1359104518794783.

Ferguson, G., Featherstone, B. and Morris, K. (2019) 'Framed to fit? Challenging the domestic abuse "story" in child protection', *Critical and Radical Social Work*, 8(1), 25–40. https://doi.org/info:doi/10.1332/204986019X15668424450790.

Ferguson, H. (2011) *Child protection practice*. Palgrave Macmillan.

Ferguson, H. (2016a) 'How children become invisible in child protection work: Findings from research into day-to-day social work practice', *British Journal of Social Work*, 47(4), 1007–23. https://doi.org/10.1093/bjsw/bcw065.

Ferguson, H. (2016b) 'Researching social work practice close up: Using ethnographic and mobile methods to understand encounters between social workers, children and families', *British Journal of Social Work*, 46(1), 153–68. https://doi.org/10.1093/bjsw/bcu120.

Ferguson, H., Leigh, J., Cooner, T.S., Beddoe, L., Disney, T., Warwick, L. and Plumridge, G. (2020) 'From snapshots of practice to a movie: Researching long-term social work and child protection by getting as close as possible to practice and organisational life', *British Journal of Social Work*, 50(6), 1706–23. https://doi.org/10.1093/bjsw/bcz119.

Fernández-González, L., Calvete, E., Orue, I. and Mauri, A. (2018) 'Victims of domestic violence in shelters: Impacts on women and children', *Spanish Journal of Psychology*, 21. https://doi.org/10.1017/sjp.2018.21.

Firmin, C. (2018) 'Contextualizing case reviews: A methodology for developing systemic safeguarding practices', *Child & Family Social Work*, 23(1), 45–52. https://doi.org/10.1111/cfs.12382.

Firmin, C., Warrington, C. and Pearce, J. (2016) 'Sexual exploitation and its impact on developing sexualities and sexual relationships: The need for contextual social work interventions', *British Journal of Social Work*, 46(8), 2318–37. https://doi.org/10.1093/bjsw/bcw134.

Firmin, C., Lefevre, M., Huegler, N. and Peace, D. (2022) *Safeguarding young people beyond the family home responding to extra-familial risks and harms*. Policy Press.

Folkes, L. (2022) 'Moving beyond "shopping list" positionality: Using kitchen table reflexivity and in/visible tools to develop reflexive qualitative research', *Qualitative Research*, 23(5), 1301–18. https://doi.org/10.1177/14687941221098922.

Freire, P. (2000 [1968]) *Pedagogy of the oppressed* (30th anniversary edn). Bloomsbury.

Fricker, M. (2009) *Epistemic injustice: Power and the ethics of knowing*. Oxford University Press.

Gabb, J. (2010) *Researching intimacy in families*. Palgrave Macmillan.

García-Sánchez, I.M. (2018) 'Children as interactional brokers of care', *Annual Review of Anthropology*, 47(1), 167–84. https://doi.org/10.1146/annurev-anthro102317-050050.

Garlen, J.C. (2019) 'Interrogating innocence: "Childhood" as exclusionary social practice', *Childhood*, 26(1), 54–67. https://doi.org/10.1177/0907568218811484.

Garthwaite, K.A., Collins, P.J. and Bambra, C. (2015) 'Food for thought: An ethnographic study of negotiating ill health and food insecurity in a UK foodbank', *Social Science & Medicine*, 132, 38–44. https://doi.org/10.1016/j.socscimed.2015.03.019.

Gatwiri, K. (2021) 'Afrocentric ways of "doing" social work', in S.M. Tascón and J. Ife (eds), *Disrupting Whiteness in social work* (1st paperback edn, pp 58–73). Routledge.

Gatwiri, K. and Ife, J. (2021) 'Teaching about vulnerability and love in social work: Lessons and reflections from two academics', *Social Work Education*, 42(3), 388–403. https://doi.org/10.1080/02615479.2021.1972962.

Geertz, C. (1993 [1972]) 'Deep play: Notes on the Balinese cockfight', in *The interpretation of cultures: Selected essays* (pp 412–53). Fontana Press.

Gembus, M.P. (2018) 'The safe spaces "in-between": Plays, performance and identity among young "second generation" Somalis in London', *Children's Geographies*, 16(4), 432–43. https://doi.org/10.1080/14733285.2017.1362498.

Gerhardt, S. (2015) *Why love matters: How affection shapes a baby's brain* (2nd edn). Routledge.

Gilbert, T., Farrand, P. and Lankshear, G. (2012) 'Troubled lives: Chaos and trauma in the accounts of young people considered "at risk" of diagnosis of personality disorder', *Scandinavian Journal of Caring Sciences*, 26(4), 747–54.

Gill, T. (2007) *No fear: Growing up in a risk averse society*. Calouste Gulbenkian Foundation.

Gill, T. (2021) *Urban playground: How child-friendly planning and design can save cities*. RIBA Publishing.

Gillies, V., Edwards, R. and Horsley, N. (2017) *Challenging the politics of early intervention: Who's 'saving' children and why* (reprint edn). Policy Press.

Goody, J. (1982) *Cooking, cuisine, and class: A study in comparative sociology*. Cambridge University Press.

Gordon, R. (2019) '"Why would I want to be anonymous?" Questioning ethical principles of anonymity in cross-cultural feminist research', *Gender & Development*, 27(3), 541–54. https://doi.org/10.1080/13552074.2019.1664044.

Gottzén, L. and Sandberg, L. (2019) 'Creating safe atmospheres? Children's experiences of grandparents' affective and spatial responses to domestic violence', *Children's Geographies*, 17(5), 514–26. https://doi.org/10.1080/14733285.2017.1406896.

Graeber, D. (2014). 'What's the point if we can't have fun?' *The Baffler*, issue 24. Available at: https://thebaffler.com/salvos/whats-the-point-if-we-cant-have-fun. (Accessed: 16 September 2025).

Grant, A., Mannay, D. and Marzella, R. (2018) '"People try and police your behaviour": The impact of surveillance on mothers' and grandmothers' perceptions and experiences of infant feeding', *Families, Relationships and Societies*, 7(3), 431–47. https://doi.org/10.1332/204674317X14888886530223.

Greenstein, A., Burman, E., Kalambouka, A. and Sapin, K. (2016) 'Construction and deconstruction of "family" by the "bedroom tax"', *British Politics*, 11(4), 508–25. https://doi.org/10.1057/s41293-016-0033-5.

Gu, J. (2014) 'A craft to call mine: Creative appropriation of Minecraft in YouTube animations', in N. Garrelts (ed), *Understanding Minecraft: Essays on play, community and possibilities* (pp 132–47). McFarland & Company, Inc.

Guedes, A., Bott, S., Garcia-Moreno, C. and Colombini, M. (2016) 'Bridging the gaps: A global review of intersections of violence against women and violence against children', *Global Health Action*, 9(1), 31516. https://doi.org/10.3402/gha.v9.31516.

Gunaratnam, Y. (2013) 'Cultural vulnerability: A narrative approach to intercultural care', *Qualitative Social Work*, 12(2), 104–18. https://doi.org/10.1177/1473325011420323.

Gupta, A. (2017) 'Poverty and child neglect: The elephant in the room?', *Families, Relationships and Societies*, 6(1), 21–36. https://doi.org/10.1332/204674315X14207948135699.

Gutin, I. (2018) 'In BMI we trust: Reframing the body mass index as a measure of health', *Social Theory & Health*, 16(3), 256–71. https://doi.org/10.1057/s41285017-0055-0.

Hackett, A., Pahl, K. and Pool, S. (2017) 'In amongst the glitter and the squashed blueberries: Crafting a collaborative lens for children's literacy pedagogy in a community setting', *Pedagogies: An International Journal*, 12(1), 58–73. https://doi.org/10.1080/1554480X.2017.1283994.

Hall, S.M. (2009) '"Private life" and "work life": Difficulties and dilemmas when making and maintaining friendships with ethnographic participants', *Area*, 41(3), 263–72. https://doi.org/10.1111/j.1475-4762.2009.00880.x.

Hall, S.M. (2017) 'Personal, relational and intimate geographies of austerity: Ethical and empirical considerations', *Area*, 49(3), 303–10. https://doi.org/10.1111/area.12251.

Hall, S.M. (2018) 'Everyday austerity: Towards relational geographies of family, friendship and intimacy', *Progress in Human Geography*, 43(5). https://doi.org/10.1177/0309132518796280.

Hall, S.M. (2019) *Everyday life in austerity: Family, friends and intimate relations.* Springer Nature.

Halliday, A.S. (2021) *Black girlhood studies collection.* Canadian Scholars' Press.

Haraway, D.J. (1988) 'Situated knowledges: The science question in feminism and the privilege of partial perspective', *Feminist Studies*, 14(3), 575. https://doi.org/10.2307/3178066.

Haraway, D.J. (2003) *The companion species manifesto: Dogs, people, and significant otherness.* Prickly Paradigm Press.

Haraway, D.J. (2008) *When species meet.* University of Minnesota Press.

Harman, J.J., Bernet, W. and Harman, J. (2019) 'Parental alienation: The blossoming of a field of study', *Current Directions in Psychological Science*, 28(2), 212–17. https://doi.org/10.1177/0963721419827271.

Harris, P. (2016) *Safeguarding Black children: Good practice in child protection.* C. Bernard (ed). Jessica Kingsley Publishers.

Hartman, S.V. (2021) *Wayward lives, beautiful experiments: Intimate histories of riotous Black girls, troublesome women and queer radicals* (paperback edn). Serpent's Tail.

Haselschwerdt, M.L. (2014) 'Theorizing children's exposure to intimate partner violence using Johnson's typology', *Journal of Family Theory & Review*, 6(3), 199–221. https://doi.org/10.1111/jftr.12040.

Haselschwerdt, M.L., Hlavaty, K., Carlson, C., Schneider, M., Maddox, L. and Skipper, M. (2016) 'Heterogeneity within domestic violence exposure: Young adults' retrospective experiences', *Journal of Interpersonal Violence*, 34(7), 1512–38. https://doi.org/10.1177/0886260516651625.

Hemmings, S. and Thompson, K. (2002) *Understanding everyday life.* T. Bennett and D.H. Watson (eds). Blackwell.

Henry, C. (2017) 'Expanding the legal framework for child protection: Recognition of and response to child exposure to domestic violence in California law', *Social Service Review*, 91(2), 203–32. https://doi.org/10.1086/692399.

Herbert, B. (2025) 'What's love got to do with it? *Live methods* and researching with children who have experienced domestic abuse and social work intervention', *Sociological Review*, 73(5), 1066–84. https://doi.org/10.1177/00380261251335490.

Hester, M. (2013) 'Who does what to whom? Gender and domestic violence perpetrators in English police records', *European Journal of Criminology*, 10(5), 623–37. https://doi.org/10.1177/1477370813479078.

Heward-Belle, S., Laing, L., Humphreys, C. and Toivonen, C. (2018) 'Intervening with children living with domestic violence: Is the system safe?', *Australian Social Work*, 71(2), 135–47. https://doi.org/10.1080/0312407X.2017.1422772.

Highmore, B. (ed) (2002) *The everyday life reader*. Routledge.

Highmore, B. (2004) 'Homework: Routine, social aesthetics and the ambiguity of everyday life', *Cultural Studies*, 18(2–3), 306–27. https://doi.org/10.1080/0950238042000201536.

Highmore, B. (2010) *Ordinary lives: Studies in the everyday* (1st edn). Routledge. https://doi.org/10.4324/9780203842379.

Highmore, B. (2014) *The great indoors: At home in the modern British house*. Profile Books.

Higonnet, A. (1998) *Pictures of innocence: The history and crisis of ideal childhood*. Thames and Hudson.

Hill Collins, P. (2016) *Intersectionality*. Polity Press.

Hochschild, A.R. (2003) *The commercialization of intimate life: Notes from home and work*. University of California Press.

Holden, G.W. (2003) 'Children exposed to domestic violence and child abuse: Terminology and taxonomy', *Clinical Child and Family Psychology Review*, 6(3), 151–60.

Holloway, S.L., Holt, L. and Mills, S. (2018) 'Questions of agency: Capacity, subjectivity, spatiality and temporality', *Progress in Human Geography*, 43(3), 458–77. https://doi.org/10.1177/0309132518757654.

Holmes, H. (2020) 'Material relationships: Object interviews as a means of studying everyday life', in H. Holmes and S.M. Hall (eds), *Mundane methods: Innovative ways to research the everyday* (pp 66–83). Manchester University Press.

Holmes, H. (2022) 'The body in personal life', in V. May and P. Nordqvist (eds), *Sociology of personal life* (2nd edn, pp 117–28). Bloomsbury Academic.

Holt, S. (2008) 'Domestic violence and child contact: Issues and dilemmas for child protection and welfare practice', in K. Burns and D. Lynch (eds), *Child protection and welfare social work: Contemporary themes and practice perspectives* (pp 180–97). A & A Farmar.

Holt, S. (2015) 'Post-separation fathering and domestic abuse: Challenges and contradictions', *Child Abuse Review*, 24(3), 210–22. https://doi.org/10.1002/car.2264.

Holt, S. (2017) *Responding to domestic violence*. Jessica Kingsley Publishers.

Holt, S. and Devaney, J. (2015) 'Understanding domestic abuse and sexual violence: Prevalence, policy and practice', in D. Healy, C. Hamilton, Y. Daly and M. Butler (eds), *The Routledge handbook of Irish criminology* (pp 70–88). Routledge.

Holt, S., Buckley, H. and Whelan, S. (2008) 'The impact of exposure to domestic violence on children and young people: A review of the literature', *Child Abuse & Neglect*, 32(8), 797–810.

hooks, bell (1987) *Ain't I a woman: Black women and feminism* (1st edn). Pluto Press.

hooks, bell (1990) *Yearning: Race, gender, and cultural politics*. South End Press.

hooks, bell (1995) *Art on my mind: Visual politics*. New Press.

hooks, bell (2004) *The will to change: Men, masculinity, and love* (reprint edn). Washington Square Press.

hooks, bell (2009) *Belonging: A culture of place*. Routledge.

hooks, bell (2015) *Black looks: Race and representation*. Routledge. https://doi.org/10.4324/9781315743226.

hooks, bell (2016a) *All about love: New visions*. William Morrow Paperbacks.

hooks, bell (2016b) *Communion: The female search for love* (reprint edn). William Morrow Paperbacks.

hooks, bell (2016c) *Salvation: Black people and love* (reprint edn). Harper Perennial.

Hope, A. (2018) 'Young children as curators', *International Journal of Art & Design Education*, 37(1), 29–40. https://doi.org/10.1111/jade.12100.

Hordge-Freeman, E. (2018) 'Bringing your whole self to research: the power of the researcher's body, emotions, and identities in ethnography', *International Journal of Qualitative Methods*, 17(1). https://doi.org/10.1177/1609406918808862.

Horton, J., Christensen, P., Kraftl, P. and Hadfield-Hill, S. (2014) 'Walking … just walking': How children and young people's everyday pedestrian practices matter. *Social & Cultural Geography*, 15(1), 94–115. https://doi.org/10.1080/14649365.2013.864782.

Houghton, C. (2006) 'Listen louder: Working with children and young people', in C. Humphreys and N. Stanley (eds), *Domestic violence and child protection: Directions for good practice* (pp 82–94). Jessica Kingsley Publishers.

Houghton, C. (2015) 'Young people's perspectives on participatory ethics: Agency, power and impact in domestic abuse research and policy-making', *Child Abuse Review*, 24(4), 235–48.

Howarth, E., Moore, T.H.M., Shaw, A.R.G., Welton, N.J., Feder, G.S., Hester, M., MacMillan, H.L. and Stanley, N. (2015) 'The effectiveness of targeted interventions for children exposed to domestic violence: Measuring success in ways that matter to children, parents and professionals', *Child Abuse Review*, 24(4), 297–310. https://doi.org/10.1002/car.2408.

Hughes, J., Chau, S. and Poff, D.C. (2011) '"They're not my favourite people": What mothers who have experienced intimate partner violence say about involvement in the child protection system', *Children and Youth Services Review*, 33(7), 1084–89. https://doi.org/10.1016/j.childyouth.2011.01.015.

Huizinga, J. (2016) *Homo ludens: A study of the play-element in culture*. Angelico Press.

Hunleth, J. (2017) *Children as caregivers: The global fight against tuberculosis and HIV in Zambia*. Rutgers University Press.

Hunleth, J. (2019) 'Zambian children's imaginal caring: On fantasy, play, and anticipation in an epidemic', *Cultural Anthropology*, 34(2), 155–86. https://doi.org/10.14506/ca34.2.01.

Hunter, K. (2019) *Institutionalised criminalisation: Black and minority ethnic children and looked after children in the youth justice system in England and Wales*. Thesis, University of Liverpool.

Hunter, K. (2022) '"Out of place": The criminalisation of Black and minority ethnic looked after children in England and Wales. *Prison Service Journal*, 258, 13–18.

Hurston, Z.N. (2010) *Their eyes were watching God*. Virago.

Icheku, V. and Graham, R. (2017) 'What social impact does exposure to domestic violence have on adolescent males? A systemic review of literature', *Journal of Healthcare Communications*, 2(1), 1–12. Available at: http://researchopen.lsbu.ac.uk/738/. (Accessed: 14 May 2017).

Jalongo, M.R. (2021) 'Pet keeping in the time of COVID-19: The canine and feline companions of young children', *Early Childhood Education Journal*, 51, 1067–77. https://doi.org/10.1007/s10643-021-01251-9.

James, A. (2013) *Socialising children*. Palgrave Macmillan.

James, A. (ed) (2014) *Constructing and reconstructing childhood: Contemporary issues in the sociological study of childhood* (3rd edn). Routledge.

James, A. and Prout, A. (eds) (2015) *Constructing and reconstructing childhood: Contemporary issues in the sociological study of childhood* (classic edn). Routledge.

James, A., Kjørholt, A.T. and Tingstad, V. (eds) (2009) *Children, food and identity in everyday life*. Palgrave Macmillan.

Jenkins, R. (2010) 'Beyond social structure', in P.J. Martin and A. Dennis (eds), *Human agents and social structures* (pp 133–51). Manchester University Press.

Jeyasingham, D. (2020) 'Entanglements with offices, information systems, laptops and phones: How agile working is influencing social workers' interactions with each other and with families', *Qualitative Social Work*, 19(3), 337–58. https://doi.org/10.1177/1473325020911697.

Johnson, G.S. (2022) 'Breach: A portolan of multimodal practice', *American Anthropologist*, 124(1), 204–11. https://doi.org/10.1111/aman.13700.

Jolly, A. and Gupta, A. (2024) 'Children and families with no recourse to public funds: Learning from case reviews', *Children & Society*, 38(1), 16–31. https://doi.org/10.1111/chso.12646.

Jordan, J. (1989) *Moving towards home: Political essays*. Virago.

Jordan, J. (2012) *Directed by desire: The collected poems of June Jordan*. Copper Canyon Press.

Jorgensen, J. (2019) 'The most beautiful of all: A quantitative approach to fairy-tale femininity', *Journal of American Folklore*, 132(523), 36–60. https://doi.org/10.5406/jamerfolk.132.523.0036.

Jupp, E., Bowlby, S.R., Franklin, J. and Hall, S.M. (2019) *The new politics of home: Housing, gender and care in times of crisis*. Available at: http://search.ebscohost.com/login.aspx?direct=true&scope=site&db=nlebk&db=nlabk&AN=2 165960. (Accessed: 10 October 2019).

Jusionyte, I. (2020) 'Writing in and from the field', in C. McGranahan (ed), *Writing anthropology* (pp 21–7). Duke University Press. https://doi.org/10.1215/9781478009160-002.

Kanyeredzi, A. (2018) *Race, culture, and gender: Black female experiences of violence and abuse* (1st edn). Palgrave Macmillan.

Kara, H. (2018) *Research ethics in the real world: Euro-Western and indigenous perspectives*. Policy Press.

Katz, C. (2001) 'Vagabond capitalism and the necessity of social reproduction', *Antipode*, 33(4), 709–28. https://doi.org/10.1111/1467-8330.00207.

Katz, E. (2014) 'Strengthening mother–child relationships as part of domestic violence recovery'. Available at: www.era.lib.ed.ac.uk/handle/1842/10423. (Accessed: 8 January 2017).

Katz, E. (2015) 'Domestic violence, children's agency and mother–child relationships: Towards a more advanced model', *Children & Society*, 29(1), 69–79. https://doi.org/10.1111/chso.12023.

Katz, E. (2016) 'Beyond the physical incident model: How children living with domestic violence are harmed by and resist regimes of coercive control', *Child Abuse Review*, 25(1), 46–59. https://doi.org/10.1002/car.2422.

Keddell, E. and Davie, G. (2018) 'Inequalities and child protection system contact in Aotearoa New Zealand: Developing a conceptual framework and research agenda', *Social Sciences*, 7(6), 89.

Kelly, L. (1987) 'The continuum of sexual violence', in J. Hanmer and M. Maynard (eds), *Women, violence and social control* (pp 46–60). Palgrave Macmillan. https://doi.org/10.1007/978-1-349-18592-4_4.

Khalili, L. (2016) 'The politics of pleasure: Promenading on the Corniche and beachgoing', *Environment and Planning D: Society and Space*, 34(4), 583–600. https://doi.org/10.1177/0263775815623538.

Kimball, E. (2016) 'Edleson revisited: Reviewing children's witnessing of domestic violence 15 years later', *Journal of Family Violence*, 31(5), 625–37. https://doi.org/10.1007/s10896-015-9786-7.

Kimber, M., Adham, S., Gill, S., McTavish, J. and MacMillan, H.L. (2018) 'The association between child exposure to intimate partner violence (IPV) and perpetration of IPV in adulthood: A systematic review', *Child Abuse & Neglect*, 76, 273–86.

Kirmani, N. (2020) 'Can fun be feminist? Gender, space and mobility in Lyari, Karachi', *South Asia: Journal of South Asian Studies*, 43(2), 319–31. https://doi.org/10.1080/00856401.2020.1716533.

Klein, J., Watson, J.L. and Bloomsbury Publishing (2019) *The handbook of food and anthropology*. Bloomsbury Academic.

Knight, A., O'Connell, R. and Brannen, J. (2014) 'The temporality of food practices: Intergenerational relations, childhood memories and mothers' food practices in working families with young children', *Families, Relationships and Societies*, 3(2), 303–18. https://doi.org/10.1332/204674313X669720.

Knight, L. (2017) 'Digital aesthetics and multidimensional play in early childhood', in C.M. Schulte (ed), *Communities of practice: Art, play, and aesthetics in early childhood* (pp 133–52). Springer Berlin Heidelberg.

Koenen, K.C., Moffitt, T.E., Caspi, A., Taylor, A. and Purcell, S. (2003) 'Domestic violence is associated with environmental suppression of IQ in young children', *Development and Psychopathology*, 15(2), 297–311. https://doi.org/10.1017/S0954579403000166.

Krasteva, G. (2021) 'Police officer filmed "choking" boy, 13, in school uniform', *Metro Newspaper*, 20 September. Available at: https://metro.co.uk/2021/09/20/met-police-officerfilmed-choking-boy-13-in-school-uniform-15287427/. (Accessed: 20 November 2022).

Lamb, K., Humphreys, C. and Hegarty, K. (2018) '"Your behaviour has consequences": Children and young people's perspectives on reparation with their fathers after domestic violence', *Children and Youth Services Review*, 88, 164–9. https://doi.org/10.1016/j.childyouth.2018.03.013.

Lamb, J., Gallagher, M.S. and Knox, J. (2019) 'On an excursion through EC1: Multimodality, ethnography and urban walking', *Qualitative Research*, 19(1), 55–70. https://doi.org/10.1177/1468794118773294.

Lapierre, S. (2008) 'Mothering in the context of domestic violence: The pervasiveness of a deficit model of mothering', *Child & Family Social Work*, 13(4), 454–63. https://doi.org/10.1111/j.1365-2206.2008.00563.x.

Lapierre, S. (2010) 'More responsibilities, less control: Understanding the challenges and difficulties involved in mothering in the context of domestic violence', *British Journal of Social Work*, 40(5), 1434–51. https://doi.org/10.1093/bjsw/bcp080.

Lather, P. (2001) 'Postbook: Working the ruins of feminist ethnography', *Signs: Journal of Women in Culture and Society*, 27(1), 199–227. https://doi.org/10.1086/495677.

Latzman, N.E., Vivolo-Kantor, A.M., Clinton-Sherrod, A.M., Casanueva, C. and Carr, C. (2017) 'Children's exposure to intimate partner violence: A systematic review of measurement strategies', *Aggression and Violent Behavior*, 37, 220–35. https://doi.org/10.1016/j.avb.2017.10.009.

Laura, C.T. (2013) 'Intimate inquiry: Love as "data" in qualitative research', *Cultural Studies ↔ Critical Methodologies*, 13(4), 289–92. https://doi.org/10.1177/1532708613487875.

Le Guin, U.K. (2002) *The dispossessed*. Gollancz.

Le Guin, U.K. (2016) *Always coming home*. Gollancz.

Lefebvre, H. (1974) *Critique of everyday life: The one-volume edition*. Verso Books.

Lefevre, M. (2018) *Communicating and engaging with children and young people* (2nd edn). Policy Press.

Lefevre, M., Tanner, K. and Luckock, B. (2008) 'Developing social work students' communication skills with children and young people: A model for the qualifying level curriculum', *Child & Family Social Work*, 13(2), 166–76. https://doi.org/10.1111/j.1365-2206.2007.00529.x.

Lefevre, M., Hickle, K., Luckock, B. and Ruch, G. (2017) 'Building trust with children and young people at risk of child sexual exploitation: The professional challenge', *British Journal of Social Work*, 47(8), 2456–73. https://doi.org/10.1093/bjsw/bcw181.

Leigh, J., Disney, T., Warwick, L., Ferguson, H., Beddoe, L. and Cooner, T.S. (2020) 'Revealing the hidden performances of social work practice: The ethnographic process of gaining access, getting into place and impression management', *Qualitative Social Work*, 20(4), 1078–95. https://doi.org/10.1177/1473325020929067.

Levendosky, A.A., Bogat, G.A. and Huth-Bocks, A.C. (2011) 'The influence of domestic violence on the development of the attachment relationship between mother and young child', *Psychoanalytic Psychology*, 28(4), 512–27. https://doi.org/10.1037/a0024561.

Levendosky, A.A., Huth-Bocks, A.C., Shapiro, D.L. and Semel, M.A. (2003) 'The impact of domestic violence on the maternal-child relationship and preschool-age children's functioning', *Journal of Family Psychology*, 17(3), 275–87. https://doi.org/10.1037/08933200.17.3.275.

Lévi-Strauss, C. (1955) *Tristes tropiques*. Penguin Books.

Liebel, M. (2020) *Decolonizing childhoods: From exclusion to dignity*. Policy Press.

Logan, T. (2017) '"If I can't have you nobody will": Explicit threats in the context of coercive control', *Violence and Victims*, 32(1), 126–40. https://doi.org/10.1891/0886-6708.VV-D-14-00187.

Lomax, H. (2012) 'Contested voices? Methodological tensions in creative visual research with children', *International Journal of Social Research Methodology*, 15(2), 105–17. https://doi.org/10.1080/13645579.2012.649408.

Lomax, H. (2015) 'Seen and heard? Ethics and agency in participatory visual research with children, young people and families', *Families, Relationships and Societies*, 4(3), 493–502. http://dx.doi.org.gold.idm.oclc.org/10.1332/204674315X14326324216211.

Lomax, H. (2020) 'Multimodal visual methods for seeing with children', in E.J. White (ed), *Seeing the world through children's eyes: Visual methodologies and approaches to research in the early years* (pp 55–71). Brill Sense.

Lorde, A. (2020) *The selected works of Audre Lorde* (1st edn). W.W. Norton & Company.

Luckock, B., Lefevre, M. and Tanner, K. (2007) 'Teaching and learning communication with children and young people: Developing the qualifying social work curriculum in a changing policy context', *Child & Family Social Work*, 12(2), 192–201. https://doi.org/10.1111/j.1365-2206.2006.00465.x.

Lugones, M. (1987) 'Playfulness, "world"-travelling, and loving perception', *Hypatia*, 2(2), 3–19. https://doi.org/10.1111/j.1527-2001.1987.tb01062.x.

Lundy, L. (2007) '"Voice" is not enough: Conceptualising Article 12 of the United Nations Convention on the Rights of the Child', *British Educational Research Journal*, 33(6), 927–42. https://doi.org/10.1080/01411920701657033.

Luttrell, W. (2020) *Children framing childhoods: Working-class kids' visions of care*. Policy Press.

Lyle, G. and Britten, T. (1983) *What's love got to do with it* [Recorded by Tina Turner]. *On Private dancer* [Album]. Capitol Records.

Macdonald, G.S. (2017) 'Hearing children's voices? Including children's perspectives on their experiences of domestic violence in welfare reports prepared for the English courts in private family law proceedings', *Child Abuse & Neglect*, 65, 1–13. https://doi.org/10.1016/j.chiabu.2016.12.013.

MacLure, M., Holmes, R., MacRae, C. and Jones, L. (2010) Animating classroom ethnography: Overcoming video-fear. *International Journal of Qualitative Studies in Education*, 23(5), 543–56. https://doi.org/10.1080/09518391003645370.

Madianou, M. and Miller, D. (2012) *Migration and new media: Transnational families and polymedia*. Routledge.

Mahmood, S. (2012) *Politics of piety: The Islamic revival and the feminist subject*. Princeton University Press.

Marshall, D.J. (2013) '"All the beautiful things": Trauma, aesthetics and the politics of Palestinian childhood', *Space and Polity*, 17(1), 53–73. https://doi.org/10.1080/13562576.2013.780713.

Marshall, D.J. (2015) '"We have a place to play, but someone else controls it": Girls' mobility and access to space in a Palestinian refugee camp', *Global Studies of Childhood*, 5(2), 191–205. https://doi.org/10.1177/2043610615586105.

Mascheroni, G. (2020) 'Datafied childhoods: Contextualising datafication in everyday life', *Current Sociology*, 68(6), 798–813. https://doi.org/10.1177/0011392118807534.

Massey, D.B. (2004) 'Geographies of responsibility', *Geografiska Annaler: Series B, Human Geography*, 86(1), 5–18. https://doi.org/10.1111/j.0435-3684.2004.00150.x.

Massey, D.B. (2005) *For space*. SAGE.

McCarthy, A. (2021) *Children and NGOs in India: Development as storytelling and performance*. Routledge.

McGavock, L. and Spratt, T. (2016) 'Children exposed to domestic violence: Using adverse childhood experience scores to inform service response', *British Journal of Social Work*, 47(4), 1128–46. https://doi.org/10.1093/bjsw/bcw073.

McGee, C. (2000) *Childhood experiences of domestic violence*. Jessica Kingsley Publishers.

McGregor, R.S. (1993) *The Oxford Hindi–English dictionary*. Oxford University Press.

McKittrick, K. (2011) 'On plantations, prisons, and a black sense of place', *Social & Cultural Geography*, 12(8), 947–63. https://doi.org/10.1080/14649365.2011.624280.

McKittrick, K. (2014) *Sylvia Wynter: On being human as praxis*. Duke University Press.

Meiners, E.R. (2016) *For the children? Protecting innocence in a carceral state*. University of Minnesota Press.

Mersky, J.P., Janczewski, C.E. and Topitzes, J. (2017) 'Rethinking the measurement of adversity: Moving toward second-generation research on adverse childhood experiences', *Child Maltreatment*, 22(1), 58–68. https://doi.org/10.1177/1077559516679513.

Mezey, G., Bacchus, L., Bewley, S. and White, S. (2005) 'Domestic violence, lifetime trauma and psychological health of childbearing women', *BJOG: An International Journal of Obstetrics & Gynaecology*, 112(2), 197–204.

Mezzadra, S. and Neilson, B. (2013) *Border as method, or, the multiplication of labor*. Duke University Press.

Miller, D. (ed) (2005) *Materiality*. Duke University Press.

Miller, D. (2008) *The comfort of things*. Polity Press.

Miller, D. (2010) *Stuff*. Polity Press.

Miller, P. (2005) 'Useful and priceless children in contemporary welfare states', *Social Politics: International Studies in Gender, State & Society*, 12(1), 3–41. https://doi.org/10.1093/sp/jxi001.

Mishra, V. (1996) 'The diasporic imaginary: Theorizing the Indian diaspora', *Textual Practice*, 10(3), 421–47. https://doi.org/10.1080/09502369608582254.

Mitchell, C. and Reid-Walsh, J. (2002) *Researching children's popular culture: The cultural spaces of childhood*. Routledge.

Mizen, P. and Ofosu-Kusi, Y. (2010) 'Asking, giving, receiving: Friendship as survival strategy among Accra's street children', *Childhood*, 17(4), 441–54. https://doi.org/10.1177/0907568209350511.

Moffatt, S., Lawson, S., Patterson, R., Holding, E., Dennison, A., Sowden, S. and Brown, J. (2016) 'A qualitative study of the impact of the UK "bedroom tax": Table 1. *Journal of Public Health*, 38(2), 197–205. https://doi.org/10.1093/pubmed/fdv031.

Mohanty, C.T. (1984) 'Under western eyes: Feminist scholarship and colonial discourses', *Boundary 2*, 12(3), 333–58.

Mohanty, C.T. (2003) '"Under western eyes" revisited: Feminist solidarity through anticapitalist struggles', *Signs: Journal of Women in Culture and Society*, 28(2), 499–535. https://doi.org/10.1086/342914.

Morrison, F. (2015) '"All over now?" The ongoing relational consequences of domestic abuse through children's contact arrangements', *Child Abuse Review*, 24(4), 274–84. https://doi.org/10.1002/car.2409.

Morrison, F., Tisdall, E.K.M. and Callaghan, J.E.M. (2020) 'Manipulation and domestic abuse in contested contact: Threats to children's participation rights', *Family Court Review*, 58(2), 403–16. https://doi.org/10.1111/fcre.12479.

Moss, D. (2010) 'Memory, space and time: Researching children's lives', *Childhood*, 17(4), 530–44. https://doi.org/10.1177/0907568209345611.

Moynagh, M. (2011) 'Human rights, child-soldier narratives, and the problem of form', *Research in African Literatures*, 42(4), 39. https://doi.org/10.2979/reseafrilite.42.4.39.

Mullender, A., Hague, G., Imam, U.F., Kelly, L., Malos, E. and Regan, L. (2002) *Children's perspectives on domestic violence*. SAGE.

Munro, E. (2004) 'The impact of audit on social work practice', *British Journal of Social Work*, 34(8), 1075–95.

Munro, E. (2011) *The Munro review of child protection: Final report, a child-centred system*. The Stationery Office.

Murris, K. (2013) 'The epistemic challenge of hearing child's voice', *Studies in Philosophy and Education*, 32(3), 245–59. https://doi.org/10.1007/s11217-012-9349-9.

Myhill, A. and Kelly, L. (2019) 'Counting with understanding? What is at stake in debates on researching domestic violence', *Criminology & Criminal Justice*, 21(3), 280–96. https://doi.org/10.1177/1748895819863098.

Neumann, M.M. and Herodotou, C. (2020) 'Evaluating YouTube videos for young children', *Education and Information Technologies*, 25, 4459–75. https://doi.org/10.1007/s10639-020-10183-7.

Nguyen, J. (2016) 'Minecraft and the building blocks of creative individuality', *Configurations*, 24(4), 471–500. https://doi.org/10.1353/con.2016.0030.

Nolas, S.-M. (2015) 'Children's participation, childhood publics and social change: A review', *Children & Society*, 29(2), 157–67. https://doi.org/10.1111/chso.12108.

Nolas, S.-M. and Varvantakis, C. (2019) 'Field notes for amateurs', *Social Analysis*, 63(3), 130–48. https://doi.org/10.3167/sa.2019.630308.

Nolas, S.-M. and Varvantakis, C. (2021) '"This parenting lark": Idiomatic ways of knowing and an epistemology of paying adequate attention', in F. Martínez, L.D. Puppo and M.D. Frederiksen (eds), *Methodologies: Unlearning, not-knowing and ethnographic limits* (1st edn, pp 45–60). Routledge. https://doi.org/10.4324/9781003103646.

Nolas, S.-M., Varvantakis, C. and Aruldoss, V. (2017) 'Talking politics in everyday family lives', *Contemporary Social Science*, 12(1–2), 68–83. https://doi.org/10.1080/21582041.2017.1330965.

Nolas, S.-M., Aruldoss, V. and Varvantakis, C. (2018) 'Learning to listen: Exploring the idioms of childhood', *Sociological Research Online*, 24(2). https://doi.org/10.1177/1360780418811972.

Nxumalo, F. (2020) 'Situating Indigenous and Black childhoods in the anthropocene', in A. Cutter-Mackenzie-Knowles, K. Malone and E. Barratt Hacking (eds), *Research handbook on childhood nature* (pp 535–56). Springer International Publishing. https://doi.org/10.1007/978-3-31967 286-1_37.

Nxumalo, F. and ross, k.m. (2019) 'Envisioning Black space in environmental education for young children', *Race Ethnicity and Education*, 22(4), 502–24. https://doi.org/10.1080/13613324.2019.1592837.

Oakley, A. (1990) *Housewife*. Penguin Books.

Oakley, A. (2005) *The Ann Oakley reader: Gender, women, and social science*. Policy Press.

Oakley, A. (2019) *The sociology of housework*. Policy Press.

O'Dell, L., Brownlow, C. and Bertilsdotter-Rosqvist, H. (eds) (2017) *Different childhoods* (1st edn). Routledge.

Ofsted (2017) *The multi-agency response to children living with domestic abuse: Prevent, protect and repair*. Available at: https://assets.publishing.service.gov.uk/government/uploads/system/uploads/attachment_da ta/file/1062330/JTAI_domestic_abuse_18_Sept_2017.pdf. (Accessed: 2 December 2022).

Øverlien, C. (2010) 'Children exposed to domestic violence: Conclusions from the literature and challenges ahead', *Journal of Social Work*, 10(1), 80–97. https://doi.org/10.1177/1468017309350663.

Øverlien, C. (2011) 'Abused women with children or children of abused women? A study of conflicting perspectives at women's refuges in Norway', *Child & Family Social Work*, 16(1), 71–80. https://doi.org/10.1111/j.1365-2206.2010.00715.x.

Øverlien, C. (2013) 'The children of patriarchal terrorism', *Journal of Family Violence*, 28(3), 277–87. https://doi.org/10.1007/s10896-013-9498-9.

Øverlien, C. (2014) '"He didn't mean to hit mom, I think": Positioning, agency and point in adolescents' narratives about domestic violence', *Child & Family Social Work*, 19(2), 156–64. https://doi.org/10.1111/j.1365-2206.2012.00886.x.

Øverlien, C. (2017) '"Do you want to do some arm wrestling?" Children's strategies when experiencing domestic violence and the meaning of age', *Child & Family Social Work*, 22(2), 680–8. https://doi.org/10.1111/cfs.12283.

Øverlien, C. and Holt, S. (2018) 'Including children and adolescents in domestic violence research', in S. Holt, C. Øverlien and J. Devaney (eds), *Responding to domestic violence: Emerging challenges for policy, practice and research in Europe*. Jessica Kingsley Publishers.

Øverlien, C. and Holt, S. (2021) 'Qualitative interviews with children and adolescents who have experienced domestic violence and abuse', in J. Devaney, C. Bradbury-Jones, R.J. Macy, C. Øverlien and S. Holt (eds), *The Routledge international handbook of domestic violence and abuse* (pp 657–70). Routledge.

Pacini-Ketchabaw, V. (2012) 'Postcolonial entanglements: Unruling stories', *Child & Youth Services*, 33(3–4), 303–16. https://doi.org/10.1080/0145935X.2012.745790.

Pacini-Ketchabaw, V. and Blaise, M. (2021) 'Feminist ethicality in child–animal research: Worlding through complex stories', *Children's Geographies*, 1–12. https://doi.org/10.1080/14733285.2021.1907311.

Page, T. (2017) 'Vulnerable writing as a feminist methodological practice', *Feminist Review*, 115(1), 13–29. https://doi.org/10.1057/s41305-017-0028-0.

Pandian, A. (2019) *A possible anthropology: Methods for uneasy times*. Duke University Press.

Parton, N. (2011) 'Child protection and safeguarding in England: Changing and competing conceptions of risk and their implications for social work', *British Journal of Social Work*, 41(5), 854–75. https://doi.org/10.1093/bjsw/bcq119.

Parviainen, J., Koski, A. and Torkkola, S. (2021) '"Building a ship while sailing it": Epistemic humility and the temporality of non-knowledge in political decision-making on COVID-19', *Social Epistemology*, 35(3), 232–44. https://doi.org/10.1080/02691728.2021.1882610.

Pearce, J. (ed) (2019) *Child sexual exploitation: Why theory matters*. Policy Press.

Peck, M.S. (2006) *The road less travelled: A new psychology of love, traditional values and spiritual growth*. Arrow Books.

Peckover, S. (2014) 'Domestic abuse, safeguarding children and public health: Towards an analysis of discursive forms and surveillant techniques in contemporary UK policy and practice', *British Journal of Social Work*, 44(7), 1770–87. https://doi.org/10.1093/bjsw/bct042.

Peckover, S. and Golding, B. (2017) 'Domestic abuse and safeguarding children: Critical issues for multiagency work', *Child Abuse Review*, 26(1), 40–50. https://doi.org/10.1002/car.2392.

Peltonen, K., Ellonen, N., Larsen, H.B. and Helweg-Larsen, K. (2010) Parental violence and adolescent mental health. *European Child & Adolescent Psychiatry*, 19(11), 813–22.

Pernebo, K. and Almqvist, K. (2016) 'Young children's experiences of participating in group treatment for children exposed to intimate partner violence: A qualitative study', *Clinical Child Psychology and Psychiatry*, 21(1), 119–32. https://doi.org/10.1177/1359104514558432.

Phadke, S. (2020) 'Defending frivolous fun: Feminist acts of claiming public spaces in South Asia', *South Asia: Journal of South Asian Studies*, 43(2), 281–93. https://doi.org/10.1080/00856401.2020.1703245.

Phadke, S., Khan, S. and Ranade, S. (2011) *Why loiter? Women and risk on Mumbai streets*. Penguin Books.

Piaget, J. (2013) *Play, dreams and imitation in childhood*. Taylor and Francis. Available at: https://public.ebookcentral.proquest.com/choice/publicfullrecord.aspx?p=1273074. (Accessed: 27 April 2020).

Pierlejewski, M. (2020) 'The data-doppelganger and the cyborg-self: Theorising the datafication of education', *Pedagogy, Culture & Society*, 28(3), 463–75. https://doi.org/10.1080/14681366.2019.1653357.

Pierlejewski, M. (2021) '"I feel like two different teachers": The split self of teacher subjectivity', *Pedagogy, Culture & Society*, 31(3), 515–30. https://doi.org/10.1080/14681366.2021.1924845.

Pink, S. (2004) *Home truths: Gender, domestic objects and everyday life* (English edn). Berg.

Pink, S. (2011) 'Multimodality, multisensoriality and ethnographic knowing: Social semiotics and the phenomenology of perception', *Qualitative Research*, 11(3), 261–76. https://doi.org/10.1177/1468794111399835.

Pink, S. (2012) *Situating everyday life: Practices and places*. SAGE.

Pink, S. (2013) *Doing visual ethnography* (3rd edn). SAGE.

Pink, S. (2015) *Doing sensory ethnography* (2nd edn). SAGE.

Pink, S., Horst, H.A., Postill, J., Hjorth, L., Lewis, T. and Tacchi, J. (eds) (2016) *Digital ethnography: Principles and practice*. SAGE.

Playing Out (2021) *Make your street a place to play*. Available at: https://playingout.net. (Accessed: 9 December 2022).

Plowman, L. and Stevenson, O. (2012) 'Using mobile phone diaries to explore children's everyday lives', *Childhood*, 19(4), 539–53. https://doi.org/10.1177/0907568212440014.

Plowman, L. and Stevenson, O. (2013) 'Exploring the quotidian in young children's lives at home', *Home Cultures*, 10(3), 329–47. https://doi.org/10.2752/175174213X13739735973381.

Plowman, L., Stephen, C. and McPake, J. (2010) *Growing up with technology: Young children learning in a digital world*. Routledge.

Potter, J. and Cowan, K. (2020) 'Playground as meaning-making space: Multimodal making and re-making of meaning in the (virtual) playground', *Global Studies of Childhood*, 10(3), 248–63. https://doi.org/10.1177/2043610620941527.

Puig de la Bellacasa, M. (2017) *Matters of care: Speculative ethics in more than human worlds*. University of Minnesota Press.

Quashie, K.E. (2021) *Black aliveness, or a poetics of being*. Duke University Press.

Radford, L. and Hester, M. (2006) *Mothering through domestic violence*. Jessica Kingsley Publishers.

Radford, L. and Hester, M. (2015) 'More than a mirage? Safe contact for children and young people who have been exposed to domestic violence', in N. Stanley and C. Humphreys (eds), *Domestic violence and protecting children: New thinking and approaches* (pp 112–30). Jessica Kingsley Publishers. Available at: www.jkp.com/uk/domesticviolence-and-protecting-children.html. (Accessed: 29 November 2017).

Richards, R. (2001) 'A new aesthetic for environmental awareness: Chaos theory, the beauty of nature, and our broader humanistic identity', *Journal of Humanistic Psychology*, 41(2), 59–95. https://doi.org/10.1177/0022167801412006.

Richie, B.E. (1996) *Compelled to crime: The gender entrapment of battered Black women*. Routledge.

Richie, B.E. (2012) *Arrested justice: Black women, violence, and America's prison nation*. New York University Press.

Robertson, L. and Wainwright, J.P. (2020) 'Black boys' and young men's experiences with criminal justice and desistance in England and Wales: A literature review', *Genealogy*, 4(2), 50. https://doi.org/10.3390/genealogy4020050.

Rohde, R. (1998) 'How we see each other: Subjectivity, photography and ethnographic re/vision', in W. Hartmann, J. Silvester and P. Hayes (eds), *The colonising camera: Photographs in the making of Namibian history* (pp 188–204). UCT Press, Out of Africa and Ohio University Press.

Rose, M. (2020) 'Pedestrian practices: Walking from the mundane to the marvellous', in H. Holmes and S.M. Hall (eds), *Mundane methods* (pp 211–29). Manchester University Press.

Rosen, R. (2017) 'Play as activism? Early childhood and (inter)generational politics', *Contemporary Social Science*, 12(1–2), 110–22. https://doi.org/10.1080/21582041.2017.1324174.

Rosen, R. and Khan, S. (2024) 'Racialising age in the UK's border regime: A case for abolishing age assessment', *Race & Class*, 66(2), 43–62. https://doi.org/10.1177/03063968241238603.

Rosenthal, D.M., Ucci, M., Heys, M., Hayward, A. and Lakhanpaul, M. (2020) 'Impacts of COVID-19 on vulnerable children in temporary accommodation in the UK', *The Lancet Public Health*, 5(5), e241–2. https://doi.org/10.1016/S2468-2667(20)30080-3.

Sahlberg, P. (2019) *Let the children play: How more play will save our schools and help children thrive*. Oxford University Press.

Saito, Y. (2017) *Aesthetics of the familiar: Everyday life and world-making* (1st edn). Oxford University Press.

Sanders-McDonagh, E., Neville, L. and Nolas, S.-M. (2016) 'From pillar to post: Understanding the victimisation of women and children who experience domestic violence in an age of austerity', *Feminist Review*, 112(1), 60–76.

Sanderud, J.R., Gurholt, K.P. and Moe, V.F. (2020) '"Winter children": An ethnographically inspired study of children being-and-becoming well-versed in snow and ice', *Sport, Education and Society*, 25(8), 960–71. https://doi.org/10.1080/13573322.2019.1678124.

Save the Children Fund (2021) '"Its time to play": Make up for those lost lockdown moments'. Available at: www.savethechildren.org.uk/what-we-do/moments-of-play. (Accessed: 26 October 2022).

Scott, S. (2009) *Making sense of everyday life*. Polity Press.

Seeberg, M.L. and Goździak, E.M. (2019) *Contested childhoods: Growing up in migrancy, migration, governance, identities*. Springer.

Seow, J. (2019) 'Black girls and dolls navigating race, class, and gender in Toronto', *Girlhood Studies*, 12(2), 48–64. https://doi.org/10.3167/ghs.2019.120205.

Seymour, C. (2019) *The myth of international protection: War and survival in Congo*. University of California Press.

Shalhoub-Kevorkian, N. (2023) *Incarcerated childhood and the politics of unchilding*. Cambridge University Press.

Shalhoub-Kevorkian, N. (2024) 'Ashla'a: Scattered body parts and the culmination of genocidal unchilding in Gaza', 18th Tom Hurndall Memorial Lecture, Cross Street Chapel, Manchester, 19 March.

Shapiro, J. (2020) *The new childhood: Raising kids to thrive in a digitally connected world*. Hodder & Stoughton.

Sharpe, C.E. (2016) *In the wake: On Blackness and being*. Duke University Press.

Sheehi, L. and Sheehi, S. (2022) *Psychoanalysis under occupation: Practicing resistance in Palestine*. Routledge.

Shepherd, E., Hoyle, V., Lomas, E., Flinn, A. and Sexton, A. (2020) 'Towards a humancentred participatory approach to child social care recordkeeping', *Archival Science*, 20(4), 307–25. https://doi.org/10.1007/s10502-020-09338-9.

Shuster, S.M. and Westbrook, L. (2022) 'Reducing the joy deficit in sociology: A study of transgender joy', *Social Problems*, 71(3), 791–809. https://doi.org/10.1093/socpro/spac034.

Sidebotham, P., Brandon, M., Bailey, S., Belderson, P., Dodsworth, J., Garstang, J. and Sorenson, P. (2016) *Pathway to harm, pathways to protection: A triennial analysis of serious case reviews 2011–2014*. Department for Education.

Siegel, J.P. (2013) 'Breaking the links in intergenerational violence: An emotional regulation perspective', *Family Process*, 52(2), 163–78. https://doi.org/10.1111/famp.12023.

Sloan-Lynch, J. (2012) 'Domestic abuse as terrorism', *Hypatia*, 27(4), 774–90. https://doi.org/10.1111/j.1527-2001.2011.01250.x.

Smith, L.T. (1999) *Decolonizing methodologies: Research and Indigenous peoples* (1st edn). Zed Books.

Smith, L.T. (2012) *Decolonizing methodologies: Research and Indigenous peoples* (2nd edn). Zed Books.

Smithson, R. and Gibson, M. (2017) 'Less than human: A qualitative study into the experience of parents involved in the child protection system', *Child & Family Social Work*, 22(2), 565–74. https://doi.org/10.1111/cfs.12270.

Spillers, H.J. (2018) 'Fugitive feminism'. Interview with Gail Lewis, Institute of Contemporary Art, London, 9 June.

Stanley, N. (2011) *Children experiencing domestic violence: a research review*. Research in Practice Dartington.

Stanley, N. and Humphreys, C. (eds) (2015) *Domestic violence and protecting children: New thinking and approaches*. Jessica Kingsley Publishers.

Stanley, N. and Humphreys, C. (2017) 'Identifying the key components of a "whole family" intervention for families experiencing domestic violence and abuse', *Journal of Gender-Based Violence*, 1(1), 99–115. https://doi.org/10.1332/239868017X14913081639164.

Stanley, N., Palmary, I. and Chantler, K. (2017) 'Introduction to special issue on "Violence against women and children in diverse contexts"', *Families, Relationships and Societies*, 6(2), 163–6. https://doi.org/10.1332/204674317X14937364476868.

Stanley, N., Chantler, K. and Robbins, R. (2018) 'Children and domestic homicide', *British Journal of Social Work*, 49(1), 59–76. https://doi.org/10.1093/bjsw/bcy024.

Stanley, N., Miller, P., Richardson Foster, H. and Thomson, G. (2011) 'A stop–start response: Social services' interventions with children and families notified following domestic violence incidents', *British Journal of Social Work*, 41(2), 296–313. https://doi.org/10.1093/bjsw/bcq071.

Stark, E. (2009) *Coercive control: The entrapment of women in personal life.* Oxford University Press.

Stearns, P. (2022) 'Pets and emotion in modern history', in K. Barclay and P.N. Stearns (eds), *The Routledge history of emotions in the modern world* (1st edn, pp 295–308). Routledge. https://doi.org/10.4324/9781003023326.

Stewart, K. (2007) *Ordinary affects.* Duke University Press.

Stewart, S. (2020) 'A mother's love knows no bounds: Exploring "good mother" expectations for mothers involved with children's services due to their partner violence', *Qualitative Social Work*, 20(3), 681–702. https://doi.org/10.1177/1473325020902249.

Stodulka, T. (2017) *Coming of age on the streets of Java: Coping with marginality, stigma and illness.* transcript.

Strathern, M. (1999) *Property, substance, and effect: Anthropological essays on persons and things.* Athlone Press.

Sutton, D.E. (2001) *Remembrance of repasts: An anthropology of food and memory.* Berg.

Taillieu, T.L., Brownridge, D.A., Sareen, J. and Afifi, T.O. (2016) 'Childhood emotional maltreatment and mental disorders: Results from a nationally representative adult sample from the United States', *Child Abuse & Neglect*, 59, 1–12. https://doi.org/10.1016/j.chiabu.2016.07.005.

Taylor, A. and Pacini-Ketchabaw, V. (2015) 'Learning with children, ants, and worms in the Anthropocene: Towards a common world pedagogy of multispecies vulnerability', *Pedagogy, Culture & Society*, 23(4), 507–29. https://doi.org/10.1080/14681366.2015.1039050.

Taylor, A. and Pacini-Ketchabaw, V. (2017) 'Kids, raccoons, and roos: Awkward encounters and mixed affects', *Children's Geographies*, 15(2), 131–45. https://doi.org/10.1080/14733285.2016.1199849.

Taylor, A. and Pacini-Ketchabaw, V. (2020) *The common worlds of children and animals: Relational ethics for entangled lives.* Routledge.

Templeton, T.N. (2020) '"That street is taking us to home": Young children's photographs of public spaces', *Children's Geographies*, 18(1), 1–15. https://doi.org/10.1080/14733285.2018.1550573.

Thiara, R.K. and Humphreys, C. (2015) 'Absent presence: The ongoing impact of men's violence on the mother–child relationship', *Child & Family Social Work*, 22. Available at: www.researchgate.net/profile/Cathy_Humphreys/publication/270597181_Absent_pre sence_the_ongoing_impact_of_men's_violence_on_the_motherchild_relationship/links/54b4b4d90cf26833efd028db.pdf. (Accessed: 25 May 2017).

Thompson, J. (2011) *Performance affects: Applied theatre and the end of effect* (paperback edn). Palgrave Macmillan.

Thorne, B. (1987) 'RE-VISIONING WOMEN AND SOCIAL CHANGE: Where are the children?', *Gender & Society*, 1(1), 85–109. https://doi.org/10.1177/089124387001001005.

Torres, J. (2021) 'Philia: The biological foundations of Aristotle's ethics', *History and Philosophy of the Life Sciences*, 43(4), 119. https://doi.org/10.1007/s40656021-00469-5.

Treanor, M.C. (2020) 'How COVID-19 crisis measures reveal the conflation between poverty and adversity', *Scottish Affairs*, 29(4), 475–92. https://doi.org/10.3366/scot.2020.0338.

Tronto, J.C. (1993) *Moral boundaries: A political argument for an ethic of care*. Routledge.

Tuck, E. (2009) 'Suspending damage: A letter to communities', *Harvard Educational Review*, 79(3), 409–28. https://doi.org/10.17763/haer.79.3.n0016675661t3n15.

Tuck, E. (2010) 'Breaking up with Deleuze: Desire and valuing the irreconcilable', *International Journal of Qualitative Studies in Education*, 23(5), 635–50. https://doi.org/10.1080/09518398.2010.500633.

Tuck, E. (2013) 'Commentary: Decolonizing methodologies 15 years later', *AlterNative: An International Journal of Indigenous Peoples*, 9(4), 365–72. https://doi.org/10.1177/117718011300900407.

Tuck, E. and Yang, K.W. (2014) 'Unbecoming claims: Pedagogies of refusal in qualitative research', *Qualitative Inquiry*, 20(6), 811–18. https://doi.org/10.1177/1077800414530265.

Turner, T. (1984) *What's love got to do with it* [Song]. On *Private dancer*. Capitol Records.

Turner, V. (2002) *The forest of symbols: Aspects of Ndembu ritual*. Cornell University Press.

Turner, V.W. (1995) *The ritual process: Structure and anti-structure*. Aldine de Gruyter.

Twum-Danso, A. (2009a) 'Reciprocity, respect and responsibility: The 3Rs underlying parent–child relationships in Ghana and the implications for children's rights', *International Journal of Children's Rights*, 17(3), 415–32. https://doi.org/10.1163/157181809X430337.

Twum-Danso, A. (2009b) 'Situating participatory methodologies in context: The impact of culture on adult–child interactions in research and other projects', *Children's Geographies*, 7(4), 379–89. https://doi.org/10.1080/14733280903234436.

Twum-Danso Imoh, A. (2022) 'Framing reciprocal obligations within intergenerational relations in Ghana through the lens of the mutuality of duty and dependence', *Childhood*, 29(3), 439–54. https://doi.org/10.1177/09075682221103343.

Twum-Danso Imoh, A. (2024) 'Challenging Global North–Global South binaries: Implications for childhood studies', in J. Wyn, H. Cahill and H. Cuervo (eds), *Handbook of children and youth studies* (pp 725–39). Springer Nature Singapore. https://doi.org/10.1007/978-981-99-8606-4_89.

Twum-Danso Imoh, A. and Okyere, S. (2020) 'Towards a more holistic understanding of child participation: Foregrounding the experiences of children in Ghana and Nigeria', *Children and Youth Services Review*, 112, 104927. https://doi.org/10.1016/j.childyouth.2020.104927.

Twum-Danso Imoh, A., Bourdillon, M. and Meichsner, S. (2019) 'Introduction: Exploring children's lives beyond the binary of the Global North and Global South', in A. Twum-Danso Imoh, M. Bourdillon and S. Meichsner (eds), *Global childhoods beyond the North–South divide* (pp 1–10). Springer International Publishing. https://doi.org/10.1007/978-3-319-95543-8_1.

Twum-Danso Imoh, A., Tetteh, P.M. and Yaa Oduro, G. (2022) 'Searching for the everyday in African childhoods: Introduction', *Journal of the British Academy*, 10s2, 1–11. https://doi.org/10.5871/jba/010s2.001.

Uprichard, E. (2008) 'Children as "being and becomings": Children, childhood and temporality', *Children & Society*, 22(4), 303–13.

Vanwesenbeeck, I., Hudders, L. and Ponnet, K. (2020) 'Understanding the YouTube generation: How preschoolers process television and YouTube advertising', *Cyberpsychology, Behavior, and Social Networking*, 23(6), 426–32. https://doi.org/10.1089/cyber.2019.0488.

Varvantakis, C. and Nolas, S.-M. (2019) 'Metaphors we experiment with in multimodal ethnography', *International Journal of Social Research Methodology*, 22(4), 365–78. https://doi.org/10.1080/13645579.2019.1574953.

Varvantakis, C. and Nolas, S.-M. (2021) 'Touching heritage: Embodied politics in children's photography', *Visual Communication*, 23(1), 119–41. https://doi.org/10.1177/14703572211039258.

Varvantakis, C., Nolas, S.-M. and Aruldoss, V. (2019) 'Photography, politics and childhood: Exploring children's multimodal relations with the public sphere', *Visual Studies*, 34(3), 266–80. https://doi.org/10.1080/1472586X.2019.1691049.

Varvantakis, C., Dragonas, T., Askouni, N. and Nolas, S.-M. (2019) 'Grounding childhood (trans)national identities in the everyday', *Children & Society*, 33(1), 68–81. https://doi.org/10.1111/chso.12299.

Velicu, I. and García-López, G. (2018) 'Thinking the commons through Ostrom and Butler: Boundedness and vulnerability', *Theory, Culture & Society*, 35(6), 55–73. https://doi.org/10.1177/0263276418757315.

Vera-Gray, F. (2016) *Men's intrusion, women's embodiment: A critical analysis of street harassment*. Routledge. https://doi.org/10.4324/9781315668109.

Vergès, F. (2021) *A decolonial feminism*. A.J. Bohrer (trans). Pluto Press.

Vizard, P., Obolenskaya, P. and Burchardt, T. (2019) 'Child poverty amongst young carers in the UK: Prevalence and trends in the wake of the financial crisis, economic downturn and onset of austerity', *Child Indicators Research*, 12(5), 1831–54. https://doi.org/10.1007/s12187-018-9608-6.

Wainright, O. (2021) 'Set children free: Are playgrounds a form of incarceration?', *The Guardian*, 25 February. Available at: www.theguardian.com/artanddesign/2021/feb/25/set-children-free-are-playgrounds-aform-of-incarceration. (Accessed: 28 October 2022).

Walby, S. (2015) *Crisis*. Polity Press.

Walby, S. and Towers, J. (2017) 'Measuring violence to end violence: Mainstreaming gender', *Journal of Gender-Based Violence*, 1(1), 11–31. https://doi.org/10.1332/239868017X14913081639155.

Walby, S. and Towers, J. (2018) 'Untangling the concept of coercive control: Theorizing domestic violent crime', *Criminology & Criminal Justice*, 18(1), 7–28. https://doi.org/10.1177/1748895817743541.

Walkerdine, V. and Pini, M. (2021) 'Girls on film: Video diaries as "autoethnographies"', in P. Reavey (ed), *A handbook of visual methods in psychology: Using and interpreting images in qualitative research* (2nd edn, pp 187–201). Routledge.

Walby, S., Towers, J., Francis, B., Balderston, S., Corradi, C., Heiskanen, M., Helweg-Larsen, K., Kelly, L., Mergaert, L., Olive, P., Palmer, E., Stöckl, H. and Strid, S. (2016) *The concept and measurement of violence against women and men*. Policy Press.

Walton, S. (2021) *Everybody needs beauty: In search of the nature cure*. Bloomsbury Circus.

Wastell, D. and White, S. (2017) *Blinded by science: The social implications of epigenetics and neuroscience*. Policy Press.

Watson, A. and Lupton, D. (2022) 'Remote fieldwork in homes during the COVID-19 pandemic: Video-call ethnography and map drawing methods', *International Journal of Qualitative Methods*, 21. https://doi.org/10.1177/16094069221078376.

Watts, L. (2020) 'Expansions: Keynote speech day 3' (conference). Research Interrupted: Methods and (Re)Design of Fieldwork in Anthropology and STS, ETHOSLab, IT University of Copenhagen, Denmark, 17 June.

Welcome, L.A. and Thomas, D.A. (2021) 'Abstraction, witnessing, and repair; Or, how multimodal research can destabilize the coloniality of the gaze', *Multimodality & Society*, 1(3), 391–406. https://doi.org/10.1177/26349795211042771.

Wells, K. and Montgomery, H. (2014) 'Everyday violence and social recognition', in K. Wells, E. Burman, H. Montgomery and A. Watson (eds), *Childhood, youth and violence in global contexts: Research and practice in dialogue* (pp 1–15). Palgrave Macmillan. https://doi.org/10.1057/9781137322609_1.

Westbrook, L. (2021) *Unlivable lives: Violence and identity in transgender activism*. University of California Press.

Williamson, T.L. (2017) *Scandalize my name: Black feminist practice and the making of black social life* (1st edn). Fordham University Press.

Willis, D., Hawkins, J.W., Pearce, C.W., Phalen, J., Keet, M. and Singer, C. (2010) 'Children who witness violence: What services do they need to heal?', *Issues in Mental Health Nursing*, 31(9), 552–60.

Winter, K., Cree, V., Hallett, S., Hadfield, M., Ruch, G., Morrison, F. and Holland, S. (2017) 'Exploring communication between social workers, children and young people', *British Journal of Social Work*, 47(5), 1427–44. https://doi.org/10.1093/bjsw/bcw083.

Wohlwill, J.F. (1976) 'Environmental aesthetics: The environment as a source of affect', in I. Altman and J.F. Wohlwill (eds), *Human behavior and environment* (pp 37–86). Springer US. https://doi.org/10.1007/978-1-4684-2550-5_2.

Woodiwiss, J. (2014) 'Beyond a single story: The importance of separating "harm" from "wrongfulness" and "sexual innocence" from "childhood" in contemporary narratives of childhood sexual abuse', *Sexualities*, 17(1–2), 139–58. https://doi.org/10.1177/1363460713511104.

Woodiwiss, J. (2018) 'From one girl to "three girls": The importance of separating agency from blame (and harm from wrongfulness) in narratives of childhood sexual abuse and exploitation', *Pastoral Care in Education*, 36(2), 154–66. https://doi.org/10.1080/02643944.2018.1464593.

Wynter, S. (2003) 'Unsettling the coloniality of being/power/truth/freedom: Towards the human, after man, its overrepresentation: An argument', *CR: The New Centennial Review*, 3(3), 257–337.

Yassine, L. (2021) 'To know is to exist: Epistemic resistance', in S.M. Tascón and J. Ife (eds), *Disrupting Whiteness in social work* (1st paperback edn, pp 91–107). Routledge.

Zeitlyn, B. (2012) 'The Sylheti *Bari* and the *Londoni* flat', *Space and Culture*, 15(4), 317–29. https://doi.org/10.1177/1206331212466080.

Index

A

academic capabilities 58
adult lens, research done through 12–13, 25
adultification 33
adverse childhood experiences (ACEs) 31
agency, children's 12, 25, 28–31, 44
Alexander, J.H. 15, 53
American Girl dolls 107–8
animals 143–6
Anjaria, J.S. 70, 71, 93
Anjaria, U. 70, 71, 93
Ann 7, 73, 86, 88, 103, 124, 125–6, 127, 144
anonymity 4, 7
Apperley, T. 112
art
  aesthetics of everyday life 98–9
  art packs 1, 17, 156, 166, 167
  digital 112
  digital creativity 112–13
  keeping safe 51
  life events artwork 138, 140
  love 129
Arthur, R. 37
assemblages 67, 70, 76, 85, 86
attachment theories 32, 121
attunement 98
austerity politics 11, 155
authoritarianism 30–1
autonomy 75

B

Back, L. 44, 63, 165
Baldwin, J. 150
banking model of education 27
Bannerji, H. 22
beauty in the everyday 94–120, 155, 164
'becoming' versus 'being' 33
bedroom tax 15
bedrooms 51, 53, 105–6
Beetham, T. 70, 162
Behar, R. 157
Bella 7
Bentham, J. 75
Berger, J. 55
Bernard, C. 34
Bhabha, H. 56
biomedical model 9, 25
birthdays 102–5
Black and minoritised children
  Child M 34
  essentialisation of children 33–4
  feminist sociology 14
  homemaking 16
  'lacking' narratives 117
  siblings 129
  surveillance 12, 19, 92
Black dolls 106–9
Black feminists
  beauty in the everyday 95–6
  cultural theories of the everyday 16
  figure of the child 13, 14, 26, 46
  fun and play 69–70
  joy and pleasure 88
  love 121
  shifting the gaze 19
blame for abuse 30, 41
blossom 97–8
bodies
  BMI (body mass index) 57
  embodied encounters with photographs 98
  embodied research methods 21
  embodied structures of violence 43
  moving to safety 53
  playgrounds 78–82
  standards of measurement 21, 56–7
boundary objects 66
Bradley, Ben 88
Brant, B. 124
Brown, A.M. 88
Buber, M. 122, 150
bullying 56–7, 131, 133
Burman, E. 3, 13, 14, 25, 26, 27, 31, 32, 33, 35, 39, 41, 42, 66
Butler, O. 61

C

Callaghan, J.E.M. 8, 14, 31, 53, 85, 99, 139, 151, 155, 164
cameras 54, 94
  see also photography
Campt, T. 19, 20, 55, 56, 98, 113, 162–3
capitalism 33, 46
  see also neoliberal ideologies
care
  affect of care 137
  children giving 60, 129–31, 142
  ethics of care 18, 159
  mothers' 147
  objects of care 147
  passive recipients of care 37
  placing children in 10
  value of care 60, 63–4
  without love 136–8
  see also love
Castañeda, C. 39–40

celebratory events 15, 56, 101–5, 148
child, definition of a 7–8
Child as method 3, 13, 14, 26–35, 38–47
child in need (CIN) 10
Child M 34, 91
child protection (CP)
  coercive system 135–6
  definition 10
  effect on mothers 57
  language barriers 63, 65
  listening to child's voice 53–4
  living and researching under shadow of 65–7
  passive/innocent child figure 41, 47
  researcher roles 65–6, 99
  risk aversion 41
  school monitoring 58
  socio-economic disadvantage 64
Child Q 33, 91
child soldier trope 36–7
childhood publics 60
childhood studies 13, 16, 30, 35, 43
Children Act 1989 12, 59
Children Act 2004 8, 12
Children First 54
children's gaze, following 20
Chin, E. 109
Chiou, L. 58
Cho, L. 49
Clark, K. 109
Clark, M. 109
climate change 140
coercive abuse 27, 28, 63, 64
collaborative seeing 20
collusion with the system 38
colonialism
  child soldier trope 36–7
  colonial gaze 19, 21, 22
  coloniality 39, 49
  disrupting the narrative of 55–6
  food 49
  idealised image of childhood 40, 41
  ignoring children's voices 42
  knowledge creation 14
  'Man' as conqueror 39
  mapping of the body 35
  'Other' 157
  passive/innocent child figure 47
  social order 2, 3, 26–7
  tropes of childhood 26–7, 55–6, 156
  see also decolonialism
confidentiality 63
Connectors Study 17, 43, 60, 71
consent 17–18, 61
contextualisation 32–3, 35, 53–4
Cooper, A. 41
co-parenting 63, 65
coping strategies 32

Corby, F. 58, 81
co-reading 21
court systems 29, 39, 54, 62, 63
covert human intelligence (CHIS) 37
COVID-19
  celebratory events 56
  impact on bedroom spaces 106
  maintaining connection with participants during 1, 15, 16, 17, 21, 156, 166–7
  play restrictions 77–8
  school closures 58
Creasy, R. 58, 81
cultural anthropology 60
cultural heritage 50
cultural ideals of childhood 30
cultural theories of the everyday 3, 14–16

D

damage narratives 3, 41–2, 84
data/statistics on frequency of domestic abuse against children 27
Davie, G. 59
de Certeau, M. 14, 45, 102
decolonialism
  decolonial scholars 13, 19, 26, 41, 45, 157
  decolonisation of social work 59
  decolonising the figure of the child 24–47
  decolonising the gaze 20
  love and decolonial research 149
Deep Play 75
deficit models 19
dehumanisation 26, 33, 34, 38–40, 99, 163, 165
Deleuze, G. 76, 85
demographics of participants 18
Dennis, F. 42, 81–2
Department of Education 10
desire 84–5
developmental psychology 32–3
deviance, prevention of 33
dhal puri 49
Di Napoli Pastore, M. 14, 15, 16, 17
digital creativity 112–13
digital inequality 58
digital technologies, connections via 51
  see also video calls
disability 35
dolls 106–9
Domestic Abuse Act 2021 8
'domestic abuse,' definition 8
domestic homicide reviews 29, 30
Dyer, H. 40, 92

E

early years child 31–3, 155
economic injustice 31–2

Index

education
  academic capabilities 58
  'good' at school 57–61
  homework 58, 59
  and the importance of play 72
  teachers 60, 62, 84, 136, 137
elitism 93
Ellis, K. 31
Elsa 5, 73, 75, 76, 77, 88, 90, 102, 110–13, 124–7, 144, 148
embodied encounters with photographs 98
embodied structures of violence 43
Emejula, A. 33
English as a second language (ESOL) 11
Enlightenment 30, 86, 121
epistemic humility 21
epistemic justice
  children's exclusion from knowledge creation 3, 154–5
  court systems 64
  figure of the child 12–14
  humanising the child 40–3
  marginalisation of children's voices 35, 40
  moving beyond the trauma lens 4
  multimodal ethnography 18, 19
escalations of violence 28
Esmeralda 5, 69, 71–7, 82–5, 92, 106–8, 114, 116, 128–9, 131, 137, 147–8, 160, 164
essentialisation of children 33
ethical dilemmas 61
ethics of care 18, 159
ethnography 1, 2, 3–4, 16–19, 43
Eurocentricity 35
everyday aesthetics 94–120
everyday life, theories of 14–16, 44–7
everyday space and safety 51–4
exhibition of photographs 61, 152–4, 161, 169
exploring 123–8
extended family 51

F

'failing to protect' children 11
fairness 56
family court systems 29, 39, 54, 62, 63
Fanon, F. 26–7, 38, 41, 42, 72, 136, 156–7
Farrugia, A. 81–2
Fassin, D. 37, 42, 99
fathers
  court systems 29, 39, 54
  playing family members off 135
  pressure on children to meet 53
  pressure to change mind about 29, 39, 54, 64
  rights of 64

Featherstone, B. 10, 11, 12, 26, 31, 32, 34, 44, 53–4, 59, 61, 136
Federici, S. 14, 55
female-only spaces 134–5
feminist theory
  addressing issue of children's exclusion from research 13, 14
  all-female groups 133–4
  domestic abuse 45–7
  and the everyday 45–6
  feminist ethics of care 18
  fugitive child trope 33
  fun and play 70
  innocent child trope 30
  unknowing 41, 157
  wider social determinants of abuse 10, 44
  see also Black feminists
Ferguson, H. 9, 15, 18, 26, 34, 44, 47, 66, 85, 105, 159
figure of the child 12–14, 24–47
fixing/rescuing children 31, 37, 38, 41
flourishing 18
food 49–51, 54, 55, 56
food parcels 87–8
free school meals 87–8
Freire, P. 27
Fricker, M. 40, 41, 155
friendships 83–5, 90–2, 112, 133, 136, 138–42
fugitive child 33–5, 155, 163
fun 155, 164
  see also play
Fung, R. 49

G

Gatwiri, K. 121, 122, 137
gaze, shifting the 19–22, 25, 40, 55, 89, 161
Geertz, C. 21, 75, 123
Gembus, M.P. 56
Gill, T. 78, 80
Gillies, V. 31
'gingerbread person' exercise 24–5
Global North/South binary 13, 26, 38–9, 162, 163, 165
  see also decolonialism
golf balls 124–5, 126
'good' at school 57–61
Graeber, D. 72
grandparents 51, 106
Guattari, F. 76, 85
Gunaratnam, Y. 157
Gupta, A. 59

H

Haraway, D. 143, 144, 145
harm narratives 9
Harris, P. 34

Hartman, S. 19–20, 165
Hartman, S.V. 35
health measured by body size 57
Herbert, B. 23, 122, 149
Highmore, B. 45, 105
Higonnet, A. 30
Holden, G.W. 28
Holmes, H. 21
home 15–16, 50–1, 53, 89, 101–5, 110–13
home decorations 102
homemaking 14, 16, 46, 105, 146
homework 58, 59
hooks, b. 13, 14, 16, 19, 46, 88, 105, 121, 122, 129, 131, 133, 135, 137, 138, 146, 148, 149, 150, 156, 163
Hope 134–5
Hope, A. 114
Horten, J. 120
household chores 14
Huizinga, J. 77, 92–3
humanising the child 40–3, 89, 150, 161, 165
humanitarian field 42
Hunleth, J. 43, 60, 131
Hurston, Z.N. 61

I
idealised image of childhood 25, 34
Ife, J. 121, 137
imagining different futures 61
imperialism 16, 27, 36–7, 40–2, 149
Indigenous communities 3
Indigenous scholars
  addressing issue of children's exclusion from research 13, 19
  beauty in the everyday 95–6
  damage narratives 84
  fun and play 70
  joy and pleasure 88
  love 149
  'not knowing and solidarity' 41
individualised narratives of safeguarding 11
inequality 12, 31, 58, 59, 70
infant determinism 31
innocent child 30–1, 35, 36, 39
insecure immigration status 34–5
intergenerational relationships 51
  see also grandparents
intersectionality 10
invisibility of children 66
'it' 79, 83

J
Jenkins, R. 58
JoJo Siwa 5, 69, 71–7, 82–5, 92, 108, 114, 128–9, 131, 160
jokes 71
Jordan, J. 146, 163

joy 41–2, 48, 67, 69, 98, 102, 114, 128
Just for Kids Law (JFKL) 37

K
Kapoor, A. 118
Katie 6, 80–1, 101–7, 113, 114, 116, 118, 129–31, 133–4, 136–40
Katz, E. 131
Keddell, E. 59
Khalili, L. 70
Khan, S. 35
kindness 60, 63–4, 136, 137
Kirk, T. 37
Kirmani, N. 70
Knight, L. 112
knowing subjects 12, 28
Kyro 6, 78–80, 94, 97–9, 111, 113, 114, 118, 137–8, 148, 160

L
Lather, P. 158
Laura, C.T. 124
Le Guin, U. 61
Lefebrve, H. 14, 44–5, 102
Lefevre, M. 29
legal framework 8–9, 27
life events artwork 138–9, 140
listening to child's voice 14, 29–30, 40–1, 53, 63, 149–50, 157, 161
listening to images 20, 55, 98, 113
lived experience, exploring children's 2, 26, 28–9, 32, 42, 44–6, 81
living well 82
locks 111
loitering with pleasure 89–92
Lorde, A. 65, 121, 122–3, 150
love 121–51, 159, 164
Lugones, M. 76–7, 85, 127
Lundy, L. 62
Luttrell, W. 15, 16, 20, 21, 55, 60, 102, 114, 147, 148

M
Macdonald, G.S. 54, 61, 64
Mahmood, S. 157
management style of social work 11
marginalised communities
  epistemic justice 42
  figure of the child 31–2, 35
  joy and pleasure 88
  researching 46, 157
  see also Black and minoritised children
Marshall, D. 95, 99
Marta 6, 134, 143, 144
materialism 63–4
Mauritian Creole 49, 62, 63, 70
mazaa 70, 71, 78, 84, 88
McCarthy, A. 21

McGee, C. 25
McKittrick, K. 117–18
meaning making 3, 15, 16, 21, 43, 56, 61, 96, 154–5, 164
Meiners, E.R. 31, 33, 40
methods 16–19, 166–9
migrant child 35
Minecraft 111–13, 168
Mishra, V. 49
Mohanty, C. 3, 13, 41, 45, 157
Montgomery, H. 43
Morrison, F. 64
mothers
  attachment theories 32
  children showing care to 131
  importance for friendships 138–9
  love 121, 146–8
  mothers' delight 89
  Mystical's relationship with 54–7
  'not good enough' 57, 121, 146, 148
  participants 6–7
  penalised for not keeping children safe 11
  scrutiny of mother's parenting 54, 57, 121, 135
  seen through eyes of oppressors 77
  'work' of creating play 86
moths 97
Moynah, M. 36
Mullender, A. 29, 44
multimodal ethnography 16–19, 43, 48, 71, 156–9
multisensory approach 20, 21
Murris, K. 41
Muslim identity 56
mutuality 122, 128, 137, 139, 140
Mystical 4–5, 48–68, 75–6, 77, 86, 102, 103, 104–5, 112–16, 118, 135–7, 142, 143, 145–6, 152, 154, 155, 159

N

names, children's 83, 84, 128–9, 159
nature photographs 114–18, 119
neoliberal ideologies 11, 53–4
neurobiology 32
NGOs 36, 37, 38, 70, 99, 165
Nicole 7, 50, 51, 54, 61–2, 63, 64, 65, 88, 103–5, 146, 152, 159
no recourse to public funds (NRPF) 34
Nolas, S.-M. 17, 43, 60, 61, 70, 71, 85, 95, 115, 118, 120, 143, 150, 156, 162
'non-children' 34
non-verbal communication 17
normalisation 46
'not knowing' 41, 136–7, 157
  see also 'unknowing'

O

Oakley, A. 14, 46, 70
object stories 169

objects of care 147
objects of memory 51
Ofsted 10
Okyere, S. 16, 43
Olajve, Benjamin 92
ongoing nature of domestic abuse 28, 63, 65–6, 135
online games 110–13
'Other' 33, 157
other families, wanting to help 62
outside in 114–20

P

Pacini-Ketchabaw, V. 144
Pandian, A. 21
parental accountability 59
parental alienation 54, 64–5
parental assessments 67
parenting, scrutiny of mother's 54, 57, 65, 67, 121, 135, 148
parenting classes 32
parents as gatekeepers 30
participant recruitment 17–18
passive recipients of abuse 9, 10, 25, 26, 99
passive recipients of care 37
passive/innocent child figure 12–14, 27–31, 36, 47, 155
paternalism 27
pathologisation 26, 29, 33, 35, 38, 41, 85, 99
patriarchy
  competition 131
  damage narratives 85
  epistemic justice 155
  fathers' rights 64
  figure of the child 22, 46, 47
  love 133, 134–6
  passive/innocent child figure 47
  power relations 77
  rejection of love 122
  social order 2, 3, 14, 16
Peck, M.S. 122
pedagogy of failure 41
Pernebo, K. 70
personhood, children's 25
pets 143–6
Phadke, S. 80, 88, 91
photography
  aesthetics of everyday life 94–120
  and beauty 96–8, 99–100
  on display in houses 113
  everyday aesthetics 94
  exhibition of photographs 61, 152–4, 161, 169
  listening to images 20, 55, 98, 113
  memories 113–14
  methods 168
  of mothers 147–8

mothers' delight in 89
multimodal ethnography 17
Mystical 54–6
nature photographs 114–18, 119
photograph books 116, 159–60, 161, 169
photographs of photographs 113–14, 148
play 86
Shelter exhibition 23, 154
sky photographs 118–20
Pini, M. 90
Pink, S. 21, 102
play
  everyday life 15, 69–93
  importance in and of itself 18, 70
  and love 123–8
  making sense of fun and play 71–2
  multimodal ethnography 17, 69–93, 155, 158, 160
  relationship-building through play 72, 75, 78, 123–8, 158–9
  'work' of creating play 86
playgrounds 77–85
pleasure, importance of 82, 88
Plowman, L. 59, 168
poetry 65
Pogi 5, 73, 86, 88–92, 102, 110–13, 123–8, 131, 137, 140, 144
policing 33, 45, 53, 59, 91
political trope, child as 14
post-separation contact 29, 39, 54, 64–5
post-traumatic stress disorder (PTSD) 37
poverty 11–12, 34, 59, 64, 131
power relations
  fathers 135
  and love 149–50
  subverting 73–5, 77
  unloving spaces 131–4
prevention of deviation 33
productivity, adult 33, 34
productivity trap, and play 72
pseudonyms 4, 7, 159
psychodynamic processes 2
psychologisation 32
psycho-medical model 25
public participation 43, 60–1, 143

R

racial marginalisation 11–12
racism 16, 31, 84–5, 92, 109
Ramadan 56, 101
Rashford, M. 88
real names 4
reason and rationalism 39
reflexivity 18, 21
refuges 134
relational agency 44
relational risk 82
relational safety 53

relationality, in play 75
relationship-building through play 72, 78, 123–8, 158–9
removal of children from parental care 10
research dissemination 159–61
research methods 16–19, 166–9
research with children, general
  lack of 2–3
researcher positionality 18
researcher roles 65–6, 99
researcher's love 148–50
Rice, Tamir 92
Richie, B. 13
risk and fun 80–2
risk aversion 41, 80–1
risk management 34, 81, 89
rites of passage 91
'river of life' 138–9, 140
Roblox 159, 168
Rohde, R. 55
Rosen, R. 35, 86
Rosie 6, 78–80, 94, 96–100, 113, 118, 119, 137–8, 148
routines and rituals 14, 15, 44–5
rule-bending/breaking 72–8
Russell, W. 78

S

safeguarding 9–12, 18, 65
safety 11, 51–4, 111, 139
Sagittarius 5–6, 91, 113, 131, 133–5, 139, 141, 143, 144
Saito, Y. 118
Save the Children 77
'science of singularity' 45
sensory objects 50–1
sensory place, home as 15
Seow, J. 109
serious case reviews 11, 12, 29, 34
sexual exploitation 30–1
Seymour, C. 36
Shalhoub-Kevorkian, N. 163
shared bedrooms 51, 53
Sharpe, C. 20, 117
Sheehi, L. 37
Sheehi, S. 37
Shelter exhibition 23, 154
Shepherd, E. 63
Shuster, S.M. 41
siblings 51, 53, 60, 66–7, 124, 125–6, 128–36, 138
sky photographs 118–20
slavery 49, 105, 117–18
Smith, L.T. 3, 13, 19, 39, 41, 45, 157
snow 114–15
social construction, childhood as 43
social hierarchies 60
social injustice 10, 32

Index

social work
  agency and blame 30–1
  attachment theories 32
  Black and minoritised children 34
  Child as method 26
  children becoming invisible in 66–7
  coercive system 136
  decolonising 59
  focus on adult perspective 2
  gaze 20
  interventions 9–12
  listening to child's voice 53–4, 61, 62, 65–6
  love 121, 149
  management style of social work 11
  not hearing voice of child 29
  and the passive child 27
  shifting gaze of 55
  unkindness of professionals 137
socioeconomic disadvantage 59, 106
socio-political contexts 11, 35, 36, 42
solidarity 41, 62, 65, 122, 129, 137, 147, 148
speculative fiction 61
Spillers, H. 40
Stacey 7
Stanley, N. 25, 26, 29, 44
Stardust 6, 143
Stenning, A. 78
stereotypes 25
Stevenson, O. 59, 168
stickers 57
Stodulka, T. 18
storage space 51
storytelling bench 115
Strathern, M. 21
Summer 6–7, 89, 94, 138
surveillance 11, 12, 20, 32, 34, 91

T

taxonomy of exposure to domestic abuse 28
Taylor, A. 144
Tdrommie 5, 111–13, 123, 160
teachers 60, 62, 84, 136, 137
Templeton, T.N. 119, 120
therapeutic interventions 70
thick description 21
'third spaces' 56
Thomas, D.A. 157
Thorne, B. 35, 40
thresholds, crossing 15
tic-tac-toe 75–6
toys 106–9
transnational identities 50
trauma lens 13, 14, 22, 25, 96, 98, 99, 114, 155
trauma recovery 32
traumatised child, figure of 37–8
trees 115–16, 117
tropes of childhood 25–40, 155

trust 29, 136, 137
Tuck, E. 3, 13, 19, 41, 42, 61, 84, 85, 109, 157, 165
Tucker, C. 58
Turner, V. 91
Twum-Danso Imoh, A. 13, 14, 15, 16, 17, 38, 43, 46, 47, 131

U

unaccompanied child migrants 35
United Nations Convention of the Rights of the Child 1989 12
'unknowing' 28, 31, 35, 39, 41–2, 155, 157, 161, 164
  see also 'not knowing'
unloving spaces 131–4
urban playgrounds 78
'urbancide' 117–18

V

value of care 60, 63–4
Varvantakis, C. 17, 50, 51, 56, 71, 85, 95, 115, 118, 119, 120, 150, 156
victims of domestic abuse, children as 8, 12
video calls 17, 71, 73, 74, 106–7, 111, 166–7
video games 112, 123, 159, 168
videos 89, 90
virtual homes 110–13
vouchers for fun 86

W

Wainright, O. 78
Walkedine, V. 90
walking 123–8, 169
walking home from school 91
Watts, L. 65
weather 94
Welcome, L.A. 157
welfare 88
Wells, K. 43
Westbrook, L. 41
White, middle-class models 32–4, 39, 40, 149
White feminism 134
White supremacy 46, 85
Women's Aid 54, 134
Woodiwiss, J. 30
woods 115
Wynter, S. 13, 39

Y

Yang, K.W. 61
Yassine, L. 149
Yoa'd Ghanadry-Hakim 37–8
YouTube 112, 160, 168

Z

Zeitlyn, B. 50, 56

www.ingramcontent.com/pod-product-compliance
Lightning Source LLC
Chambersburg PA
CBHW051542020426
42333CB00016B/2059